MARYLAND

CALENDAR OF WILLS

1744-1749

VOLUME 9

Continuing the series begun by Jane Baldwin Cotton

F. Edward Wright

D1303321

WILLOW BEND BOOKS
2007

WILLOW BEND BOOKS

AN IMPRINT OF HERITAGE BOOKS, INC.

Books, CDs, and more—Worldwide

For our listing of thousands of titles see our website
at
www.HeritageBooks.com

Published 2007 by
HERITAGE BOOKS, INC.
Publishing Division
65 East Main Street
Westminster, Maryland 21157-5026

Originally published by
Family Line Publications
(1991)

International Standard Book Number: 978-1-58549-185-8

INTRODUCTION

The first volume of *THE MARYLAND CALENDAR OF WILLS* was
published by Jane Baldwin in 1904. The purpose of her work, as
expressed in her introduction, was to meet the need of students
of history and genealogists. She expected that her compilations
would also assist in tracing titles to properties.

Embracing the same goals as Jane Baldwin and following a
similar format we continue the series from where she ended her
work. The series resume in liber 23 of the Prerogative Court
series in 1744 (date of probate).

The Prerogative Court wills consist of 41 volumes and
represent the totality of wills of the counties (with some
omissions). In those instances where the county copies were
destroyed by fire, such as those of Calvert and Dorchester Wills,
this series is all the more important. On the other hand the
wills for some counties can be found in three forms, housed at
the Maryland State Archives: the original as written for the
testator, the county recording, and the Prerogative Court
recording. The experienced researcher will not be surprised to
find differences in the three versions.

Since the advent of Baldwin's compilations there have been
additional publications of Maryland's probate records. In 1933
James M. Magruder, Jr. gave us, *Index to Maryland Colonial Wills,
1634-1777*, an alphabetical listing of the testators, date of
probate, county, liber (book) and folio (page) number. Since
then Ruth Dryden has published a series of abstracts of the
county wills for Worcester and Somerset, supplemented by works of
Sharon Jones and Vernon Skinner covering periods omitted by
Dryden. *Harford County Wills 1774-1800* was recently completed by
Ralph H. Morgan, Jr. Raymond Clark, Jr. published abstracts of
the Calvert County Wills for the period, 1654-1700 (taken from
the Prerogative Court records). Abstracts of Montgomery County
Wills have been published in two volumes, 1776-1825 and 1826-
1875. These were compiled by the team of Mary G. Malloy, Jane
Sween and Janet D. Manuel. Specific indexes to testators have
been done for Anne Arundel and Baltimore Counties. The Prince
George's County Genealogical Society has completed an Index to
the probate records of Prince George's County, Maryland, 1696-
1900. The value of another series of probate records, has been
greatly enhanced by the efforts by Vernon L. Skinner, in his on-
going series, *Abstracts of the Inventories of the Prerogative
Court of Maryland*.

The resumption of the publication of Prerogative Court Wills
was greatly aided by the work done by Annie Walker Burns and her
assistants. Abstracts of the wills, beginning with Liber 24 were
done some years ago under the direction of Annie Walker Burns.
Copies were made and distributed to a few repositories. We began
the process by copying her versions and comparing this copy with
the original Prerogative Court records. Many errors were
corrected in the Burns' version, and as time allowed the names of
slaves were added. (The names of slaves were also omitted from
Baldwin's work.) Difficulties in spelling and interpretations of
the wording have been resolved to a high degree.

We attempted to interpret the intention of the will while

avoiding involved and lengthy provisos and other entangled arrangements. In all such cases the names of individuals have been copied. When the meaning of the will was obscure we have avoided giving an interpretation.

Following the Baldwin format we show the date of the drawing of the will followed on the next line by the date the will was proved (date of probate). The reader should note that the Gregorian calendar was not adopted until sometime after 14 September 1752. The numbers at the foot of the will refer to liber (book) and folio (page).

Abbreviations used:

A. - acres
bet. - between
dau. - daughter
ex. - executor
extx. - executrix
hr. - heir
sd. - said
wit. - witnesses (In the earlier wills the terms testis and testes were used.)
young. - youngest
The other abbreviations should be obvious.

F. Edward Wright
Westminster, Maryland 1991

JONES, LEONARD, Dorchester Co.,   24th June, 1743
    To son LEONARD and JAMES JONES, uppermost pt. of "Friends
Assistance."
    To son DANIEL my dwelling plantation, being pt. of "Friends
Assistance."
    To daus. SARAH, ELIZABETH and UNICE, personalty.
    To ISAAC JONES, dau ANNE JONES, dau ANNE NELSON, dau MARY
DASHIELD, dau SARAH OLWENT, dau PRISCILLA COOPER, dau JANE
McCLUER, dau ISABELLA JONES, dau REBECCA NOBOBBE, each 1
shilling.
    To three sons, LEONARD and DANIEL (sic).
    To wife ELIZABETH, sole extx., my dwelling plantation for
duration of widowhood, personalty.
    To son JAMES.
    Residue of estate to four daus: SARAH, ELIZABETH, UNICE and
SOPHIA.
Test: THOS. HICKS, BENJAMIN RECORDS, CATHEWOOD HOST.
    Widow claims her thirds.
                                                   23. 600

WILLIAMS, WILLIAM, Dorchester Co.   9th Apr. 1744
    To son EDWARD, 100 A. of "Biter Bite," and personalty.
    To son WILLIAM, personalty.
    To dau. MARGARET, personalty.
    To son RICHARD, 50 A. of "Bitter Bite."
    To son EZEKIEL, 50 A. of "Bitter Bite."
    To dau MARY ANNE, 10 shillings.
    To son JAMES, personalty.
    To son ALLEN, personalty.
    To wife MONAKY, sole extx., residue of estate.
Test: John Browne, Robert Polke, Wm. Bradley.   23. 603

EDGAR, HENRY, Dorchester Co.   11th Aug, 1744
    To wife RUTH, my dwelling plantation and all my personal
estate for life or widowhood. At her decease, personal estate to
be divided among children, WILLIAM, HENRY; all my other children.
Wife sole extx.
Test: John Gootee, Richard Lane, Lewis Griffin, Jr.
                                                   23. 605

RICHARDSON, WILLIAM, Anne Arundel Co.   18th day, 9th mo., 1741;
    To wife MARGARET, coextx., use of my now dwelling plantation,
and other lands during her widowhood, she to allow son DANIEL to
live on any one pt. (for location see will.)
    To son JOSEPH, lands (see will) and personalty.
    To son DANIEL, coextx., 120 A., and personalty.
    To son RICHARD, land in Baltimore Co., bought of Richard
Owings and Charles Dorsey, "Owings adventure" and "Owings
addition," 450 A., plus personalty.
    To son THOMAS.
    To son NATHAN, 350 A. of "United Friendship" in Baltimore Co.,
bought of Dr. Samuel Chew, personalty.

To son THOMAS, 558 A. "High Spaniola" in Cecil Co., plus
personalty.
　To grandsons WILLIAM AND RICHARD, sons of son JOSEPH,
personalty.
　To dau SARAH HILL, her children, HENRY and MARGARET,
personalty.
　To SAMUEL THOMPSON, son of AUGT. and ELIZABETH, personalty.
　To ELIZABETH RICHARDSON, dau of my bro. JOSEPH, personalty.
　To Joseph Galloway 5 pounds for Quakers of West River
　To bro. JOSEPH, wearing apparel.
　To dau SOPHIA GALLOWAY.
Test: Nicholas Watkins, John Ross, Thomas Sprigg. 23. 606

DONALDSON, THOMAS, Anne Arundel Co.　　　　28th Nov, 1743
　　　　　　　　　　　　　　　　　　　　　　17th Dec, 1742
　To WILLIAM MATHERLY, son of my espousal wife MARY DONALDSON,
25 pounds and personalty when is of age.
　To son THOMAS, wearing apparel, personalty.
　To son JOHN to continue with his mother-in-law, my present
wife, personalty at 21.
　To wife to have 1/3 of estate, sole extx.
Test: Wm. Kirkland, Richard Taylor, Daniel Pierce. 23. 610.

WILSON, JAMES, Annapolis, labourer.　　　　4th Feb, 1743
　　　　　　　　　　　　　　　　　　　　　　19th May, 1744
　Residue of estate (after debts are paid) to Thomas King of
Annapolis, shoemaker, ex.
Test: Thos. Williamson, Robert Shaw, James Hendry. 23. 612.

BURCKHEAD, NEHEMIAH, Anne Arundel Co.　　　6th June, 1744;
　　　　　　　　　　　　　　　　　　　　　　26th July, 1744.
　To wife, 1/3 of my estate, real and personal.
　To eldest son Nehemiah, "Wells Hills."
　To son SAMUEL, coex., pt. of my dwelling plantation adj. land
of Seaborn Tucker.
　To sons John, coex., and Mathew, remainder of my land, to be
equally divided among them.
　To granddau SARAH WATERS, personalty.
　To granddau SARAH BIRCKHEAD
　To ELIZABETH WATERS.
Test: Dr. John Hamilton, Richard Randall, Wm. Brereton.
　　　　　　　　　　　　　　　　　　　　　　23. 613.

BURMAN, SAMUEL, Annapolis, butcher　　　　24th Jan, 1743
　　　　　　　　　　　　　　　　　　　　　　11th Oct, 1744
　To wife, ANNE, all my estate, sole extx.
Test: Geo. Chambers, Hannah (H) Chambers, Mary (M) Ellis
　　　　　　　　　　　　　　　　　　　　　　23. 615-616

WOODWARD, THOMAS, Baltimore Co., cooper　　2nd June, 1743
　　　　　　　　　　　　　　　　　　　　　　25th Sept, 1744
　To son JOHN, now in England, "Hogs Nortin" and "Shoemakers
Lot," lot in Baltimore Town.
　To wife MARY, now with child - if a son to have "Shoemakers
Lot" and lot in Balto, and to be named THOMAS.

All my personal estate to be divided among my child., JOHN,
ANNE, MARY and unborn child.
Extx.: wife MARY.
Test: Mary Anne (N) Harris Walker, Christopher Gardiner at
probate called Mary Ann Harrison.   23. 617-618

REYNOLDS, JOHN, Talbot Co.   21 Aug, 1744
                                         26 Oct, 1744
To son ROBERT, 1 sorrel mare.
To wife SARAH, pt. of "Reynolds Point," bet. land of James
Hopkins and Samuel Hopkins, sd. tract about which John Leonard
and I were at law.
To JONATHAN HOPKINS, pt. of "Reynolds Point" which I sold him.
Extx.: wife SARAH.
Test: Nicholas Benson, Thomas Robson, Henry Robson.
                                         23. 619-620

SWEAT [SURAT?], VARTY [sic] [Talbot Co.] 20 July, 1744
                                          26 Oct, 1744
Dau to be of age at 14, personalty; if my wife remarries,
residue of estate to sons CHARLES, NAM (?) and MARY, wife,
        and my father JOHN SURAT, sole ex.
Test: William (M) Walner, Mary Sweat, Ann (W) Walner
                                          23. 620-622

LINGAN, MARTHA, Calvert Co., gentlewoman 27 Sept, 1744
                                          29 Oct, 1744
To son THOMAS, personalty, ex.
To son GEORGE, personalty, ex.
To son SAMUEL, personalty.
To dau ANN, personalty.
To dau ELIZABETH CHAPMAN, personalty.
To dau MARY, personalty.
Codicil 27 Sept, 1744, son THOMAS and son-in-law ELISHA HALL,
personalty.
Test: Mary Smith, Wm. Holland, Wm. Chapman. 23. 622-624

DEVEROW, ELEANOR, Prince George's Co.   12 Dec, 1743
                                          19 Nov, 1744
To granddau RUTH CLARY, dau of DANIEL CLARY, personalty,
residue of estate.
To granddau MARY CLARY, dau of DANIEL CLARY, personalty.
To dau ELEANOR CLARY, personalty.
To grandson WILLIAM CLARY, personalty.
To son-in-law DANIEL CLARY, residue of estate.
Test: Caleb Litton, Daniel (DC) Chandlee, Grace Litton.
                                          23. 624-625

CARTER, WILLIAM, Charles Co., planter.   12 Feb, 1743
                                          10 Mar, 1743
To wife SOPHIA, sole extx, my dwelling, plantation and all my
movable estate.
To son WILLIAM, personalty at death of mother.
To dau JANE BIRKHEAD, pt. of "Bridge Town" for life, then to
son WILLIAM, personalty.

4

To dau ELIZABETH, wife of late THOMAS THOMAS, personalty.
Residue of est. to be divided by wife among all my child.
Test: Thomas North, Wm. Brooke, Luke Adams.
23. 625-628

CHUNN, JOHN, Charles Co.   29 Dec, 1743
                                                  25 Oct, 1744
     To eldest son RICHARD, 112 A., pt. of "Morrises Mount," bought
from Wm. Coode and Joseph Allen.
     To third son ANDREW CHUN, ex., 1/3 of "Brotherood" - land
given to John Chunn.
     To fourth son PEREGRINE CHUNN, 1/3 of "Brothwood."
     To sons RICHARD, JOHN, ANDREW, PEREGRINE; to daus MARY ANN,
ELIZABETH, LYDIA, JUDITH and DOROTHY, personalty, residue of
estate.
Test: Samuel Amery, Samuel (L) Leve, Jr.   23. 628-631

BURTON, WILLIAM, Queen Anne's Co.
                                                  13 Sept, 1744
     To wife JULIANA sole extx, residuary legatee.*
     To dau RACHEL CARMAN, 1 shilling.
     To JOHANA JAGO, personalty.
     To MARGARET PINDER, dau of dau MARGARET PINDER, personalty.
     To JOHN LEWIS, personalty.
     *at her death, estate to bro-in-law JOHN JOHNSON, he to pay my
grandson WILLIAM BURTON, 1200 pounds of tobacco a year until he
comes of age.
     Cousin JOHN WOODALL, son of JOHN WOODALL.
Test: James Brown, John Higgins, John Hollandsworth.
                                                  23. 631-633

COLEMAN, MORDECAI, of Prince George's Co.   20 Mar, 1740

     To bro JOSEPH, personalty.
     To SPICER OWEN (?), residue of estate.
Test: Charles Couts, James (E) Jones.   23. 633

SHANKS, JAMES, Calvert Co., schoolmaster.   3 Apr, 1744
                                                  14 Nov, 1744
     To be buried at Christ Church, Calvert Co.
     Friend Dr. JAMES SOMERVELL, sole ex, personalty.
     Mother CHRISTIANA FORDICE, if alive.
     Sisters JENNET and MARGARET SHANKS, living in parish
Fordonshire of the Meins (?).
     Three god children: JAMES JOHNSON, REBECCA MACKALL, ELIZABETH
STATER.
Test: Robert Skinner, Jno. Somerville, Barbara B. Boyde.
                                                  23. 633-635

HUNGERFORD, JAMES, Calvert Co.   10 July, 1744
                                                   3 Dec, 1744
     To son EDMUND, personalty.
     To dau JANE, personalty, 20 pounds sterling at 16 or marriage.
     To wife, 1/3 personal estate.
     To nephew JAMES HUNGERFORD.

To niece ELIZABETH CLARE, dau of my sister, HANNAH CLARE.
To nephew, JAMES CLARE.
Wife, extx.
Bros. Benjamin and Edmund Hungerford, trustees.
Test: John Clare, William Forde, Robert Greves, Jr.
                                                23. 635-637

PHILLIPS, JOHN, Calvert Co.   7 Sept, 1744
                                          11 Dec, 1744
   To wife, whole estate for life, then moveable estate to be
divided between my 3 child., JOHN, SARAH and SOLOMON.
To son JOHN, 1/2 my land.
To son SOLOMON, residue of land.
To WILLIAM CRANFORD, personalty.
Wife extx.
Test: James Dorsey, Wm. (X) Tayman, Thos. (T) Morsell, John
Davis Scarff, Mary (M) Leach.   23. 637-638

CRANALL, FRANCIS, Anne Arundel Co., St. James Parish

                                          30 Nov,' 1744
   To son FRANCIS, personalty.
   To dau ESTHER GOTT, personalty.
   To son WILLIAM, personalty.
   To son ABEL, personalty.
   To dau ANN GOTT, personalty.
   To son JOSEPH, residue of estate, sole ex.
Test: Jacob Franklin, Abel Hill.   23. 639-640

HALL, EDWARD, SR., Anne Arundel Co.   19 Mar, 1742/3
   To son EDWARD, coex., 1/2 my div. plantation cont. 300 A.
   To daus JANE and SARAH HALL, residue of my dwelling pl. until
they marry, personalty.
   To son JOHN, coex., residue of plantation at marriage or death
of daus.
Test: Richard Warfield, Sr., Sophia Dorsey, Jehosophat Rawlings.
                                          23. 640-642

HARRIS, BENJAMIN, Calvert Co., gentleman.   1 Dec, 1744
                                            24 Dec, 1744
   To neighbor JOHN TUCKER, personalty.
   To niece SARAH HARRISON, dau of RICHARD HARRISON, personalty.
   To wife SARAH, all my lands.
Test: Jo Hamilton, Richard Roberts (Quaker), John Stallings, Jr.,
Nathaniel Dare.   23. 642-643

WRIGHT, JOHN, Baltimore Co.   29 Nov, 1744
                                          3 Jan, 1744
   To cousin JOHN ORAM, "Maidens Choice" 225 A., personalty.
   Bro COOPER ORAM, ex.
Test: George Bailey, Oliver Cromwell, Zabez Bailey.

RYAN, DENNIS, Anne Arundel Co.   7 Sept, 1744
                                          3 Jan, 1744
   To dau SECILIA, personalty at age 18 or marriage.

6

To son-in-law WM. FISHER, personalty; at age 21, 5 pounds.
To son-in-law ABRAHAM FISHER, at age 21, 5 pounds.
To son-in-law MARTIN FISHER, at age 21, 5 pounds.
To dau-in-law, MARTHA FISHER, at age 21, 5 pounds.
Residue of estate divided between wife ELEANOR and dau
SECILIA.
Test: Abraham Simmonds, William Simmonds, Margaret Simmons.
                                              23. 645-647

JOHNSON, AFFRADOZI, Worcester Co.   3 Feb, 1743
                                           5 Oct, 1744
     To son GEORGE, 200 A. my divided pl., "Rochester," bought from
Mr. John Godden.
     To son THOMAS, 87 A. pt. of "Friend's Choice" in Somerset Co.,
bought of William Whittington.
     To son PURNELL.
     To son SAMUEL, residue of "Friend's Choice."
     To grandson SAMUEL DENNIS, personalty.
     Residue of estate to child., SARAH, PURNELL, ex., GEORGE, ex.,
THOMAS, and SAMUEL.
Test: Isaac Morris, John Scarborough, James Martin.
                                              23. 647-648

HOPKINS, SAMUEL, Worcester Co.   22 May, 1744
                                           28 Nov, 1744
     To grandson, LEVIN HOPKINS, land (for desc. see will).
     To son-in-law, EZEKIEL WISE, 60 A.
     To RICHARD AYRES and his wife SARAH, land.
     To son SAMUEL, residue of land, to be sole ex.
Test: Jno Scarborough, Hampton Hopkins, Matthew Selby.
                                              23. 846-650

Notation in margin that the will of Selby Claywell of Worcester
Co. was here omitted being recorded in Liber DD #3, f.248, f.649.

HENDERSON, THOMAS, Anne Arundel Co., Westminster Parish.
                                           12 June, 1741
                                           10 Jan, 1744
     To son THOMAS FRISBY HENDERSON, my div. plantation, "Bear
Neck."
     To son WILLIAM, "Jacob's Improved Purchase."
     To son GEORGE, "Henderson's Meadows."
     Wife, personalty; sole extx.
     Estate to be divided among my 6 child.: THOMAS FRISBY,
WILLIAM, GEORGE, SARAH, FRANCES (X) CORDELIA.
Test: Edward Tenton, Abraham (X) Frizell, Joseph (IP) Pumphrey.
                                              23. 650-651

ANDREWS, ALICE, Anne Arundel Co.   7 Sept, 1744
                                           12 Jan, 1744
     To friend, FRANCES MAPP, of Anne Arundel Co., personalty,
coex.
     To bro RICHARD CLIPSHAM, all my estate.
     To SAMUEL SMITH, ESQ., ..Anne Arundel Co., resid. leg. with
coex.

Test: John Howard, John Stewart, Jno. Cavendish.   23. 651-653

MURPHY, JOHN, Baltimore Co. [Will recorded Liber CC No. 2, f.783]
  12 Jan, 1744, Anne Lovelace one of the subscribing witnesses
to his will swore she saw him sign the will.
                                                  23. 653

TOLLEY, JAMES, Baltimore Co.   16 Oct, 1744
                                           2 Nov, 1744
  To my wife, if she delivers a child born in wedlock, all my
lands, then to said child, personalty, coex.
  To my nephew, WALTER TOLLEY, JR., personalty.
  To my niece ELIZABETH TOLLEY, personalty.
  To my niece, MARY TOLLEY, personalty.
  To my niece, SOPHIA TOLLEY, personalty.
  To my bro WALTER TOLLEY, personalty, coex.
  To my sister MARY TOLLEY, personalty.
Test: Roderick Cheyne, Js. Starkey, Abigail Cook. 23. 654-655

HOOKER, THOMAS, Baltimore Co.   14 Dec, 1743
                                           7 Nov, 1744
  To wife ELENER, tract "Elener's Lookout" for life, then to son
JOHN.
  To son SAMUEL, 1 shilling.
  To son RICHARD, 1 shilling
  To son JOHN, personalty.
  To dau RUTH, personalty.
  To dau EDETH, personalty.
  To son BENJAMIN, portion of estate.
  To each of BENJAMIN CARR'S child., 1 shilling, each.
Test: Nicholas Haile, Moses Merryman, Elexious (EL) Lemmon.
                                                  23. 656-657

TOLLEY, MARY, widow of JAMES, Baltimore Co. 20 Oct, 1744
                                             9 Nov, 1744
  To sister, FRANCES HAMMOND DORSEY, personalty.
  To sister of my dec'd. husband, ELIZABETH MILLER, personalty.
  Bro-in-law John Hammond Dorsey, ex.
Test: Roderick Chayne, Jonathan Starkey, Jacob Starkey.
                                                  23. 657-659

SIMPSON, ANDREW, Charles Co.   2 Nov, 1744
                                          3 Dec, 1744
  To son THOMAS, personalty.
  To son JOSEPH GREEN SIMPSON, personalty.
  To dau ANN CLARK, personalty.
  To grandson, JNO. SEMMES, son of CLEBURN SEMMES, 5 shillings.
  To dau MARY, personalty.
  To dau CLARE, personalty.
  To wife JULIANA, personalty and residue of estate, sole extx.
Test: Jos. M. Semmes, Wm. Hugan.   23. 659-660

CLUBB, JOHN, Charles Co.   25 June, 1737
                                          18 Dec, 1744
  To wife ANNA, 1/3 of my personal estate, coex.

To son, PHILIP, 100 A., pt. of "Hopewell," 12 pence.
To son, MATTHEW, 100 A., residue of "Hopewell," and residue of
my personal estate, coex.
To dau ELIZABETH WEDDING, 95 A. "Maiden's Pleasure" and 12
pence.
Test: Ralph (R) Marlo, Mary (M) Willett, Charles Willett.
                                          23. 660-662

SMOOT, BARTON, Charles Co., gentleman   22 Sept, 1744
                                             16 Jan, 1744
     To wife, ANNE, my divided plantation, and 200 A. of land at
Port Tobacco, "Skipten," 100 A. near Charles Baker's "Fishpond."
     To son BARTON, 200 A. "Brant's (?) Cliffs"; also "Mt.
Clipsham," containing 68 A.; also 100 A. Marsh land - at his
death to testator's grandson HENRY SMOOT, then to GEO. SMOOT.
     To son ISAAC, "Smoot's Delight" 88 A; "Smoot's Swamp" 50 A.;
"Smoot's Swamp Addition" 55 A.; "Lomax Addition" 68 A.
     To son WILLIAM, "Barton's Hope" 100 A.; pt. of Daniel's Mount
25 A.; "Monday's Disappointment" 100 A.
     To son THOMAS
     To wife ANNE, 1/3 of my personal estate.
     Residue of estate to be divided among my four sons and dau:
THOMAS, BARTON, ISAAC, WILLIAM, dau ELIZABETH GUYTHER.
Test: Philip Dorney, Tobias Coohagen, Margaret Coohagen.
                                          23. 662-664

QUINLY, MARGARET, Anne Arundel Co., St. James Parish.
                                             1 Jan, 1744/5
                                             4 Feb, 1744
     To be buried at my dwelling plantation
     To son SAMUEL SCOTT, my dwelling plantation, "Deaver's Range."
If he dies without lawful issue, to my son SABRETT SCOTT.
     To son SABRETT SCOTT, personalty.
     To dau SARAH SCOTT, personalty.
     To son THOMAS SCOTT, and dau MARGARET TROTT or SCOTT, residue
of estate.
Test: John (J) Powell, John (X) Trott, George Macquire.
                                          23. 665-666

                                             3 Nov, 1744
Alice Lee of Talbot Co., Spinster. made oath that
CATHARINE NEWMAN, widow of JOHN NEWMAN, dec'd on 21 Nov last said
she desired that Nicholas Goldsborough of Talbot Co. to
administer her estate and have the care of eldest dau Elizabeth
and youngest dau Mary if the wife of John Cox would not take the
said Mary. Dau Sarah to the care of John Cox's wife.

COLLISON, ELIZABETH, Talbot Co.   2 Nov, 1741
                                             2 Dec, 1744
     To son WILLIAM, all my estate, ex.
Test: John Lowe, Wm. Webb Haddaway, Thos. Smith. 23. 667-668

WILLIAMS, JACOB, Talbot Co.   1 Dec, 1744
                                             11 Jan, 1744
     To bro MATTHEW, personalty.

To JAME (JAINE?) PITTS, personalty.
To WILLIAM SHELD, personalty, coex.
To wife Rachel residue of estate, coex.
Test: John Sweat, James (IS) Sanders.

23. 668-669

DEEN, JAMES, Somerset Co.   26 Mar, 1743/4
                                         23 Oct, 1744
    To (wife?) MARY, being with child, my whole estate, sole extx.
    To child, unborn, "Deen's Venture."
    To bro CHARLES, "Gladstone's Industry."
Test: John Beadley, Thomas (T) Huffinton, Samuel Badley.

23. 669-671

BLUER, JAMES, Somerset Co.   2 Feb, 1736/7
                                         21 Oct, 1744
    To JAMES BLUER of RICHARD, personalty.
    To JAMES BLUER of SAMUEL, personalty.
    To JAMES BLUER of SARAH, personalty.
    To wife MARGARET, 1/3 of my estate.
    To the children she bears me, lawfully begotten, residue of
estate.
Test: Levin Gale, Wm. Murray, Wm. Drumond.   23. 671-673

DASHIEL, ROBERT, Somerset Co., gentleman   11 May, 1744

    Personal estate to wife (ESTHER) and daus., JANE and ESTHER.
    My wife to have the care of bringing up my two daus.
Test: Geo. Dashiel, John Handy, Michael Dashiel.   23. 673-674

WALKER, THOMAS, Somerset Co.   29 Dec, 1744
                                           12 Jan, 1744
    To JACOB SAILY, for his child. begotten on the body of my dau
ELIZABETH GAILEY (?), my dwelling plantation.
    He to pay COL. GEORGE GALE and MATTHEW GALE, 175 pounds.
    To dau MARY RICHARDSON, coextx, 300 A. of land, pt. of
"Coskaway"; personalty.
    To dau SARAH FLETCHER, coextx, 250 A., "pt. Caskaway";
personalty.
    To dau JANE LUCAS, 250 A. of said tract; personalty.
    To dau REBECCA WALKER, 150 A. of said tract.
    To granddau BETTY DAY SCOTT, 100 A. of said tract; personalty.
    To dau ELEANOR WALKER, my lot in White Haven town; personalty.
    To RICHARD WALLAS, of Dame's Quarter, land he has paid me for.
    To child. of my dau ELIZABETH SAILY, land in Sussex Co.,
Delaware.
    To granddau MARY FLETCHER
    To dau ANNE WALKER, personalty.
    Grandson SAMUEL CHASE, at age 21
Test: George Dashiels, Patrick Stewart, Thos. (D) Miller, Gilbert
Stewart.

23. 674-677

JONES, JAMES, Somerset Co., schoolmaster   22 Dec, 1744
                                            25 Jan, 1744
    To wife SARAH, sole extx., 1/3 of my movable estate.
    To son ISAAC, my dwelling place and 50 A.
    To son JAMES, 50 A.
    Residue of estate to be divided among all my child.
Test: John Rickards, Joseph Callaway, Wm. Walker.
Widow accepts the will and relinquishes any claim by will.
                                            23. 678-679

LLOYD, ALICE, Queen Anne's Co.   6 Apr, 1739
                                             4 Dec, 1744
    To sister, ANNE TILGHMAN, my share of tract, "Gropes," given
me by my mother.
    Sister MARGARET WARD
    To cousin PHILEMON BLAKE, confirmation of deed for 570 A. (for
desc., see will) I lately made over to him.
    To cousin, MARY CARROLL, daughter of CHARLES CARROLL by my
cousin DOROTHY, dec., residue of "Lloyd's Meadow Resurveyed," and
"Lloyd's Meadows Addition." In default of her hrs, to her
younger bro JOHN CARROLL, and hrs, then to her eldest bro CHARLES
CARROLL, and hrs, then to my cousin, JOHN BLAKE.
    To PHILEMON BLAKE, son of my cousin PHILEMON, personalty.
    To cousin JOHN BLAKE, personalty.
    To cousin HENRIETTA MARIA ROBINS, cousin ANN LLOYD, now the
wife of my cousin ROBERT LLOYD.
    To cousins ANN and HENRIETTA MARIA EARL, daus of MR. JAMES
EARL, each 10 pounds.
    To cousins, JOHN and PHILEMON BLAKE, sons of my sisters,
HENRIETTA MARIA BLAKE, dec., residue of estate. To be execs.
Test: David Melville, Thomas Kendall, Richard Bennett, Mich or
Nich Fletcher.   23. 679-682

WINCHESTER, JACOB, Queen Anne's Co, Kent Island
                                            29 Nov, 1744
                                            31 Jan, 1744
    To son ISAAC, personalty.
    To son, JACOB, personalty.
    To daughter, SARAH, personalty.
    To child my wife goes with personalty.
    To wife MARY, extx, her thirds. Residue of estate to four
child., afsd.
Test: Joseph Sudler, Andrew Price, James Harvey. 23. 682-684

ROSS, WILLIAM   9 Mar, 1743/4
                                           10 Mar, 2743
Note: Will begins, "I, WILLIAM ROSS. . .but is signed, "THOS.
ROSS."
    To FRANCIS BOSTICK, overseer of RICHARD YOUNG, exec.,
personalty.
    To JACOB LUSBY, personalty.
    To BENJAMIN TASKER, Esq., personalty.
Test: B. Rogett, Francis (B) Bostick.   23. 684-685

BEDDARD, RICHARD, Worcester Co., gentleman   5 Nov, 1744
                                       19 Jan, 1744/5
    To wife ANNE, my dwelling plantation for life, then to
BENJAMIN DAVIS, sole extx.
    To BENJAMIN DAVIS, land he now lives on.
    To dau SARAH BEDDARD, personalty.
    To dau JERASHA BEDDARD, personalty.
Test: John Evans, Gammage Evans, Zachariah Bold.
                                       23. 685-687

GREEN, BOWLES, Kent Co.   29 Nov, 1730
                                     10 Nov, 1744
    To son JOHN, all my land and houses, personalty, to be raised
by kinsman, WM. WRENCH.
    To wife MARY, personalty, other half my personal estate,
coextx.
    WM. WRENCH of Queen Anne's Co., coex.
    Memo: Wife MARY to have all my land for her widowhood.
Test: Peter Green, Robert Green, Jonathan Whitworth.
                                       23. 687-688

THOMAS, WILLIAM, Kent Co.   28 Sept, 1744
                                     12 Jan, 1744
    To son WILLIAM, my dwelling plantation, including tracts
Kedgerton, also "Thomas' Purchase." If he dies before age 18,
land to dau, MARY THOMAS.
    To cousin, WILLIAM THOMAS, son of my bro HENRY.
    Personal estate to son and dau, afsd.
    Wife SARAH, to have use of lands for her widowhood.
    Wife SARAH, and cousin RICHARD GRESHAM, join execs.
Test: Nicholas Pearce, Sr., Wm. Trew, Jr., Nicholas Neal.
                                       23. 689-691

O'NEAL, LAWRANCE, Kent Co., weaver.   9 Jan, 1744/5
                                     27 Jan, 1744
    To daughter, MARGARET O'NEAL, personal estate
    To my loving housekeeper, ROSAMOND REYNOLDS. . .
    To my friend, HENRY SPENCER, sole exec.
Test: Thos. Cowper, Mathias Day.   23. 691-692

BALL, JANE, Kent Co.   20 Dec, 1744
                                       2 Feb, 1744
    To my dau MARGARET KELLY, and son JAMES KELLY, all my estate.
    Bro WILLIAM MOODE of Philadelphia, to have care of my son
JAMES.
    Execs. dau Margaret, and Abraham Milton
Test: Nicholas Pearce, Sr., James Claypoole, Edward Brown.
                                       23. 693-694

REYNOLDS, EDWARD, Calvert Co.   26 Feb, 1739
                                       14 Dec, 1744
    To dau MARY WILLSON, 50 pounds.
    To grandson, EDWARD WILLSON, 150 pounds.
    To grandson, REYNOLDS ALLEN, 130 pounds at age 18.
    Residue of my estate to son THOMAS, sole exec.

12

Test: Wm. (W) Kidd, James Weems, Gebrial Parker.
23. 694-695

CURRENT, ANN, Calvert Co.   23 Jan, 1744/5
                                              2 Feb, 1744
    Bro GARARD DIXON and THOMAS SHEPHARD to see I have Christian
burial.
    To dau ELIZABETH CURRENT, being 9 years of age, on 15 July
next, personalty.
    To dau SARAH CURRENT, personalty.
    Property at John Benans (Bevans?).
Test: J. Rigby, John Smith.   23. 695-696

HASSETT, DINA, Calvert Co.   22 Jan, 1744
                                             12 Feb, 1744
    Bro -in-law THOMAS GOLSBERY, to raise my dau GRACE PHILIPS
until she comes of age.
    Two sons MICHAEL and JOHN HASSETT, to be raised by JOHN
CULLPEPPER till they reach age 19.
Test: Thomas Gassaway, Dina (T) Pearce, Thomas Brittin.
                                             23. 697

PIERCE, RICHARD, Calvert Co.   20 Jan, 1743
                                             12 Feb, 1744
    To granddau GRACE PHILLIPS, personalty.
    To son WILLIAM PIERCE, personalty, he to raise sons, RICHARD
and JOHN, until they are of age.
    Son-in-law THOMAS GOLDSBERY, exec.
Test: Thomas Elsbury, Richard Trewton, Sam'l Bennett.
                                             23. 697-699

DICKINSON
DICKISON, STEVEN, Calvert Co.   7 May, ----
                                             16 Feb, 1744
    To dau-in-law MARY EDMANS, personalty.
    To dau-in-law CATERAN EDMANS, personalty.
    To WILLIAM HUTSON, personalty.
    To wife ANN, residue of my personal estate, sole extx.
Test: John Brooke, Sarah Brooke.   23. 699-700

A'PRICE, EDW. A. JR., St. Mary's Co.   7 Oct, 1744
                                              8 Nov, 1744
    Wife ANN A'PRICE.
    Child. mentioned, not named.
    Bros. THOS. A'PRICE, JAMES A'PRICE, mentioned.
    ANN A'PRICE, extx.
Wit: Thos. Metton, John Temper, John Wood.
                                             24. 1

BEDMAN, JOHN, JR., St. Mary's Co.   9 Aug, 1744
                                             12 Nov, 1744
    Child. mentioned, names not given.
Wit: Robert Mosley, Benj. R. Bedman, Geo. Crashill.
                                             24. 2

CISSELL, WM., St. Mary's Co.. planter.   22 Jun, 1742
                                             28 Nov, 1744
     Child.: ARTHUR CISSELL, LUKE CISSELL, MARGARET THOMPSON, ANN
EDWARDS, MATHEW CISSELL, ELIZABETH (wife of Charles Payne), CLARE
BARTON; grand-children: WM. CISSELL (Son of JOHN and his mother
Elizabeth Neall), WM. CISSELL (son of WM. and CLARA, his wife),
     To grandau ELINER (dau of son ARTHUR), land bet. Arthur's
plantation and the plantation whereon John Harden now lives.
     To son ARTHUR CISSELL, plantation he now lives on, pt. of 100
A. called "Scotland."
     To son Luke, other pt of "Scotland," 50 A., it bein obtained
by Judgment in chancery by Daniel Dulay.
     To dau MARGARET THOMPSON, plantation she now lives on.
Mentions John Thompson, Charles Neale and Charles Payne.
     To dau ANN EDWARDS, plantation she now lives on.
     To son MATTHEW, 50 A., pt of "White Acre," the plantation he
now lives on, given by my father's will and 20 A. called
"Cissells Improvements."
     To WM. CISSELL, son of WM. CISSELL and CLARE his wife, 1 sh.
     To ELIZABETH WIFE OF CHARLES PAYNE, land bet. Wm. Cissell's
and Ann Edwards' land and deeded from her brother Wm. Cissell's
land.
     To dau CLARE BARTON, 1 A. now in possession of Wm. Cissell son
of John.
     To NEALL (sic) wife of Charles Neal, access to Wm. Cissell's
land.
     Exs. Arthur Cissell, Luke Cissell, Mathew Cissell, Edward
Cissell, Marg. Thompson.
Wit: Cath. Russell, Margaret Pye, Wm. Russell.   24. 2-4

SOTHERON, JOHN JOHNSON, St. Mary's Co.   9 Oct, 1744
                                                5 Dec, 1744
     Wife ELIZABETH SOTHERON, dwlg. plantation, to return to her
son GREENFIELD on her death.
     To son HENRY G.
     Exs., Samuel Sotheron, Richard Sotheron (bros) and appointed
as trustees over son Henry C. who is not to enjoy his estate
until age 21.
Wit: Leonard Clark, John Briscoe.   24. 4-5

CHENEY, CHARLES, Senr., Anne Arundel, Planter.
                                                11 Feb, 1744
     To my son CHARLES CHENEY, 1 s. sterl.
     To my son JACOB CHENEY, 1 s. sterl.
     To my son GREENBURY CHENEY, clothes.
     To my dau MARY PICKETT, 1 s. sterl.
     To my sons MORDICAI and ISAAC CHENEY and my daus RACHEL and
ELIZABETH CHENEY, all my pt moiety of a tract called "The North
Addition" lying and being in Anne Arundel Co., and a tract called
"Cheney's Resolution," and a tract called "Indian Range," lying
in sd county to my sons and daus; MORDICAI, ISAAC, RACHEL and
ELIZABETH CHENEY. My wife AGNES CHENEY, the third pt of tracts
of land above mentioned.
Wit: John Jacobs, John Hooper, Thos. Cheney.   24. 5

WOODWARD, ABRAHAM, Anne Arundel Co.   26 Jan, 1744
                                            1 Mar, 1744

To my son WILLIAM WOODWARD
To my 5 child. REBEKKAH, MARTHA, ABRAHAM, THOMAS and PRISCILLA
WOODWARD, 2/3 of my whole estate.
To my wife PRISCILLA WOODWARD, 1/3.
To my son, WILLIAM WOODWARD, all my interest that I have in
Great Brittain which is dependency to come from my dec'd father
WILLIAM WOODWARD of Great Brittain.
Extx. wife Priscilla and dau Rebekkah Woodward.
Wit: Gerrard Hopkins, Joshua Gaither.   24. 7

WILLETT, EDWARD, Prince George's Co.   16 June, 1743
                                          11 Feb, 1744

To my eldest son NINIAN WILLETT, 5 s. sterl. and the
plantation which he now lives on, which sometime ago gave him by
a deed of gift, which may be found among the records of Prince
George's Co. Courts.
To my son EDWARD WILLETT, 5 s. sterl. and 60 A. being pt of
the tract of land Jones (?) or James (?) lives on and made over
to him by a deed of gift, sometime ago. I give my son THOMAS
WILLETT and hrs tract called "Lick Hill" belonging to me.
To my son WILLIAM WILLETT, I give tract called "Beal's Craft"
of 43 A. and 87 A of tract called "Bealington" being pt where I
now live.
To my son JAMES WILLETT, all remaining tracts of land called
"Bealington" with his 2 bros, EDWARD and WILLIAM WILLETT.
To my dau ANN SWAN, all that tract called "Ryley's Plains"
adjoining to the land of Cuthberd Anderson, 172 A., and I give to
the sd Ann Swan, the acre of land I bought of Mr. Stodart in the
town of Mount Calvert.
Mentions sons THOS., WM., and JAMES and dau ANN SWAN tract called
"Little Dear" that I bought of Thomas James and tract called
"Horse Race" that I bought of Ephriam Beal.
Exec. son WM. WILLETT.
Wit: James Gibson, Wm. Harper, Edward Risten.
                                          24. 8

RIGGS, JAMES, SR., Prince George's Co.   21 Aug, 1744
                                          4 Mar, 1744

To wife ELIZABETH RIGGS, estate to be divided amongst my
child., JAMES, JOHN, EDMON, SARAH RIGGS and JANE CRAMPHIN.
To my dau SARAH RIGGS, furniture and etc.
After my wife's decease, give son EDMOND RIGGS some slaves.
Wife ELIZABETH, extx.
Wit: Samuel Riley, Matt Sparrow, Thom. Lucas, Jr.
                                     24. 10

JONES, LEWIS, Talbot Co., carpenter   15 Feb, 1744
                                          15 Feb, 1744

To my son JAMES, my land called "Duty Wines" (?); addition and
pt of tract "Triangle" on east side of a creek called Bear Point
Creek, on the road leading to Mr. Robt. Lloyd's plantation.
To my son LEWIS JAMES, remainder of said tract.

Wife, extx., if my wife is deceased, then my friend Richard
Gibson to act as admin.
Wit: John Willson, Sarah Willson, Frans Cook.
Note: Richard Gibson refuses admin.   24. 11

ATCHISON, JOHN, Prince George's Co.   22 Feb, 1744
                                              14 Mar, 1744
    To my wife, MARY ANN ATCHISON, whole of my personal estate.
    To my dau, ELIZABETH MC FALL
    Extx, my wife.
Wit: John Stoddert, Robert Gordon, William McClash.
Then came Capt. John Stoddart, and the other 2 witnesses and
probated the will.
                                                          24. 12

SELBY, NATHAN, Prince George's Co.   28 Feb, 1744
                                               4 Apr, 1745
    To my sons, WILLIAM and NATHAN, my land called "Toogood,"
equally.
    To my son, JOHN, slaves.
    To my wife, EASTER SELBY, extx.
Wit: John Orme, Thos. Selby, Newcom Brobvin, James Hollyday.
                                                          24. 13

KNIGHT, STEPHEN, Kent Co.   18 Oct, 1742
                                               21 Mar, 1745
    To my wife, ANNE KNIGHT, extx, my estate both real and
personal in Kent Co. or elsewhere, except hereafter stated.
    To my grandson, JOHN LEACH KNIGHT, my house and lot in
Chestertown.
    Design that by leaving my estate to my wife, that she shall
lay claim to dower, to my plantation that was at Boho.,
[Bohemia?) in Cecil.
    To my son, WILLIAM, my plate that is engraved with my coat of
arms and chest to him and hrs forever; my personal estate and
slaves in Cecil to my sd son.
    To my dau MARY STOKES, slaves.
    To my 2nd dau, SARAH PHILIPS, slaves.
    To my 3rd dau, CORDELIA KNIGHT, slaves.
    To my 3 daus, 10 pounds sterl.
Wit: James Watson, John Watson, Elizabeth Peavoll (or Teooll ?)
                                                          24. 14

HOWARD, ANN, Charles Co.   5 Oct, 1744
                                                6 Oct, 1744
    Child.: SARAH, MARY ANN
    To sister PRUDENCE SAUNDERS, 1 suit apparrell, saddle and
furniture.
    To sister MARY POORE, 1 suit apparrell.
    Desire that trusty friend, Joseph Lancaster and wife Jane,
have bringing up and educating daus. SARAH and MARY ANN, and that
their share of estate shall be paid them at age of 16 or on the
day of marriage.
    Ex. Jos. Lancaster.

Francis Hamusley, Justice of Peace, made oath that he read above
will to Ann Howard and asked her if she approved. She replied,
"Yes." Asked if she would sign it, answered she would, but after
taking pen was unable to do so and requested sd. Hamusley to sign
for her, which he did.

24. 15

COLEMAN, THOMAS., Charles Co.   19 Feb, 1743
                                                  2 Oct, 1743
    To son THOMAS, tracts, "Redding" and Homely."
    To dau CATHARINE SAMWAYS COLEMAN, pt of tract "Homely," and
for want of issue then to THOMAS COLEMAN, son of John Brightwell,
and for want of issue to my son THOMAS.
    To dau MARTHA, 6 A. and dwlg house and remaining pt of tract
"Redding" and remaing pat. of "Homely."
    Slaves to divided bet. my 6 ch.: Thomas, Ursilla, Elizabeth,
Martha, Martha and Catharine.
    Ex. Thos. Coleman, Martha Coleman
Wit: John Briscoe, Joseph Barker, Luke Adams.   24. 16

GOLFLING, THOS., St. Mary's Co.   27 Apr, 1740
                                                  21 Feb, 1744
    Wife ELIZABETH, extx., all my estate.
Wit: John Adams, Philip Scirven, Roger Copsey, David Hughes
                                                       24. 18

AESQUITH, ELIZABETH, St. Mary's Co.   10 Sep, 1749
                                                  22 Feb, 1744
    Estate to be divided equally bet. son GEORGE and dau ANN.
    Ex. Geo. Aisquith, son
Wit: Hugh Hopewell, Jr., Eliz. Hopewell   24. 19

BLUMFIELD, JAMES, St. Mary's Co.   15 Jan, 1744
                                                  5 Mar, 1744/5
    To son-in-law, Matthew Daft, tract, "Crucked Billt," land on
Eastern Shore in Dosset Co. near Great Choptank.
    Ex., Mathew Daft, son-in-law.
Wit: Enoch Combs, Nicholas Mills, Cuth. Greenwell.
                                                       24. 19

BAGGLEY, SAMUEL, St. Mary's Co.   10 Jun, 1744
                                                  5 Mar, 1745
    DRAYDEN BAGGLEY, wife, extx., all my lands but if she dies
without issue then to godson THOMAS READA, son of THOMAS READA,
and my brother BENJAMIN READA.
    To my wife's brother THOMAS BOND, 1 slave.
Wit: Thos. West, John Spragg, James Pascoe.   24. 20

WATTS, WILLIAM, St. Mary's Co.   23 Dec, 1744
                                                  5 Mar, 1745
    Child.: WILLIAM, THOMAS, GEORGE, DANIEL, ELIZABETH.
    JANE WATTS, wife, extx.
Wit: Geo. Clark, Jno. Blackeston, Jno. Clark.   24. 20

GANYOTT, CHARLES, St. Mary's Co.   11 Nov, 1744
                                    6 Mar, 1744/5
   To JOHN DENT, neighbor, tract of land, called "Zoak by
Chance."
   To son CHARLES, remainder of tract and "Ganyott's Lott," and
to have 3 years schooling after age 10.
   To eldest dau MARY, 2nd dau CONSTANTIA, 3rd dau MARGARET.
   To son who may be born to ELIZABETH GANYOTT, wife, within 9
months of my death.
   SAMUEL MITCHELL, servant man, to be set free at expiration of
nine years' service.
   Desire that bros.-in-law John Fenwick and Ignatius Fenwick, be
empowered to see that provisions of will are fulfilled.
   ELIZABETH GANYOTT, wife, extx.
Wit: Edw. Cole, Wm. Lucas, Chas. Lucas.   24. 23

 HEBB, THOMAS, St. Mary's Co..   14 Jan, 1744
                                  13 Mar, 1744/5
   To son EDW. HILLARD HEBB, tract where I now live.
   To sons WILLIAM and JOHN, leased land, "Scotland."
   To son William tract bought of John Noble, formerly taken up
by David Wheatley.
   Mentions ch., JANE JENKINS, ANNE BAXTER, LUCRETIA HEBB.
   Grand-son FRANCIS BEAN
   Elizabeth Rule, sister; Edward Hebb, son; William Hebb, son.
exs.
Wit: Will Hebb, Thomas Perring, David Hebb, Jos. Hebb.
                                    24. 25

BALL, BENJAMIN, Dorchester Co., (who was the son of BENJAMIN BALL
of Calvert Co., Md.)   23 Jul, 1744
                                 2 Jan, 1744
   In consideration that my eld son THOMAS BALL, has a plantation
given him by his grandfather, THOMAS HICKS, I give him no part of
my land.
   To my sons, BENJAMIM AND LEVIN, to be equally divided betw.
them, the 36 A. pt of "Taylor's Ramble" which Edmondson is to
convey to me by my hrs or assigns, and "Ball" to the 50 A. lying
in Dorchester Co. to demand as pt of my personal estate and made
sale of by my extx. and all other lands of mine in Calvert Co. or
elsewhere.
   To my wife, ELIZABETH, as a legacy, cattle.
   To my son, THOMAS, slaves.
   Note: Mentions "my 4 children": THOMAS, BETTY, BENJAMIN and
LEVIN; wife ELIZABETH HALL"
Wit: Elizabeth Hicks, Mary Hicks, Roger Pitt, John Hicks.
                                    24. 26

ROSS, Edward, Dorchester Co.   18 Feb, 1739
                                  18 Feb, 1744
   To son JOHN ROSS, remaining pt of tract called "Rosse's
Venture," out of which I sold 50 A. to James Crameen (?), and
what remains not taken away by Edward Willobes land and at
decease of his mother.

To son EDWARD ROSS, 100 A. out of land called "Stewart's Vineyard."
To dau SARAH ROSS, 50 A. out of afsd. land.
To dau MELESEW ROSS, my dwelling plantation with the remaining pt of tract afsd.
Wife MARY, extx.
Appoint my bro PETER ROSS, and my son EDWARD ROSS, to have care of my dau MELISEWS' estate in her minority.
Wit: Thos. Peirson, John Bartlett, James Carameen.   24. 28

BRONOCK, THOMAS, Dorchester Co.   28 Jan, 1744/5
                                         14 Mar, 1744
To my LEVISEY FRANCESS, slaves.
To grand-son, EDWARD BRONOCK, son of EDWARD BROOK, tract called "Bronack's Adventure," lying in Dorchester Co. on Fishing Creek, on west side of a fresh called Gates Creek.
To sd. grand-son, EDMOND BORONOCK, in case my sd grand-son EDMOND BRONACK, should die without issue, then my will is that the said land should go to his bro THOMAS and hrs.
To son PHILLEMON BRONACK, half of a tract called "Timber Neck," beginning at the first bounder; also give him pt. of trace "Harwood," adjoining William Phillips and if PHILLEMON has no issue, then to my son HENRY BRANNOCK.
To son THOMAS BRONNOCK, 3 s.
To son WILLIAM BRONNOCK, 3 s. in full of his portion.
To dau MARGARET EVENS, wife of CURTIS EVINS, 3 s. in full of her pt. of my estate.
To dau MARY MEEKINGS, wife of JOHN MEEKINGS, 3 s.
Wife FRANCES BRANNOCK, and son JOHN BRANNOCK, exs.
Wit: Thos. Woolford, Wm. Kennerly, Thos. Mace.   24. 29

OGLEBY, JOHN, Cecil Co.   19 Jan, 1744/5
                                         4 Feb, 1744
To wife RACHEL, the third of my remaining estate.
To son JAMES OGLEBY, remaining estate except 10 pounds currency, which I give to my bro GEORGE'S child., JANE OGLEBY and DARCUS OGLEBY, in Ireland, and if they ever come in the country, the 10 pounds is to be paid equally between both by John Cockrane and JAMES OGLEBY who are executors of my will.
Leave my son in the care of his uncle JAMES OGLEBY, to be educated.
Wit: ROBERT NEELEY, PATRICK MACHAM.   24. 31

BLEACK, JOHN, of Detet (Detel, Delet ?), Cecil Co. 14 Mar, 1744
                                         15 Aug, 1744
                                         19 Sep, 1744
To son GEORGE BLEACK, after decease of my wife, ELIZABETH BLEACK, my land and houses.
To son JOHN BLACK, 5 pounds.
To dau REBECCA BLEACK, a bed.
To dau MARGARETT BLEACK, cattle.
Wife, extx.
Wit: Signed sealed published and pronounced and declared by the sd. Richard Harrison, Henry Jackson, Edward Jackson.

Note that I leave to my dau REBECCA BLEACK, the ruggs that
belongs to the said bed is written at the foregoing will.
Richard Harrison and Henry Jackson, 2 of the witnesses, say they
saw testator JOHN BLEACK, sign the will.   9 Sep, 1744, Richard
Harrison, Henry and Edward Jackson say they saw him sign same.
24. 32

WALKER, HUGH, Cecil Co.   22 Dec, 1744
                                                11 Mar, 1744
    To son HUGH WALKER, plantation I now live on in Cecil Co.
    To son SAMUEL WALKER, 100 pounds current money.
    Order that my son HUGH pay to my wife, MARGARET, the sum of 30
pounds current money.
    To son SAMUEL the sum of 25 pounds current money afsd. to be
paid by my son HUGH, provided that he the afsd. SAMUEL, his hrs.
and executors do give and surrender, peaceable possession of the
afsd. plantation lying in Virginia, with deed and writing
thereunto belong with my son HUGH or his order.
    To dau ANNE, 10 pounds money, provided her husband, WILLIAM
DAIREES (DAVIESS?), my son-in-law.
    To dau FRANCES, 25 pounds money to be paid by my son HUGH.
    Appoint my son SAMUEL WALKER, and my son-in-law, WILLIAM
MACKY, execs. and Messrs. Andrew Barry and Michael Wallace,
overseers, over my child. and execs.
    If HUGH dies without issue, my 2 pts. of the plantation in
Cecil Co., Maryland and the plantation in Virginia, shall descend
to my son SAMUEL.
    To daus ANNE and FRANCES, the other third pt.
Wit: Andrew Hall, John Edmiston, Geo. Lawson.   24. 33

AKINSON, ISAAC, Worcester Co., planter   25 Dec, 1744
                                           13 Jan, 1744/5
    To wife TABITHA, my plantation or tract of land in the Indian
Town, lying on the east side Nasingo Creek and called, "Choice."
At her decease, sd tract to be sold and money divided bet. my 4
daus: SOPHIA, HANNAH, MARY and RACHEL.
    To wife, 25 pounds due me by bond from Robert Layfield,
Somerset Co., she paying unto my 4 child. above named 10 pounds
each.
    Robert Layfield, has my bond.
    Appoint Angelo Atkinson and John White, of sd. county,
guardians.
Wit: Caleb Beavans, Hanna White, Chas. King.   24. 36

BURTON, WILLIAM, Worcester Co.   ---------
                                             1 Feb, 1744/5
    To grand-son ROBERT BURTON, being son of WILLIAM BURTON, the
one-half pt a moiety called "Hopewell," lying in the county and
on the north side of the Indian River, to be divided, and if he
die without issue, the land to fall to his bro JOHN RUSSELL
BURTON.
    To grand-son, WILLIAM BURTON, being son of WILLIAM BURTON, the
other half paid, known by name of "Hopewell," and if WM dies
without issue, to descend to his bro JOHN RUSSELL BURTON.

To grand-son JOHN RUSSELL BURTON, being the son of WILLIAM BURTON, 50 A. pt. of tract "Conclusion" and pt. of tract "Folly," lying on the westward pt of the sd. 2 tracts and binding on Shiloes Branch.

To grand-dau ELIZABETH BURTON, the dau of WM. BURTON, the other half pt. of a slave.

To son RICHARD BURTON, use of plantation he now dwells upon of 405 A. and use of 200 A. upon the north side of the head of Broad Kill Creek, and use of 15- A. of marsh that I purchased of Frances West.

To grand-son WILLIAM BURTON, son of RICHARD BURTON, the plantation whereon his father now dwells, of 405 A. to be possessed by him after his father's and mother's decease, and 15 A. of marsh, which I purchased of Frances Woolf.

To grand-son EBENEZER BURTON, son of RICHARD BURTON, 200 A. in Sussex Co., and on north side of head of Broadkill Creek.

To son JOHN BURTON, the plantation whereon I live, of 400 A. called "Brooked Project"; also, one mill on Swan Creek and 150 A. thereunto belonging, which I bought of Robert Lady and lying in Sussex Co.; also the upper part of the island.

To dau CATHARINE MORRIS, use of the land and plantation whereon she and her husband now dwell, 340 A. called "Chance"; also, slaves.

To 3 grand-sons: WILLIAM, JOHN and JOSHUA MORRIS, sons of my dau CATHARINE, the plantation whereon their father and mother now live at the decease of their mother.

To dau ELIZABETH BURTON, use of the land I purchased of Abraham Ingram of 400 A. adjoining William Maples line which I bought of Babtist Newcomb during his life.

To grand-son, WOOLLSEY BURTON, of dau ELIZABETH, the land I bought of Abraham Ingram, of 400 A., adjoining Wm. Naples line.

To dau SARAH INGRAM, land on north side of Sheep Pen Branch called, "Rich Island," and 150 A. whereon they now dwell, being north pt. of land called "Conclusion."

To 6 child.: RICHARD BURTON, JOHN BURTON, JOSHUA BURTON, CATHARINE BURTON, ELIZABETH BURTON and SARAH INGRAM, the profits and ground rents, of land called "Worurck(?)," which was laid out for a town, beginning from the river and running 100 poles in length back and from William Waples line, up the river.

To wife FRANCIS BURTON, use of my dwelling plantation, and the island during her widowhood, and use of all my slaves.
Wit: Benj. Salmon, Elizabeth Duffe, Joseph Carter.   24. 37

CLAYWELL, PETER, Worcester Co.   26 Dec, 1742
                                        15 Feb, 1744/5
To son SHADRICK CLAYWELL and hrs., 250 A. in the Indian Town, called, "Security" whereon he now lives.

To son THOMAS CLAYWELL, slaves.

To son PETER CLAYWELL, slaves.

To dau ELIZABETH HILL, 1 slave.

To dau COMFORT PAGE, 1 slave.

To dau MARY BOUND, 5 pounds money.

To son SOLOMON CLAYWELL, and hrs., plantation I now live on called "New Yermouth" 200 A., In case my son SOLOMON should die without issue, then land to my 2 sons THOMAS and PETER CLAYWELL.

To wife LUCRETIA CLAYWELL, remainder of estate, and appoint
wife and son PETER CLAYWELL, exs.
Wit: Alexa. Bunch, John Rope, Sr, or John Pope, Wm. Duer.
24. 41

WILDMAN, JOHN, Parish of Stepeny, Co. of Middlesex, weaver.
(Probated in Worcester Co., Md.)   8 Feb, 1732
                                                    22 Feb, 1744/5
   My wife CATHARINE WILDMAN, extx.
Wit: Calb. McAlster, Wm. Wildman, Samuel Wilcocks, Jr., *vera
copia*, Per Benton Hanes, Deputy Comr.   24. 43

HAMPTON, MARY, Somerset Co.   26 Feb, 1741
                                                   13 Dec, 1744
   To son ROBERT JENKINS HENRY, my several tracts of land in
Somerset Co.: tract "Mary's Lot" and "Henry's Addition,"
including 200 A. purchased by me of my bro ROBERT KING; one tract
called "Lembrick"; names of other tracts: "Cyprus Swamp,"
"Conveyance," "Cyprus Neck," "Highland," "Whitely," "Dickenson,"
"Hope," "Goose Marsh," "Cow Marsh," "Providence," "Friend,"
"Assistance" and my gristmill near William Stephen's Ferry, and 1
other gristmill at Rehoboth Town, and all my lots in sd. town,
and one moiety of a lot in Snow Hill Town, and half of the Stone
House on sd. lot, being No. 2, and moiety of tract called
"Pershore," in Delaware Bay, near Horn [Hore] Kill Creek in
Sussex Co., for benefit of my sd. son ROBERT JENKINS HENRY.
   To son JOHN HENRY, land called "Spring Hill," in Somerset Co.
and "Golds Delight," adjacent bought of John Mathewson, and
"Buckland" and "Sister's Gift," which I purchased of Robert King,
my bro, and tract "Jasemine."
   Gives tract "Ignoble Quarter" to Revd. Thomas Fletcher.
   To bro ROBERT KING, 10 pounds money.
   To 2 nephews, sons of sd. bro., and nephew and niece, sons and
dau of my sister, ELEANOR BALLARD, dec'd, 20 s. current money.
   To Mr. Edward Round and wife Katherine Round, 20 s.
   To Elizabeth Jones, wife of Wm. Jones, of Menikin, 1 slave.
   To Mary Jones, dau of Wm. Jones, some cattle.
   My son ROBERT JENKINS HENRY
Wit: Archibald White, Wm. White, Jno. Baker., who probated the
will.   24. 44-47

COLLENS (COLENS), WILLIAM, Somerset Co.   29 Feb, 1743/44
                                                  20 Mar, 1744
Wife ELIZABETH COLENS (?) COLLINS (?)
Wit: Isaac Mitchell, Wm. Boland.   24. 47

JONES, WILLIAM, Calvert Co.   16 Oct, 1744
                                                   18 Apr, 1745
   To MRS. ELENER DAVALL dau of HENRY DAVALL (probably meant
DUVALL) of Portland Mannor, one slave. (The name appears as
ELENER DARNAL in another line.)
   To MARTHA GRIFFITH, some cattle.
   To PHILIP DARNAL, SR., mourning gloves and etc. His estate in
England or Maryland or elsewhere to be equally divided bet. my

good friends Thomas Diggs and Henry Darnall of Portland Mannor, execs of this will.

(Signed: WILLIAM JONES, HALL CREEK)
Wit: Lewis Griffith, John Griffith.   24. 47

BEALL, VERLINDER, Prince George's Co.   29 Mar, 1745

    To grand-dau, VERLINDER, the dau of my son JOSIAH, 1 slave.
    To dau LUCY, 20 pounds money.
    To 2 daus HANNAH and VERLINDER, my 6 youngest child.: BAZEL, LUCY, JOHN, HANNAH, VERLINDER and CLEMENT.
    Appoint my son JOSIAH and dau LUCY execs., they to educate my son CLEMENT with Christian faith.
Wit: James Edmonston, Geo. Cook, Mary Edmonston.   24. 48-49

BROOKE, THOMAS, of Prince George's Co.   7 Dec, 1738
                                  29 Mar, 1745

Mentions my son WALLER, tract "Content" and "Brooks Content," and lot in Upper Marlborough.
    My wife LUCY BROOKE, she to have "Brookefield" and "Addition To Same."
Mentions "mortgage by my father or myself."
Wit: Elener Beall, Samuel Beall, Richard Brooke.   24. 50

WADE, ZACHARIAH, Prince George's Co.   13 Dec, 1744
                                   8 Apr, 1745

    To son ZACHARIAH, "Stoney Harbour," north side Tinkers Run and "Wade's Adventure."
    Reserving to MARY, my beloved wife, her dower (page 52).
    To dau MEEK, 100 A. of "Stoney Harbor" which land was bequeathed to him by his father, ROBERT WADE.
    To daus ANN and MARY ANN, "Wade's Adventure," lying near the head of Piscattaway Creek, 150 A., which I purchased of Robert Wade, Jr.
    To dau MEEK, 1 horse which came of Richard Wade's mare and was broke and gaited by Alexander Norton. (Pgs. 52 & 53)
    My late dau ELIZABETH, the wife of Richard Harrison, was provided for when married to sd. Harrison, now dec'd.
    To JOSEPH, the son of sd. Harrison, money for mourning ring.
    To VIRLINDER, the dau of sd. Harrison, also by my sd. dau ELIZABETH, when she is age 16 or on her dat of marriage.
    To grand-son GEORGE WADE, 20 s.
    To JOHN, the son and SARAH, the dau of my late bro, dec'd.
Wit: John Tolson, Step. Pickering, James Kendall.
8 Apr, 1745 came MARY WADE, extx, and declared she was determined to have her thirds of dec'd's estate and would not abide by the devise as in the will.   24. 51-53

NORRIS, MARY, Prince George's Co.   31 Aug, 1738
                                   15 Apr, 1745

    To son BENJ. NORRIS
    To grandson WILLIAM NORRIS, son of my son BENJAMIN NORRIS.
    To grand-son JOHN NORRIS, son to my son BENJ. NORRIS, 1 slave.
    To grand-dau ANNE NORRIS, dau of my son BENJAMIN NORRIS
Wit: John Addison, John Locker, Jr.   24. 54

BUCKLEY, RICHARD, of Queen Anne's Co., St. Luke's Parish,
planter.   27 Sep, 1744
                                            7 Feb, 1744
    To dau RACHEL BUCKLEY, my dwelling plantation, 50 A. "Buckley
Delight" for 10 years.
    To dau MARY ANN BUCKLEY
    To dau ISBAL BUCKLEY and FRANCES BUCKLEY, unto RACHEL and MARY
ANN BUCKLEY, until the age of 18.
    To dau ISBEL, FURNITURE.
    To dau FRANCES BUCKLEY, 1500 pounds tobacco.
    I leave JOSEPH BUCKLEY in care of Thomas Lee of Tulley's Neck.
    To son RICHARD BUCKELY, JR., 1 s.
Wit: John Burk, John Smith, Thomas Burn.
                                            24. 55

POWELL, JAMES, St. Luke's Parish, Queen Anne's Co.
                                           17 Feb, 1745
                                           28 Feb, 1744
    To dau _____ Higgens, cattle.
    To Michael Higgens, clothing.
    To 2 daus MARGARET POWELL and SARAH POWELL
    My wife MARY ANN, extx.
Wit: Thos. Harper, Benj. Harper, Amey N. Powell.
                                            24. 57

ELLIOT, BENJAMIN, Kent Island, Queen Anne's Co.
                                           25 Mar, 1742
                                           21, Mar 1744
    To dau REBECCA ELLIOTT, slave
    To son BENJAMIN ELLIOTT, slaves.
    To my unborn child, and if sd. child should not live, the
property to my son BENJ., land in the forrest of Chester on Red
Lyon Branch, being tract called "Slaughter's Town."
    To wife MARY ELLIOTT,
Wit: Christe Granger, William N. Rabbels, Jas. Harvey.
                                            24. 57

WEEKS, JOHN, St. Luke's Parish, Queen Anne's Co.
                                           15 Sep, 1742
                                            4 Apr, 1744
    To wife HESTER WEEKS
    To eldest son JOHN WEEKS, 52-1/2 A.
    To young. son STEPHEN WEEKS, 52-1/2 A., land beginning at end
of 100 perches for length and from the end of the south line for
breadth, 84-1/3 of a perch west and from the end of the west line
north, 100 perches and from the end of the north line with a
straight line to the first beginning on the south line of where
his bro, JOHN WEEKS', ends and to my sd. son STEPHEN WEEKS,
remainder of what land of Mount Pleasant I now hold lying bet.
"Tilghman's Discovery" and Chester River.
    To son MATTHEW WEEKS, tract "Enjoyment," and he and my son
STEPHEN to be exs.
    To dau MARY POWELL, 1 s. sterl.
    To dau ALICE DEFORD, 1 s.
Wit: Robert Gould, James Gould and Benj. Gould.   24. 59

DULANY, WILLIAM, Wye, Queen Anne's County, planter

- - - - -

11 Apr, 1745

To son WILLIAM DULANY, my home plantation called "Standford" 200 A., and 30 A. called "Mount Mill" thereunto adjoining.

To dau ELIZABETH DULANY, liberty of living and abiding on my home plantation.

To 2 sons MICHAEL DULANY and DANIEL DULANY, my plantation called "Pustico (?)" standing in the eastern side of Tuckahoe Creek containing 200 A., of land to be divided; to son MICHAEL DULANY, 100 A.; to son DANIEL, the other 100 A.

To dau ELIZABETH DULANY, my plantation "New Nottingham."

To son THOMAS DULANY, 1 s.

WILLIAM DULANY, ex.

Wit: Wm. Farrell, John Farrell, Jno. Browne.   24. 61

TRAYMAN, THOMAS, Talbot Co.   - - - - - -

14, Mar, 1744

To dau ELINOR TRAMAN, 1 slave.

To wife MARY TRAMAN, 1/3 of my estate.

To dau ELINOR TRAMAN, remainder of estate.

Wit: Wm. White, Wm. Sharp (Quaker).

24. 63

HARRISON, JOHN, Talbot Co.   17 Jul, 1744

19 Mar, 1744

To wife MARY HARRISON, slaves to be divided bet. my wife and my dau FRANCES HADDOWAY, and grand-dau SARAH HADDOWAY.

To bro ROBERT HARRISON, my great coat.

Son-in-law, WILLIAM WEB HADDOWAY, ex.   24. 63

DULIN, JOHN, Talbot Co., planter.   19 Feb, 1744/5

29 Mar, 1745

Appoint wife MARY, extx.

Wit: Thomas Ellis, Wm. Carr, John Angley.   24. 65

OLDFIELD, HENRY, Talbot Co.   3 Mar, 1744/5

29 Mar, 1745

To wife SARAH OLDFIELD, my dwelling plantation at her decease; plantation called "Summerly," to my son BARBER.

Mentions my daus MARY WARD, REBECCA BOSWICK and DEBORAH CHANCE; my sons and daus hereafter named: BARBER, RACHEL, HENERY, JOHN and SARAH.

Wit: Daniel Chapman, Samuel Hambelton, Mary Hambelton, Mary Chambers, J. Goldsborough.   24. 66

MARTIN, SAMUEL, Talbot Co., planter.   19 Mar, 1744

23 Feb, 1745

To son THOMAS MARTIN, land called "Jurdin's Hill" and upper range in Talbot Co., and in case of no hrs., the same to go to JOHN MARTIN, son of WM. MARTIN.

To bro DANIEL MARTIN, my clothing and my books of navigation and my instruments.

To son and wife, my personal estate, expenses to be equally divided bet. them.
I constitute my wife and bro WM. MARTIN, to be exs.
Wit: James Dickinson, Elizabeth Richardson, Sarah Stueart(?), Bridgit Norton.   24. 68

NEALL, ANNE   4 Apr, 1745
                                                    24 Apr, 1745
Henry Woods and Robert Curge, being Quakers, make affirmation that they were present Sundry times in the last illness of ANNE NEALL, one of the daus of FRANCIS NEALL, dec'd, in which illness she died, who stated she desired her bro FRANCIS NEALL, JR. should have what estate belonged to her of her grandfather WILLIAM FERRALL, dec'd; that she gave her wearing apparel to be divided bet. her sister SUSANNAH NEALL and SARAH MORGAN, wife of Enoch Morgan, and also what was coming to her of her father, the afsd. FRANCIS NEALL. His personal estate, she gave to JOANNA HARRISON, wife of JAMES HARRISON.

Wit: Henry Woods, Anne Neall, Robert R. Curge   24. 69

DUDLEY, SAMUEL, Talbot Co., planter.   31 Mar, 1745
                                                    10 May, 1745
     To wife MARY DUDLEY, my dwelling plantation and all my other land during her life; then
     To son RICHARD DUDLEY and hrs.
     To bro THOMAS DUDLEY, "Broad Lane" which was contained by my father's estate, whose name was THOMAS DUDLEY'S last will.
     To THOMAS DUDLEY, son of JAMES DUDLEY, late of Talbot Co., dec'd., my claim of "Dudley's Inclosure" according to the intent and purpose mentioned in my grandfather, RICHARD DUDLEY'S will.
     Balance to my 3 child.: SAMUEL DUDLEY, THOMAS DUDLEY, REBECCA DUDLEY.
     Appoint wife, MARY DUDLEY, and RICHARD DUDLEY, exs.
Wit: Thos. Kelld, Jno. Nedels, Charles Manship.   24. 70

NEALL, FRANCIS, Talbot Co., planter   - - - - - -
                                                    10 May, 1745
     To sons, FRANCIS NEALL and SAMUEL NEALL, 'Hickery Ridge" on the west side of "Melords Manour" and adjoining, to be equally divided.
     To son JONATHAN NEALL, for want of such hrs.
     To wife ANNE NEALL, land "Hickory Ridge" in sd. Mannor, which I bought of said Lord, 137 A. being my dwelling plantation. She not debarring my son SOLOMON NEALL of being on sd. plantation if he stand in need of it, and at her death, the same to pass to son SOLOMON NEALL, but for want of such hrs., same to fall to son JONATHAN NEALL.
     To wife ANNA NEAL, slaves.
     Mentions the other nine of his child.: FRANCIS, ANNE, SARAH, SUSANNA, SAMUEL, SOLOMON, FORTUNE, HANNAH, RACHEL and JOHNATHAN, the rest of the money.
     To dau MARY EDMONDSON, 5 s.
     To dau ELIZABETH FAIRBANK, 20 s.
     To dau JOANNA SHERWOOD, 2 s. sterl.

To son JONATHAN NEAL, 1 slave.
Wife, ANNE, extx.
Wit: Edward Neall, John Regester, John B. Masson. Edward Neall
and John Regester, 2 of the witnesses, were Quakers.
24. 71-73

BATCHELDOR, ELIZABETH, Talbot Co.   10 Mar, 1744
                                             10 May, 1745
     To son JOHN BURGESS, the plantation that I now live on, being
pt. of tract called "Beaver Neck," containing 149 A., which my
father JOHN BERRY, bought of my uncle THOMAS BERRY, lying on
north side Choptank River, Talbot Co.
     To son GEORGE BURGESS, 100 A., being pt. of land that my
father JOHN BERRY, bought of Robert Grundy to his hrs. forever.
     To dau ELIZABETH BATCHELDOR, 50 A. of land, being pt. of tract
called "Broad Lain" bought of Robt. Grundy.
     My friend Thomas Dudley, shall bring up my 3 child.: JOHN
BURGESS, GEORGE BURGESS and ELIZABETH BATCHELDOR, in a Godly and
sober manner. Sd Thomas Dudley to have use of my land until my
son JOHN BURGESS comes to age 21, it being for the maintaining
and educating of my 3 child.
     To my 3 child., my land in Dorchester Co., 1 tract, "Com by
Chance," equally divided.
     Appoint my friend Thomas Dudley, as ex.
Wit: Samuel Dudley, Thomas Powell, James Bell.   24. 74

ALEXANDER, WILLIAM, late of that pt. of the Kingdom of Great
Brittain, called Scotland, but now of Cecil Co. in the province
aforesaid, merchant.   20 Jul, 1738
                                             17 May, 1745
     To wife ARAMINTA ALEXANDER
     To sister, MARGARET CLELAND, of the parish and town of
Whithern Shire of Galloway and Kingdom of Scotland, give out of
the afsd. sum of 400 pounds sterl. In 12 months after the
decease of my wife, sd. sister to have whatever of his estate
that is in Scotland.
     To cousin MARY DONALDSON, in parish of Kirkcoubright in the
Stewartry of Galloway in the Kingdom of afsd, 100 pounds sterl.
I confirm a certain instrument of writing commonly called "A
Marriage Settlement," bet. me and my sd. wife ARAMINTA, bearing
date 25th day of July 1738, and also a deed of gift from my wife,
unto her son, EPHRAIM AUGUSTINE HERMON of the same date to all
intents and purposes as if they were here fully expressed.
Wit: Wm. Wye, John Roberton, David Alexander; probated by Mrs.
     Araminta Alexander, the widow and extx.   24. 75 - 77

ARMSTRONG, JOHN, Christ Church Parish, Calvert Co.
                                             29 Nov, 1743
                                             16 Apr, 1745
     To dau RHENES ARMSTRONG, slaves.
     To wife, my 2 plantations; one called "Island Creek," and the
other called "Peddington."
     To son EDWARD, plantation called "Island Creek Neck."
     To son JAMES, "Peddington," at decease of my wife.
Wit: Samuel Bennett, Francis Spencer.   24. 77 - 78

FREAZER, DANIEL, Calvert Co. 7 Feb, 1744
 20 Apr, 1745
    To son JAMES FRAZER, land I now live on called "Heel Hall,"
which I bought of William Beanes.
Wit: James Duke, James Duke, Jr., Benj. Duke. 24. 78 - 78

MANNERS, MARY, Calvert Co. 4 Apr, 1745
 4 May, 1745
    Child. share equally in everything that is mine. Appoint
bro JAMES RICHARDSON, ex.
    Mr. Walker Smith have jurisdiction over effects and see that
my children be justly done by.
Wit: Jo Hamilton, Jno. Bond (Quaker), Roger Brooke.
 24. 80

BOWLEY, DANIEL, Baltimore Co., merchant 17 Mar, 1744
 3 Apr, 1745
    His houses and lots in the town of Baltimore to be sold and to
be equally divided bet. wife, ELIZABETH BOWLEY, and her unborn
child.
    Wife, extx.
Wit: George Buchanan, Wm. Rogers, Nichs. Rogers. 24. 80 - 81

SCOTT, DANIEL, Baltimore Co. 13 Mar, 1744
 15 Apr, 1745
    To wife ELIZABETH SCOTT, my dwelling plantation, "Scott's
Improvement, enlarged," 390 A., and 100 A. adjoining that I
bought of Michael Taylor, being pt. of tract called "Burr" during
her life.
    To son Daniel SCOTT, after my wife's decease, the same, and
100 A. "Scott's Close" which I bought of James and Edward Meeds.
    To son JAMES SCOTT, tracts on west side, north fork Winter's
Run: "James Forrest, 216 A.; & "Add'n to James Forrrest," 340 A.
    To son ACQUILA SCOTT, 5 tracts, 400 A., pt. of "Beal's Camp,"
200 A. pt. of "Scott's Hopewell"; "Trust" being the tract that my
old quarter is settled on of 100 A.
    To son DANIEL SCOTT, land "Scot's Improvement," Negro Mingo
and his wife Marria.
    To wife ELIZABETH SCOTT, slaves: Sambo, Hercules, Phillis and
Pegg.
    To son JAMES, dau HANNAH, wife of Edward Norris, dau SARAH,
wife of Thomas Wheeler, dau MARTHA, wife of Daniel Maccoma, dau
MARY SCOTT, grand-dau ELIZABETH SCOTT, dau of DANIEL SCOTT and
Hannah his wife, grand-son DANIEL SCOTT, son of JAMES SCOTT and
Ann his wife, grand-dau MARTHA SCOTT, dau of AQUILLA SCOTT and
Elizabeth his wife, dau MARY SCOTT, son DANIEL SCOTT.
Wit: Robert Makilivain, Samuel Durham, James Whittiker. 24. 81.

COALE, THOMAS, Baltimore Co. 25 Apr, 1745
 22 My, 1745
    To son WILLIAM COALE, 420 A. "Bonds Last Shift."
    To dau SARAH COALE, and in case she dies before age 21,
leaving no issue, then to my nephew, ACQUILA MASSEY.
    To nephew, JOHN COLLIER MASSEY and my dau SARAH, 10 slaves.

To son WILLIAM, dau SARAH, nephew AQUILA MASSEY, the still
with all its appurtenances.
To nephew JONATHAN COLLIER MASSEY, furniture.
I assign my bro-in-law SAMUEL RICHARDSON, ex. and guardian of my
child., with power to remove them into the county where he
resides.   24. 85 - 86

CROMICHEL, JOHN, St. Mary's Co.   12 Jan, 1744
                                                  11 Mar, 1744/5
     Child.: MARY, ELIZABETH, ANN CROMICHEL.
     Bros.: PHILIP MERRIL, LUKE MERRILL
     PRISCILLA CROMICHEL wife, extx.
Wit: Rich. Barnhouse, Chas. Smith   24. 87

READMAN, JOHN, St. Mary's Co.   4 Mar, 1745
                                                  8 Mar, 1745
     Child.: JAMES, JEREMIAH, JOHN, BENJAMIN, MARTHA, MARY LURTY,
ELIZABETH ADAMS, THOMAS, ELEANOR COX.
     To son JAMES, dwelg plantation and tract, "Small Hopes."
     To son Jeremiah, "Small Hopes," 50 A.
     REBECCA READMAN wife, extx.
Wit: Thomas Readman, Elizabeth Phips   24. 89

CHEVERELL, Clement, St. Mary's Co., planter.   14 Jan, 1744
                                                  29 Apr, 1745
     To son CLEMENT, personalty.
     To dau HANNAH.
     To grandson, WILLIAM OARE, cow, and to JOHN OARE 1st calf and
next calf to MARY OARE.
     Wife JANE.
Wit: John Daffon, Faith Daffon.   24. 90

PICKERL, JEREMIAH, St. Mary's Co.   28 Apr, 1745
                                                  6 May, 1745
     To JOHN HADACK, bequeath all belongings; hr. to estate.
     No relationship mentioned; ex.
Wit: Thos. Forrest, Francis Hutchins.   24. 91

NOTTINGHAM, STEPHEN, St. Mary's Co.   23 Apr, 1745
                                                  7 May, 1745
     Child.: ATHANATIUS, son, to be declared of age at 20, dwlg
plantation, "Nevet's(?) St. Anns."
          MARY, ANNE, MATHIAS.
     Athanatius Nottingham, ex.
Wit: Ignatius Greenwall, Mark Jarboe.   24. 92

BEAN, JOHN, St. Mary's Co.   26 Mar, 1745
                                                  20 May, 1745
     Child.: JOHN, BENJAMIN, JOSHUA, ROBERT, PHILIP, ELIZABETH,
FAITH.
     To son JOHN BEAN, JR., plantation where I live, being pt of
"Friends Congoneon," and "Beans Thurofare."
     To son BENJAMIN, rest of "Friends Congonean."
     MARY BEAN wife, extx.
Wit: Pat Forrest, Wm. C. Forrest, Anne Alstone.   24. 93

MATTENLY, JAMES, St. Mary's Co.   3 May, 1745
                                    28 May, 1745
   Child.: ANNE, ROBERT, PETER, JOHN, JAMES, THOMAS
   Land to sons James and Thomas.
   Bros.: Thomas Mattenly, Luke Mattenly, exs.
Wit: John Sheircliffe, Peter --?, Clement Hill.
                                    24. 95

HORSEY, JOHN, Somerset Co.   1 Feb, 1744
                                  29 Feb, 1744/5
   To son, WILLIAM HORSEY, plantation whereon I dwell.
   To dau BETTY, pt. of tract "Sarahs Joy."
   To Isaac Horsey, son of Revell Horsey, late of Somerset Co.,
give afsd. land .
   To wife and child., personal estate, my wife to have land
until WILLIAM comes to 21.
   Wife RACHEL and her brother, JOSHUA MITCHELL, exs.
Wit: Heber Whittingham, John Mathew, Margaret Harris. 24. 96

DASHIELL, MATTHIAS, Somerset Co.   23 Feb, 1744/5
                                    23 Mar, 1744
   To JOHN STUART, son of REBECCA STUART, 150 A. "Long Hill"
where his mother now lives.
   To Capt. Caprill King, 100 A. "Gordons Delight."
   To William STUART, my god-son, a slave, and in case WM. STUART
dies before of age, then his brothers and sisters have benefit of
sd. slave.
   To ANNE STUART, the child of REBECCA STUART, a slave, and if
she dies before of age, then to BETTY STUART.
   To THOMAS, JOSEPH and BENJAMIN DASHIELL, the sons of GEORGE
DASHIEL, 10 pounds.
   To Margaret Wale, 40 pounds, and at her decease, to return to
my sister REBECCA STUART'S child., and all accounts of sd.
Margaret Wale shall appear to be due to be paid her without the
exact forms of proving according to law.
   To Benjamin Handy, my houlster caps with silver fringe and the
pistols.
   To Robert Handy, a ring.
   To George Duglass, Lawer [lawyer?], a pt. of JAMES DASHIELS,
JR'S. estate who died in year, 1734, now in possession of Capt.
Caprill King, in the value of 20 or 30 pounds.
   To BETTY STUART, dau of REBECCA STUART, 1 slave, and if she
dies, same to go to her younger bro WILLIAM STUART.
   To sister, REBECCA STUART, 1 gold ring, marked "H.D."
   To bro WILLIAM DASHIEL, the remainder of my estate, and
appoint him as ex.
Wit: Day Scott, Thomas Winder, Clement Dashiel. 24. 97

BUSHAW, GILES, Somerset Co.   16 Mar, 1738
                                    23 Mar, 1744
   To Jasett Bushaw, tract "Hogs Down," dividing it from land of
Growes Bordam, and if sd. Jasett Bushaw dies without hrs., the
same
To his sisters, Anne Bushaw and Elenor Bushaw.

To Graves Bordman, 40 A. of sd. "Hogg Down," lying bet. 2 branches dividing it from the land of Thomas Goslin, dividing it from the land of Jasset Bushaw.
To Samuel Bordman, land.
To my cousin, SARAH BORDMAN, 20 s.
To Priscilla Goslin, dau of Elizabeth Goslin.
To Frances Goslin, a little skillett.
The balance of my estate to be divided bet. Elenor Goslin, Elizabeth Harron, SARAH BORDMAN, Wine Cornish and Sarah Bushaw and Mary Bushaw, Anne Bushaw and Elenor Bushaw, the daus of Andrew Bushaw and Thomas Bushaw and Sarah Hardy.
Jasett Bushaw, in case he gets the sd. land, must pay to Thos. Collier, 10 s.
To Peterkin that married Elizabeth Nutter, a slave, in lieu of what I was to give him.
Wit: Thos Collier, Matthew Goslin, Thomas Goslin. 24. 99

PRIOR, THOMAS, Somerset Co.   15 Dec, 1744
                                               19 Apr, 1745
    To wife ANNE, all my land and estate, at her death
To my child.
    To son SAMUEL PRIOR, land on easternmost side of a river dam.
Wit: I. C., Sinah Scott, John Cahoon.

CONNER, JOHN, Somerset Co.   4 Oct, 1743
                                               27 Apr, 1745
    To son, ELIJAH CONNER, my wife ELIZABETH CONNER, son WILLIAM CONNER, dau SARAH LONG, son JOHN CONNER, son LEVIN, dau MARY LANGFORD, my movable estate, to be divided amongst my 7 child.; after decease of my wife, ELIZABETH CONNER, viz: John, Levin, Mary, Elizabeth, Rachel, William and Elijah.
Wit: Bele Maddox, Purnell Outten, Wm. Rutter.
                                               24. 102 - 104

MARTHUESS, PATRICK, Somerset Co.   25 Feb, 1744
    To son WILLIAM MARTHUESS   14 May, 1745
    To dau MARY POLLETT or PULLETT.
Wit: Whittington King, James Collings.
The name of Patrick Martheus is spelled "Mathews" in the probate.
                                               24. 104 - 105

HANDY, JOHN, Somerset Co.   16 Dec, 1744
                                               28 May, 1745
    To son JOHN HANDY, my dwelling plantation, including land I bought of George Twiller, that was alienated me by Benjamin Venable, and in case he should die without issue, same to my son CHARLES HANDY, and all the land I bought of Francis Persons which was alienated to me by James Lawling on south side Naticoke River, called "New Scotland," 400 A., but in case of death of son JOHN, without issue, my son CHARLES, should possess what I leave to my son JOHN; that my son SAMUEL HANDY should have land at head of Nanticoke.
    To son LEVIN HANDY, tract called "Lott" containing 200 A.
    To dau ESTHER DASHIEL, 1 slave.
    To dau PRISCILLA HANDY, 1 slave.

To dau ANNE HANDY, 40 pounds money.
To dau MARY HANDY, 1 slave.
Mentions friends, Isaac Handy and George Dashiel, who are
to have charge of CHARLES, SAMUEL and LEVIN HANDY to be bound out
to such trade as they think fit.
My wife, JANE HANDY.
Abraham Dear mentioned.
My 7 child.: JOHN, PRISCILLA, ANNA, CHARLES, SAMUEL, LEVIN, and
MARY HANDY.
Wit: George Dashiell, Wm. Murray, Hester Anne Hodson.
24. 105 - 107

EDGAR, SAMUEL, Annapolis   14 Dec, 1744
                                            29 Apr, 1745
George Stewart, physician, of Annapolis, ex., who is to sell
the contents of trunk marked, "A.E.," and give money to Mrs.
Willilam Bowden, merchant, of Seething Lane, Tower Street,
London.
To Mrs. Roger's Children, I leave all my clothing.
Wit: Peter Buchanan and John Inck.   24. 108

BATTEE, FARDINANDO, Anne Arundel Co.   - - - - - -
                                            29 Apr, 1745
Wife ELIZABETH, son FARDO BATTEE, 2 sons, SAMUEL and JOHN,
lands I hold by a lease out of His Lordship's Mannor, of 100 A.
To wife, ELIZABETH, and 4 child., JOHN, ELIZABETH, DINAH,
FARDO BATTEE, 24 pounds each.
Wife and son SAMUEL, exs.
Wit: Thos. Spring, Thos. Sparrow, John Talbott.   24. 109 - 110

MILL, Thomas of Anne Arundel Co.   7 Apr, 1745
                                            29 Apr, 1745
To dau Mary, land, and if she dies without hrs. then to
Benjamin Gardner.
Benjamin Gardner, ex.
Wit: Philip Pettibone, John Gardner, Mary Gording.

MC CUBBIN, SAMUEL, Anne Arundel Co.   16 Mar, 1744/5
                                            12 Jun, 1745
To grand-son, SAMUEL LANE, son of Joseph Lane, and hrs. all
the money that lyes in England in sd. SAMUEL'S name, and desire
my sd. grand-son SAMUEL LANE, consult and take the advice of my
friends, Henry and Philip Darnall, in the management of their
affairs.
To my daus. ELIZABETH WEST and RACHEL LANE, they
To be the extxs.
Wit: James Deals, Thos. Vernon and Edward Carter   24. 111 - 113

KENT, ABSOLOM, Calvert Co.   21 Apr, 1745
                                            27 May, 1745
To wife ELIZABETH, slaves, and at her decease, to my son
ABSOLOM KENT.
To dau. ELEANOR, now wife of Thomas Byhen, and if she dies,
then to my brother, JOHN KENT'S child.
To son ABSOLOM KENT, 2 slaves.

4 of the best hogsheads of tobacco in my tobacco house to be shipped to Joseph Addams, merchant, in London.
    To dau. ELEANOR BYEN, 2 slaves.
Wit: Robert Yoe, Daniel Frazier and John Young.   24. 113 - 115

MEDWAY, GEORGE, Charles Co.   28 Mar, 1745
                                                     5 Apr, 1745
    God-child.: JAMES MONCASTER, Jr., son of Wm. Moncastor.
        GEORGE BURCH, son of John Burch.
        ANNA SMITH, dau. of Simon Smith.
        JOHN HATCH.
    Servant woman, MARGARET BICKNELL, be free.
    Bequests to JOHN GRIMES and EDWARD KELLOTT.
    John Hatch, Edw. Kellott, exs.
Wit: none listed.   24. 116

DAVIES, THOMAS, Charles Co.   8 Apr, 1745
                                                     7 May, 1745
    To Edward Perrie, 70 A. land.
    Edward Perrie, ex.
Wit: Rob. Davis, John Bird.   24. 116

STEWARD, JAMES, Charles Co.   24 Apr, 1745
                                                     8 May, 1745
    Henry Goodrich, son of Francis Goodrich.
    JOHN HANSON, JUN.
    John Hansen, ex.
Wit: Edm. Portens, William Hansson, Jr., Thomas Matthews, Jr.
                                                    24. 117

KELLY, BRIAN, Prince George's Co.   5 Jan, 1742
                                                     3 May, 1745
    To my eldest son JOSEPH KELLY, 100 A. "Dispute" and
"Advantage" at the discretion of William West and John West, to
see sd. land laid out for him.
    To my son BENJAMIN KELLY, after my wife's decease, my dwelling
plantation "Two Brothers."
    To son THOMAS KELLY, 100 A.
    Wife MARY KELLY to live and reside upon tract called "Two
Brothers."
    Wife, extx.
Wit: John West, James LaMar and William West.   24. 118

NEALL, ANN, widow of FRANCIS NEALL, Talbot Co., dec'd.
                                                    27 Apr, 1745
                                                    10 May, 1745
    To dau FORTON NEALL
    To my six child.: SAMUEL, SOLOMON, FORTEN, HANNAH, RACHEL and
JONATHAN NEALL.
    My friend John Goldsborough, and my son SAMUEL NEALL, exs.
Wit: Edward Neall, Henry Woods, Joseph Price, James Berry.
                                                    24. 120

WEST, LOTAN, Talbot Co.   21 May, 1745
                                                 14 Jun, 1745
    Wife, HANNAH WEST, son GEORGE, and son HENRY WEST, dau ANNE
RATHEL.
HANNAH, GEORGE, HENRY and ANNE, exs.
Wit: Cornelius Brady, Foster Armstsrong.
We hereby renounce the administration and executenship on our
pts. and behalves on the within written will, 14 June, 1745;
signed: GEORGE W. WEST, HENRY WEST, DAVID RATHEL and ANN RATHEL,
and I hereby make my election and will not stand by the will,
within, but fly to my third part of my deceased husband's estate;
signed: HANNAH WEST   24. 121

WILLSON, THOMAS, Talbot Co.   27 Apr, 1745
                                                 - - - - - -
    To bro. JAMES WILLSON, land in Dorchester Co. "Brotherly
Kindness."
    To bro. JOSEPH WILLSON, 30 pounds money.
    To bro. GEORGE WILLSON, 30 pounds of my personal estate.
    To cousin SARAH WILLSON, 25 pounds of my personal estate.
    To bro. WILLIAM WILSON, my dwelling plantation.
Wit: Michel Malony, Jr., Wm. Stuard, Aaron Parratt.
                                                 24. 123-125

REYNOLDS, EDWARD, Calvert Co.   1745
                                                 9 Jul, 1745
The following probate taken at the request of JOSEPH WILSON,
before his Hon. Commissary General, was ordered to be recorded in
the Book of Wills for this present year, 1745.
July 9, 1745, came James Weems, one of the subscribing witnesses
to the within will, on oath sd. that he saw testator EDWARD
REYNOLDS, sign and seal sd. will.
(This will is in Liber DD No. 2, Folio 488(?) or 694(?); the 488
being crossed out and 694 interlined).

YEWELL, CHRISTOPHER, Queen Anne's Co.
                                                 11 Mar, 1744/5
                                                 30 May, 1745
    To wife and child.: viz: son SOLOMON COOPER YEUELL, unto James
Frute (?) to be and remain with him, the sd. JAMES, until the sd.
Solomon Cooper [YEUELL] shall be age 21.
    Son CHRISTOPHER, and dau SARAH, I leave unto William
Fitzpatrick of Talbot Co., CHRISTOPHER to remain with Wm.
Fitzpatrick, until age 20 and SARAH until age 16.
    Son ESEAS, I leave unto care of my bro. SOLOMON YEUELL, until
age 21.
    Appoint my wife ABYAH (Abijah?) YEWELL, extx.
Wit: I. Loockerman, John Lewis, Soll. Wattkins.   24. 126

VANDERFORD, WILLIAM, Queen Anne's Co.   1745
                                                 24, June, 1745
    To sons JOHN VANDERFORD and JAMES VANDERFORD
    Wife REBECCA VANDERFORD
Wit: Charles Vanderford, William Vanderford, Jr. 24. 127 - 128

CHAPELL, JAMES, Calvert Co.   1745
                                           17 Jun, 1745
     To wife MARY CHAPPLE, the last son JAMES CHAPPLE, remaining
pt. of my estate, and if he die without issue, to fall to my bro.
CHARLES CHAPPLE, provided he be found within 2 years of my son's
decease, and if he be not found, then to Bradley Bowers.
     Friend, William Thornbury, and son JAMES, exs.
Wit: Thomas Gatwood, Benj. Scrivener.   24. 129

BAKER, JOHN, Calvert Co.   ----
                                            6 Jul, 1745
     To my child.: sons ISAAC, JOHN, NATHANIEL, and daus. PRISCILLA
ANNE and REBECCA, and their hrs., my estate after decease of my
wife., my son ISAAC.
Wit: Hen. Cowan.
This is to certify, July 5, 1745, that ISAAC BAKER, the eldest
son of JOHN BAKER, dec'd. does not intend to concern about
administering upon his father's estate. Signed: ISAAC BAKER, JR.
                                                       24. 130

RICHARDSON, BENJAMIN, Spring Street of the Parrish of St. Paul
Shadwell, in the county of Middlesex, mariner, New Chief Mate on
Board The William of London for Maryland, being in bodily health
and sound mind and memory and considering the perils and dangers
of the Seas and other uncertainties of this transitory life,
makes the following will:
                                           10 Feb, 1729
     MARY RICHARDSON, wife
     Interlined: William Williams at the Plough and Cherrytree at
Blackwall, Anne Williams his wife; Samuel Toye clerk of Madam
Crawley's works at Blackwall.
Wit: Wm. Legard, Pet. St. Elvoy, Henry Stevens.   24. 131

USLEY or USLER, WILLIAM, Kent Co.   10 Oct, 1744
                                           20 Apr, 1745
     To wife HANNAH USLEY, one-fourth pt. my estate, besides her
3rd.
     To child.: CATHERINE, MARY and JOHN, balance.
     As for my son WILLIAM USLEY, I desire he have no pt., only 1
s. sterl.
     Wife, extx.
Wit: Obadiah Fisher, Wm. Willshaw, Robert Wiltshare.
                                                       24. 133

CLAY, THOMAS, Chestertown Merchant.   Oct, 1744
                                           24 May, 1745
     To mother ANNE BOLTON, 1 slave.
     To bro. JOHN BOLTON,
     To my friend Thomas Ringold, Jr., of Eastern Neck, all the
volumes I have in Rapins (?), History of England.
     To wife MARY CLAY
Wit: Jno. Webb, James Anderson, Jno. McCracken.   24. 134

RILEY, NICHOLAS, KENT CO. 15 Apr, 1745
25 May, 1745
    To son NICHOLAS RILEY, JR., my land on Sassafras River.
    To son BENJAMIN, my dwelling plantation, after decease of wife, MARY, to my child.
    To 3 daus.: REBECCA, SARAH and ELIZABETH
    To son NICHOLAS, 500 A. lying in Pennsylvania called "Greenfield."
    To dau. ELIZABETH, 60 A. called "Pearces Rambles" in Kent Co., after decease of Thomas Richfoot; also give to my dau. ELIZABETH, 10 pounds money.
    To son HEZEKIAH, who is not capable of maintaining himself
    To John Riley, son of Isaac Riley, a horse.
Wit: Nicholas Smith, Benjamin Palmer, John Riley. 24. 135 - 136

PEARCE, GIDEON, JR., Kent Co. 1 Feb, 1744
25 May, 1745
    To wife BATRICE PEARCE
    To son WM. PEARCE,
    To son GIDEON PEARCE, lot of land in George [Georgetown?] Number One.
    To son THOMAS PEARCE, lot of land in Georgetown, Number 2.
    To dau. MARY PEARCE, 1 slave.
    To dau. BATRICE PEARCE, slaves.
    Wife, extx.
Wit: G. W. Forester, Lewis Williams, Wm. Pearce. 24. 138

DEW, ROBERT, Kent Co. 4 Jun, 1745
15 Jun, 1745
    To John Wallace, Scotchman, my friend, my brown mare.
    Mentions Samuel Norris; John Wallace's house, where some of his belongings were; Collins Ferguson's; some cattle at Wm. Smith's in Cecil Co. He had many cattle, mentions how they were branded.
    To John Cragg, 1 colt.
    To James Gray, the debt due him.
    Mentions Thomas Atkinson, to Wm. Hall, 1 mare; the debt from Wm. Johnson and debt of John Brown of Cecil Co.; account of Sutton Burgin.
    Ex., friend Collin Ferguson.
Wit: Thos. Cowper, Roger McCartey, James Wood. 24. 139

BOON, JAMES, Queen Anne's Co. 17 Apr, 1745
16 Jul, 1745
    To wife PHEBE
    To son WILLIAM BOON, plantation which I leased to Thomas Fisher, where he now lives.
    To son JACOB BOONE, plantation where I now live, after my wife's decease.
    To son THOMAS BOON, 3rd pt. of my lands, equally divided among the three.
    After my wife's 3rd is taken out, balance to my 4 child.: WILLIAM, JACOB, MARGARET and THOMAS.
    Wife extx.
Wit: Thos. Foster, Jacob Boon, Benjamin Boon. 24. 142

36

ROBERTSON, PATRICK, Queen Anne's Co.   ----
25 Jul, 1745

Wife JANE ROBERTSON
To sons PAT and ALEX ROBERTSON, the 4 tracts of land called
"Fully Barden" and "Fully Bardens Addition."
To grand-son, ROBERTSON STEVEN, to my dau. MARGARET, slaves.
To grand-son ROBERTSON STEVEN, tract "Hunting Tower"; if he
shd. die without hrs., but if ESOBEL STEVEN should have another
son, I leave to him and my dau ISABELL, if ISABELL shd. die
without male issue, leave to my grand-dau. CHRISTIAN STEVEN, the
whole north side of the horepond branch.
Mentions: my dau MARGET, and my grand-son ROBERTSON STEVEN
To my dau CHALMER, tract "Blair Casle."
Sons Pat and Alex Robertson, exs.
Wit: Henry Burt, John Swift and Richard Swift.   24. 143 - 145

RICKETTS, ELIZABETH, Kent Co.   15 Mar 1742/3
5 Aug, 1745

To dau ELIZABETH COURSEY, 500 A. "Bateman Content" as appears
by patent, provided she makes 200 A. to my son JOSEPH RICKETTS.
To dau ELIZABETH COURSEY, 25 pounds money.
Mentions: my grand-dau. ELIZABETH COURSEY, and if she die
before of age, to fall to my grand-dau. BLANCH COURSEY.
Sons: Henry Coursey, Joseph Ricketts, exs.
Wit: David Stanwood, Samuel Watters, Abel Bell.   24. 146

HAYWARD, THOMAS, Dorchester Co.   10 Jan, 1744/5
22 Apr, 1745

To wife MARGARET HAYWARD, land called "Hopewell."
Wife extx.
Wit: Wm. Wheatly, Thomas Russell, Henry Wall.   24. 147

STEVENS/STEPHENS, WILLIAM, Dorchester Co.   13 Dec, 1745
4 May, 1745

To son EDWARD STEVENS, my right and property in a bond of
writing obligatory past by John Cooks, dec'd.
To bro. EDWARD STEPHENS, dec'd., for the annual payment of 600
pounds of tobacco during the life of sd. William Stevens.
To 2 daus. BETTY STEPHENS and NANCE STEPHENS, all the land I
now live on called "Laybrook." To them, the sd. BETTY and NANCE
STEPHENS, and their hrs., to be equally divided bet. them when
dau. NANCE arrives to age 16.
To son EDWARD, my 3 slaves.
To dau. BETTY STEVENS, dau NANCE STEVENS, slaves.
Friend, John Eccleston, and son, Edward, exs.
Wit: John Trippe, James Hooper, Benj. Wheeland, Henry Hooper.
Codicil, which reads about the same, dated 28 May, 1744.
Wit: John Trippe, James Hooper, Thos. Williams. Probated 4 May,
1745   24. 148 - 150

RUMBLY, JOHN, Dorchester Co.   16 Feb, 1744/5
14 May, 1745

To son JOHN RUMBLY, the 2nd, my gold ring.
To wife PRISCILLA RUMBLY, my dwelling plantation.

Appoint wife extx.
Wit: David Rogers, Thomas Walter, Hugh Cannon.   24. 151 - 152

HARPER, WILLIAM,   11 Feb, 1744/5
                                             24 May, 1745
    To son WILLIAM HARPER, tract called, "Harper's Adventure."
    To son BEAUCHAMP HARPER, the other half of the Mill Tract,
with a tract called "Harper's Luck."
    Wife MARGARET HARPER.
Wit: Solomon Turpin, John Anderton, Bartholomew Twyford.
                                                 24. 152

MERPHY or MORPHY, DANIEL   8 Apr, 1745
                                             2 Jun, 1745
    Sister ELLIN MORPHEY
    Father-in-law SAMUEL COBAN, ex.
Wit: Zachariah Nichols, John Nicolls.   24. 153 - 154

ADAMS, WILLIAM, Dorchester Co., planter   26 Mar, 1745
                                             12 Jun, 1745
    To eldest son EZEKIEL ADDAMS, tract of land called "The
Folley," whereon THOMAS ADDAMS now lives, of 100 A.
    To 2nd son _____ ADDAMS, my dwelling plantation.
    My wife MARY, and my bro. THOMAS ADDAMS, exs.
    I leave my bro. THOMAS, Trustee to take care of my 2 sons if
their mother should remarry.
Wit: Thomas Clifton, Jacob Gray, Anne Makemorry.
A copy of Wm. Addams' Day Book of a list of debts due to him, 25
Mar, 1745, is copied at length and several names are here shown.
                                                 24. 154

RUMBLY, JOHN, Dorchester Co.   27 Feb, 1744
                                             12 Jun, 1745
    To wife ANNE, dau. NANCY, dau. MARY, dau. BETTY, son JACOB,
the plantation whereon I now live; son EDGAR
Wit: Wm. Addams, John Pritchett Fisher, James Vaulx.
                                                 24. 157

PATTISON, ST. LEEGAR, James Island, Dorchester Co.
                                             8 Jan, 1744/5
                                             14 Jun, 1745
    To eldest dau. ELIZABETH DAVISON, that tract of land I now
live on called "Pattison's Folly," of 130 A. lying on James
Island upon the Bay side in Dorchester Co.
    Wife MARY PATTISON; 3 child.: daus. ELIZABETH PATTISON,
PENELOPE PATTISON, MARY PATTISON
    Appoint wife MARY PATTISON and her father, JOHN PATTISON, exs.
Wit: Peter Bell, Wm. Abbot, Matthew Bebbe.   24. 158

MAC DANIEL, WILLIAM, Dorchester Co.   16 Apr, 1745
                                             14 Jul, 1745
Jane Dunawan and James Hayes make oath that were sent for by
WILLIAM MAC DANIEL, who sd. that his will was that his 2 daus.
ELINOR and ELIZABETH MAC DANIEL should have cattle.
Wit: James Hayes and James Dunawan.   24. 160

CREEK, JOHN, Dorchester Co.   30 Jan, 1741/2
                                 24 Jul, 1745

    To son JOHN, my carpenter's tools.
    To dau. ANNE, furniture.
    To dau. SARAH, dau. and dau. REBECCA HUST.
    If JOHN die without hrs., then to his sister ANNE.
    Wife SARAH CREEK, extx.
Wit: Wm.. Langral, Mary Dicks, Anne Langrall.
                                   24. 161

ROYALL, THOMAS, Dorchester Co.   24 Jun, 1745
                                  2 Aug, 1745

    To son THOMAS ROYALL, land, "Cumberland."
    To son ELIJAH ROYALL, my dwelling plantation.
    To son SAMUEL ROYALL, he to secure 50 A. for his bro. THOMAS
ROYALL.
    Wife MARY ROYALL, extx.
Wit: James and Thomas Brown, Phillip Dell.   24. 162

SLYE, MARY, St. Mary's Co.   10 Dec, 1744
                                  7 May, 1744

    To Mrs. Livers.
    To dau Mary Lancaster.
    To dau Henrietta Plowden, negroes.
    To dau Anne Nealle.
    To grandau Mary Nealle, Jr., cattle.
    To Mary Miles.
    To son George Sly, ext., rest of estate.
Wit: Philip Key, Anne Carroll.   24. 163

WARREN, THOMAS, St. Mary's Co.   13 Mar, 1744/5
                                 4 Jun, 1744/5

    Child.: MARY KITTING, SUSANNA STRONG, MONICA HILL, GEORGE.
    Grand-child.: heirs of ELIZABETH MATTINGLY, dec'd.
    To MARY KITTING, dau., 1 heifer, provided her husband delivers
my young horse to GEORGE WARREN.
    George Warren, ex.
Wit: Thos. Spalding, Leonard Mattingly, Edward Mattingly.
                                     24. 164

GREEN, JOHN, St. Mary's Co.   11 May, 1744
                                    22 Jul, 1745

    Child.: JOSEPH, THOMAS, MOSES.
    Wife (name not given), extx.
Wit: John Conally, John Thomas, Wm. Jones.   24. 165

O'BRYAN, TERRENCE, Cecil Co.   30 Mar, 1745
                                    11 May, 1745

    That son JOHN, son JAMES
    To child., excluding grand-child., and recommend that my
child. remain with their mother as long as they are not married.
Wit: Joshua George, Edward Mears or Edward Means. 24. 166

HODSHON, SOLOMON, Cecil Co.   22 May, 1745
                                           30 May, 1745
   Wife GRACE
   Young. dau. ANNE
   My late Master, Mr. Thomas Colvil, to have guardianship of sd.
dau.
Wit: Thos. Stewart and Peter Lawson.   24. 167

JAMES, HOWELL, Cecil Co., millwright   22 Nov, 1743
                                            25 Jun, 1745
   Wife SARAH
   4 daus.: ANNE, HANNAH, SARAH and PRISCILLA
   Son WILLIAM JAMES, but if he die, then to son BENJAMIN, and if
he die, then to return to son JOHN JAMES.
Wit: Lambert Willmer, Daniel Nowland, John Hutchison.
                                            24. 168 - 172

RYLAND, JOHN, SR., Cecil Co.   20 Mar, 1739/40
                                            22 Jul, 1745
   To wife MARY, my dwelling house, the one-half of my land in
Kent Co.
   To son THOMAS RYLAND, remaining lands called "Mulberry Mould"
and "Mullberry Dock."
   To dau MARY PENINGTON, after death of my wife, chest of
drawers and etc.
   To Elizabeth Severson, wife of Thomas Saverson, some cattle.
   Son JOHN RYLAND, my sons-in-law RICHARD and BARTLET SMITH and my
wife, exs.
Wit: James King, Charles Leack, John Lodowick Aklehart.
                                            24. 172-174

KENNET, MARTIN, Worcester Co.   7 Dec, 1744
                                            1 Apr, 1745
   To son LABEN KENNET, 125 A., the plantation whereon I now
live.
   To son MARTIN KENNETT, "Cornhill."
   To dau. RHODIAH KENNETT, 75 A.
   Son LABEN KENNET, dau RHODYAH, 2 cows.
   Dau. AREADAH KENNETT
   That Samuel Hopkins and David Johnson be Trustees to my will.
   Wife Bridget Kennett, extx.
Wit: John Turville, Nathan Brittingham, Samuel Hopkins.
                                            24. 174

HEATHER, EPHRAIM, SR., Worcester Co.   7 Oct, 1743
                                            4 Apr, 1745
   To son EPHRAIM HEATHER, plantation whereon I now live, the
same belonging and the right of the lease from Parker Selby.
   To dau. MARTHA HEATHER, cattle.
   Remainder to my child.: Viz: EPHRAIM, ANNE, RACHEL, MARTHA,
MARY and RUTH, and in case any of my daus. that are married shd.
die, then their child. shd. have their pt.
Wit: Richard Blizard, Henry H. Smock, Ed. Bound.
                                            24. 176

ALLEN, FRANCIS, Worcester Co.   22 May, 1744
                                                 17 May, 1745
    That Mr. John Landon be satisfied the debt due by my dec'd.
son JOHN.
    To son FRANCIS, the use of the plantation and tract he now
lives upon, being same tract I bought of Walter Lane.
    To son WILLIAM, son MOSES, son JOSEPH, wife MARY, (ELEANOR,
MARY and ELIZABETH, also his child.), my land in Nasswattux.
    Mentions: plantation belonging to Abraham Gibbs and Angelo
Atkinson.
    My friend, Thomas Hayward, my son-in-law Jacob Hindman, my
wife, exs.
Wit: John Dennis, Cornelius Dickeson, George Benson.
                                                    24. 178

TAYLOR, JOSEPH, Worcester, gentleman.   15 Dec, 1744
                                                 7 Jun, 1745
    To my bro. JAMES TAYLOR, 200 A, "West Ridge," in Accomack Co.,
VA.
    To bro. JOHN TAYLOR, 20 pounds, cash, which is in the care of
John Cillum.
    To bro. SAMUEL TAYLOR, 100 A. out of tract "West Ridge" in
Accomack Co. and 100 A. in Somerset Co., MD.
    To bro. MATTHIAS TAYLOR, a gun at Henry Graham's and 30 s. in
Samuel Malson's care and corn in John Bufinton's hands
    To Mary Greane (?), 6 s. and corn in Wm. Brown's hands.
    To Henry Graham, for taking care of me in my illness, the
horse which is in Benj. Reccord's care, and the saddle in Samuel
Melson's care.
Wit: Andrew Sanders, Lame (Lans?) James, Henry Graham.
                                                    24. 180

DISHAROON, LEWIS, Worcester Co.   8 Apr, 1745
                                                  7 Jun, 1745
    To son, LEAVING DISHAROON, 100 A. "Holder's (Holsom?) Folley,"
about 6 miles from the fork of Wicomico River.
    To grand-dau., MARY DISHAROON, 1 horse.
    To son LEAVING DISHAROON, personal estate.
    To grand-dau. JANE DISHAROON, dau. of JOHN DISHAROON, stock.
    To 3 grand-daus.: MARGARET, ELIZABETH and ELLANOR DISHAROON,
daus. of JOHN DISHAROON, stock.
    Appoint son LEAVING DISHAROON, ex.
Wit: Benj. Handy, Rencher Robards and Archibald Smith.
                                                    24. 182

SEDWICK, BENJAMIN, Calvert Co., merchant.   29 Dec, 1743
                                                  5 Aug, 1745
    To son BENJAMIN (JR), "Bullen's Right," lately purchased of
Robert Jarman and John Jarman, 375 A.
    Mentions: Wm. Whittington's land; wife BETTY, unborn child,
    daus., MARY, BETTY and ANNE SEDWICK.
    Wife, extx.
Wit: Ellis Slater, Chaney Sedwick, Ja White.   24. 183 - 186

BLACKSTONE, THOMAS CAPT.   16 May, 1741
                                           21 May, 1741
  Samuel Spurrier, Ex.
  Appoint bro-in-law Richard Blackstone of London, mariner, my
true attorney to receive of David Lawson of Patapsico in
Maryland, merchant, what goods and etc. belonging to me. 1743.
Wit: Samuel Gray, Henry Seymour, Wm. Holloway, published in
London.
  In the name of God Amen, I THOMAS BLACKSTONE of the Parrish of
St. John in Southwork in the county of Surrey, mariner:
  To wife MARY BLACKSTONE, some furniture.
  To bro. RICHARD BLACKSTONE, my messuage or tennement and 2 A.
of land or thereabouts lying at Maryland in America, and to him
mall that my sloop or vessell called "The Dolphin" Burthen about
20 tons now lying in Maryland.
  To bro-in-law HUGH COLEMAN, my cloth coat and my slave or
negro servant, Thos. Lawson, and my goods and effects at Maryland
houses and etc. shall be sold and the money to go to my wife,
MARY, and my honored mother, MARY COLEMAN.
  To bro-in -law SAMUEL SPURRIER, of sd. Parish of St. John in
Southwark, Victualler, and my sister, SUSANNA DARBY, equally
divided bet. them, 4 pts.
  Appoint bro-in-law, SAMUEL SPURRIER, ex.
Wit: Wm. Sanders, Thomas Poultney, Abraham Harman.

John by Divine, Providence, Archbishop of Canterbury, Private of
all England and metropolitan, do by thee presents make known to
all men, that on the 21st day of May, 1741 at London before the
Worshipfull, Edward Kinaston, Doctor of Laws, Surrogate of the
Right Worshipful, John Bettesworth, Dr. of Laws, Keeper or
Commissary of our Prerogative Court of Canterbury, lawfully
constitute the last will of THOMAS BLACKSTONE, late of the
Parrish of St. John, Southwark in the county of Surry, dec'd, was
proved and etc.
Wit or Deputy Registers: Wm. Legard or Segard (?), Pat. St. Eloy,
Hen. Stevens.   24. 186 - 189

WEST, BENJAMIN, Prince George's Co.   9 Nov, 1744
                                            27 Jun, 1745
  To son JOSEPH WEST, 170 A.
  To dau. SARAH WEST, my dwelling plantation.
  My mother to have a living out of my estate.
  Bro. JOHN WEST, ex.
Wit: Nath. Wickham, Jr., James Derry, Kennedy Farrell.
                                            24. 190 - 191

ELLIS, OWEN, Prince George's Co.   4 Sep,1743
                                            14 Aug, 1745
  Wife MARY ELLIS
  Estate to be divided bet. my 6 child: son JOHN ELLIS, son
JOHNATHAN ELLIS, son OWEN ELLIS, JR., dau. ELIZABETH ELLIS, dau.
MARY ELLIS, dau. JANE ELLIS.
  Friends, Henry Truman and John Lawson, exs.
Wit: John Johnson, Samuel Warren, John Gates.   24. 191 - 195

SANTEE, NATHANIEL, Talbot Co.   25 Aug, 1742
                                                 26 Jul, 1745
    To son CHRISTOPHER SANTEE, land, "Adventure."
    To son JAMES SANTEE, tract, "The Golden Grove," lying nigh Wey
Bridge in Queen Anne's Co., 96 A.
    Wife SARAH SANTEE.
    To son JOSEPH SANTEE, slaves.
    Wife SARAH and friend Alexander Jordan, exs.
Wit: Richard Barrow, Thomas Cooper, Priscilla Howard.
                                                 24. 195 - 196

POWELL, JOHN, Anne Arundel Co., near Herring Bay 28 May, 1745
                                                  8 Jul, 1745
    To dau. ELIZABETH POWELL, land that my bro. WILLIAM POWELL,
possesses, and the land where I now live, and the plantation I
rent to James Trott, 200 A., known by name, "Gory Banks."
    Mentioned: wife, but not her name.
Wit: James Trott, Wm. Stone, Abraham Tangueray (?).
                                                 24. 197

PIPER, CHRISTOPHER, Somerset Co.   24 Mar, 1744
                                                 28 May, 1745
    To son CHRISTOPHER PIPER, JR., my dwelling plantation.
    To son MATTHEW, plantation I bought of William Mears (?),
lying at head of Quantico Creek.
    To dau. ANNE PIPER, slave.
    To dau. MARY PIPER, slave.
    Dau. SARAH GILES
    Wife RACHEL PIPER
    Child.: CHRISTOPHER, MATHEW, ANNE, MARY and ELEANOR.
    Friends, Henry Lowes and Hewit Nutter, Trustees.
Wit: John Gosle, Robert Hard, Joanna W. Goslee.
                                                 24. 198 - 199

WINDER, THOMAS, Parish of Stepney, Somerset Co.
                                                 9 Mar, 1744/5
                                                 28 May, 1745
    To dau. MARY, and my unborn child, my plantation.
    Wife ELEANOR.
    Nephew WINDER JACOBS
Wit: Chrisr. D. Jackson, Joseph Venables, David Polk.
May 28, 1745, then came ELENOR WINDER, widow of THOMAS WINDER,
and made her election.   24. 199 - 200

RECORDS, JOHN, Somerset Co.   29 Jan, 1744/5
                                                 21 Jun, 1745
    To son THOMAS RECORDS, my dwelling plantation, 100 A., which I
bought of Wm. Elgin and 50 A., "Whetstone," given to me by Philip
Carter adjoining sd. plantation and 100 A. called "Partners
Choice," which I have Philip Records' bond for making over the
same to him.
    To son THOMAS RECORDS, 10 pounds money.
    To son PHILIP, 50 A., pt. of "Shippard's Crook."
    To son JOHN RECORDS, 10 A.
    To son JOSEPH RECORDS, 20 A.

To son PHILIP RECORDS, 1 s.
To dau. MARY RECORDS, and dau. ELIZABETH CANNON, 1 s. sterl.
To son SAMUEL RECORDS, 1 s.
TO my 4 child.: SUSANNA BOUNDS, JAMES, THOMAS and MARY
RECORDS, remainder of estate.
Thomas Records, ex.
Wit: Thomas Cary, Thomas Jackson, Wm. Augston, Ambrose Riggen.
24. 201 - 202

GOSLEE, JAMES, Kent Co. *[Somerset Co.]   17 May, 1745
                                           21 Aug, 1745
    To wife, MARY GOSLEE, son JAMES GOSLEE, son LEVIN GOSLEE, 85
A.
    To daus.: SARAH, SUSANNA and ELIZABETH GOSLEE, my personal
estate.
Wit: Joshua Jackson, Wilson Ryder and James Astin.
* Recorded in error at the Prerogative Court. It should read
Somerset Co.   24. 202

GUNBY, JOHN, Somerset Co.   24 Oct, 1744
                                           29 Aug, 1745
    To JAMES GUNBY, my tract, "Kirk's Purchase" and "Gunby's
Venture."
    To wife SARAH GUNBY, 1/3 of my personal estate.
    To son KIRK GUNBY, 1 s. sterl.
    To dau. PRISCILLA GUNBY, 1 s. sterl.
    To dau. GRASIANNAH LANE, same.
    To dau. ARDREY ADAMS, same.
    To SUSANNA TAYLOR, same.
    To grand-son, JAMES GUNBY, and my dau. SARAH GUNBY, and my
dau. RACHEL GUNBY, remaining pt. of estate.
    Wife and James Gunby, exs.
Wit: Chas. West, John Horsey, Thos. Bell and Michael Roach.
                                           24. 204

TIBBELS, JOHN, of St. Michaels Parrish, Talbot Co.
                                           22 May, 1745
                                           23 Aug, 1745
    Wife ANNE, son THOMAS, son JOHN, daus.: MARY and ANNE.
    Wife extx.
Wit: Thomas Winchester, Sarah Wise, Robert Newcom
                                           24. 205 - 206

PORTER, PHILEMON, Talbot Co.   13 Sep, 1745
                                           11 Jul, 1745
    To wife ELIZABETH PORTER, 30 pounds money.
    To dau. RACHEL PORTER, slaves.
    Young. dau. LUCEY PORTER
    Friend, John Blake, and my wife, exs.
Wit: Wm. Roberts, John Craddock, Robert Willson.   24. 206

MACKDANIEL, DANIEL, Charles Co.   25 May, 1745
                                           13 Aug, 1745
    Child.: DANIEL, THOMAS, WILLIAM, ESTER.
    CATRON RYLE, cousin.

Wife ANNE MACKDANIEL, extx.
Wit: Thos. Freeman, John Moore.   24. 207

BURNS, MICHAEL, St. Mary's Co.   29 Apr, 1745
    1 May, 1745
Dau. MARY BURNS.
Will not written, but declared verbally in presence of Solomon
Jones and Robert Holton, who made oath to same.
    24. 210

JOHNSON, JOHN, St. Mary's Co.   14 Jan, 1744
    2 Apr, 1745
  Child.: PETER, THOMAS, JOHN, LEONARD, SUSANNA
Wife (name not mentioned), and Peter Johnson, exs.
Wit: John Temple, Mary Temple, John Cook.   24. 210

WATERS (WAYTERS), THOMAS, St. Mary's Co.   12 Mar, 1744/5
    28 May, 1745
  Child.: MARY WALLER(?), PENELOPE, SEWELL, THOMAS, ELIJAH,
JOSEPH.
Elijah Waters, ex.
Wit: William Tilor, Roger Copsey.   24. 211

BUSSEY, HEZEKIAH, St. Mary's Co.   30 Jun, 1745
    26 Jul, 1745
Land in Prince George's County to be sold to discharge debts.

Rachel Bussey wife, extx.
Wit: Hugh Hopewell, Jr., Robt. Greves, Henry Carey.   24. 213

GIBSON, JOHN, St. Mary's Co.   8 Apr, 1745
    6 Aug, 1745
  Child.: SUSANNA, ELIZABETH, JOSHUA, WILLIAM, MATHEW, JEREMIAH,
JOHN.
Alice Gibson wife, and William Gibson son, exs.
Wit: John Bond, James Dunbar.   24. 214

BOULT, THOMAS, St. Mary's Co.   13 Jun, 1745
    8 Aug, 1745
ELIZABETH BOULT wife.
Child.: JOHN, THOMAS, ANNE, KENELIN, SUSANNA HOBB, ANN.
Grand-child.: JOSHUA WATTS, KENELEN BOULT WATTS, ELIZABETH
BOULT, dau. of THOMAS.
Kenelin Boult, Susanna Hobb, Anna Boult, exs.
Wit: David Bennett, Wm. Phippard (Hippard?), William Ball.
    24. 215

AUSTIN, HENRY, Calvert Co.   18 Jan, 1743
    31 Aug, 1745
To son SAMUEL AUSTIN, half of my estate.
To HENRY and ELINOR AUSTIN, son and dau. of HENRY AUSTIN,
dec'd, the other half, but if either die before of age, then
their pt. to HENRY AUSTIN, son of SAMUEL AUSTIN.
To wife JANE AUSTIN, slaves, and at her decease, sd. slaves to
ELIZABETH, the dau. of SAMUEL AUSTIN.

To MARY, the dau. of SAMUEL AUSTIN, slaves.
To Elizabeth Lyle, dau. of William Lyle, 2 ewes.
To grand-son HENRY AUSTIN, son of HENRY AUSTIN, slaves.
To grand-dau. ELINOR, slaves.
Wife and son, SAMUEL AUSTIN, exs.
Wit: Wm. and Elinor Lyles. 24. 209

GASSAWAY, THOMAS, Anne Arundel Co. 25 Mar, 1745
28 Sep, 1745
Wife SARAH, extx.
Wit: Thos. Sappington, Anthony Smith, John Watkins.
24. 216

STILL, GEORGE, Kent Co. 17 Mar, 1744
26 Oct, 1745
To GEORGE TILLARD, eldest son of Edward Tillard and Elizabeth
Tillard his wife, 50 A. next adjoining his own land, which he had
by deed of gift from William Thomas, and on the north pt. of mine
unto sd. GEO. TILLARD.
To EDWARD TILLARD and ELIZABETH TILLARD his wife, 50 A. next
adjoining his own land, which he had by deed of gift from William
Thomas, and on the north pt. of mine unto sd. GEO. TILLARD.
To EDWARD TILLARD and ELIZABETH his wife, remaining pt. of my
lands in Kent Co.
Then my will is to JOHN TILLARD, 2nd son of EDWARD TILLARD and
ELIZABETH his wife.
Wit: Geo. Denning, Jr., Charles Breward, Nichs. Smith.
24. 218

STAPLES, HENRY, Kent Co. 3 Oct, 1686
1 Mar, 1686
To JOSIAS JACKSON and DAVID DAVISON, 200 A. "Killy Longfort"
on Langfords Bay.
That the Indian woman servant, named JOAN, at the expiration
of 15 years, be a free woman, and she be paid 800 pounds
tobacco.
To SIMON WILMER, and his wife REBECCA
To WIFE ANNE STAPLES
Wit: Joseph Lambert, Elizabeth Kellor, Humphry Jones.
Probated before Judge for Probate of Wills and granting Admr.
that HENRY STAPLES, late of Kent Co., dec'd., was at St. Mary's
in common form proved.
Wit to probate: Henry Darnall and Clement Hill. 24. 219

TAYLOR, JOHN, Baltimore Co. 19 Mar, 1745
20 Apr, 1745
To son CHARLES TAYLOR, tract "Chexens Purchase," where his
uncle George Simmons did live being one-half of what I hold.
To son JOHN, the other half.
To son THOMAS, tract bought of Wm. Deal, and tract "Taylor's
Good Luck."
To dau. ELIZABETH, slave, the land I bought of Joseph Ellidge,
desire to be sold.
To dau. HANNAH
Wife, extx.

46

Wit: Richard Robinson, Thomas Bond, Jr., Daniel Dunning.
24. 221

GRIFFITH, SAMUEL, SR., Baltimore Co.   14 Mar, 1744
                                              24 Jun, 1745
   To eldest son LUKE GRIFFITH, tracts: "Refuse," "Abbet's
Forrest," "Williamson's Hope."
   To daus.: MARY GRIFFITH, ELIZABETH and SARAH
   To son SAMUEL GRIFFITH, my now dwelling plantation.
   To wife MARY, that my lands in Calvert Co. and Anne Arundel
Co., be sold and piece of land in Baltimore Co., head of
Gunpowder River, "Polecat Neck," be sold; balance to be divided
bet. my 7 child., at decease of their mother.
   Wife and friend, SOLOMON HILLEN, exs.
Wit: John Matthews, James Phillips, Francis Holland
                                              24. 222

HOWARD, EDMOND, Baltimore Co.   19 Apr, 1745
                                              24 Jun, 1745
   To RUTH HOWARD, my dwelling plantation "Howard's Fancy"; at
her decease, to my son JOSHUA HOWARD.
   To dau. RUHANNAH HOWARD, upper pt. of tract "The Reserve."
   To son CHARLES HOWARD, 100 A., pt. of tract "Cornelius and
Mary's Lott."
   To dau. REBECCA HOWARD, 100 A., the lower pt. of "Reserve."
   To son JOSHUA HOWARD, 100 A. pt. of "HOWARD'S FANCY."
   To dau. MARY HOWARD, slaves.
   To dau. JOHANNAH HOWARD, stock and slaves.
   Wife, RUTH HOWARD, extx.
Wit: Thos. Norris, Step. Heart Owings, Lewis Jesse (?).
                                              24. 223 - 225

WALLACE, RICHARD, Somerset Co.   15 Feb, 1744
                                              14 Oct, 1745
   To wife GRACE WALLACE, land lying bet. Crab Creek and Dam
Quarters Creek,, during life.
   To daus. MARY WALLACE and MARGARET WALLACE
   Son JAMES WALLACE, pay to his bro. RICHARD WALLACE, 10 pounds
sterl.
   To son THOMAS WALLACE, 150 A. which lyeth in the forrest of
Wikcomoco River, Somerset Co.
   To son MATTHEW WALLACE, my land on S. W. side Crabb Creek.
   Child.: JOHN WALLACE, RICHARD WALLACE, THOMAS WALLACE,
ELIZABETH LYNN, JAMES WALLACE, DAVID WALLACE.
   To grand-son JOHN WALLACE, son of OLIVER WALLACE, 1 s. sterl.
Wit: Thomas and Francis White.   24. 225

PARKER, TABITHA, Worcester Co.   12 Aug, 1745
                                               4 Oct, 1745
   To son GEORGE PARKER, slaves.
   To son PHILIP PARKER, slaves.
   To son CHARLES PARKER, slaves.
   To grand-dau. TABITHA PARKER, dau. of my son SAMUEL PARKER,
slaves.
   To dau. SARAH DENNIS, furniture.

To dau. ELINOR DENNIS, large chest.
To afsd. 2 daus., 3 pewter dishes and etc.
To grand-son JOHN TURNER, slaves.
To grand-son CHARLES PARKER, son of JOHN PARKER, cattle.
To daus.: TABITHA NICHOLAS, ELINOR DENNIS and SARAH DENNIS
Son GEORGE PARKER ex.
Wit: Elizabeth Truit, Rachel Nicholas, Isaac Norris.
                                                24. 227

ASKIN, VINCENT, Charles Co.   11 Jan, 1745
                                      22 Oct, 1745
    JOHN, REBECCA, SARAH, ELIZABETH, MARY, and ORDARY ASKIN,
child. of GEORGE ASKIN, but relationship of GEORGE is not
mentioned.
    Sister SARAH ASKIN.
    Mulatta Man called JOHN DOVE, his freedom.
    James Middleton, Ignatius Gardiner, exs.
Wit: Francis Bryan, James Kuch, Joseph Glaze.   24. 229

LEWIS, GEORGE, Charles Co.   - - - - - -
                                      4 Nov, 1745
    ELIZABETH SHERWIN, MARY HUNTER, daus. of Johnathan Hunter,
both living in Liverpool, county of Lancashire.
    JOHN COURTS and wife.
    (Does not mention relationship of any of above.)
    John Courts, ex.
Wit: Jos. Wilson, Thos. Howard.   24. 230

CRAXSON, JOHN, Charles Co.   16 Apr, 1744
                                      19 Nov, 1745
    To cousin JOHN BURGESS, son of SAMUEL BURGESS and ELIZABETH,
his wife, my slave.
    To cousin SUSANNA HAISLIP, wife of Henry Haislip
    Mentions: JOHN, son of Samuel Burgess; to cousin JOHN BURGESS
and THOMAS BURGESS, his bro.
    SAMUEL BURGESS ex.
Wit: James Ross, John Johns, John Stephenson.   24. 231

WARREN, SAMUEL, Prince George's Co.   25 Sep, 1742
                                      27 Aug, 1743
    To wife ROSE, my plantation.
    To son SAMUEL, at decease of his mother, my plantation.
    My dau., ELIZABETH.
Wit: Jonathan Ellis, John Johnson, Susanna Johnson.
                                                24. 232

ORCHARD, JOHN, Prince George's Co.   1 Aug, 1745
                                      - - - - -
    To my 2 sons-in-law, JOSEPH RYON and NATHANIEL RYON, my
personal estate.
    JOSEPH RYON ex.
Wit: Virlinda Nash.   24. 234

BEUSEY, SARAH, Prince George's Co.　　　25 Aug, 1745
　　　　　　　　　　　　　　　　　　　　15 Oct, 1745
　　To son EDWARD BEUSEY, slaves.
　　To son SAMUEL BEUSEY,
　　Mentions: sons-in-law, JOSEPH RICHARDSON and GRIFFITH DAVIS,
and his dau., ANNE DAVIS.
　　To grand-dau. MARY RAY, slaves.
　　Son JOHN BEUSEY ex.
Wit: Henry Smith, Daniel Beusey, James Ray.　　　24. 234 - 235

DALEY, JOHN, SR., Queen Anne's Co.　　　24 Jul, 1743
　　　　　　　　　　　　　　　　　　　　4 Oct, 1744
　　To son JOHN DALEY; my son WILLIAM DALEY, my dau. KATHERINE
KIERAN, grand-son JOHN KIERAN, son of dau. KATHERINE, son RICHARD
DALEY, my wife ANNISTICO DALEY.
　　To 2 sons JAMES and RICHARD DALEY, cattle, slaves and money.
　　Son JAMES ex.
Wit: Sarah Sweatnam, Joseph Sweatnam, David Lindsey.
　　　　　　　　　　　　　　　　　　　　　　　　24. 235

DAVIS, THOMAS of St. Paul's Parish, Queen Anne's Co.
　　　　　　　　　　　　　　　　　　　　31 Jul, 1745
　　　　　　　　　　　　　　　　　　　　17 ---, 1745
　　To son JOHN DAVIS, all plantation and land whereon I live,
which lies bet. my land and Mathias Dockery; at his decease, to
my dau. SARAH MOORE, and if they die without issue, to my nephew
THOMAS DAVIS, son of bro. JOHN DAVIS.
　　To dau-in-law ESTHER DAVIS, 100 A. "Content" toward George
Smith's branch, and at her death, to RACHEL DAVIS, dau. of sd.
ESTHER DAVIS.
　　To nephew THOMAS DAVIS, son of bro. JOHN DAVIS, one tract
called "Addy House," 68 A.
　　Wife ELIZABETH DAVIS
　　To CHARLES BISS, some cattle.
　　To nephew THOMAS WALKER, cattle.
　　To dau. SARAH MOORE, slaves.
Wit: Henry Webb, John Baley, Jr., Thomas Wilkinson.
　　　　　　　　　　　　　　　　　　　　　　　　24. 237

MEREDITH, WILLIAM, Queen Anne's Co.　　　24 Feb, 1738/9
　　　　　　　　　　　　　　　　　　　　14 Nov, 1745
　　To son WILLIAM, my great church Bible as a legacy.
　　To eldest dau. MARY, 1 dz. plates.
　　To dau. ELIZABETH, dishes.
　　To son JOHN, my fiddle, as a legacy.
　　To young. dau. MARGARET, 10 pounds money.
　　To wife ANNE MEREDITH, stock.
　　To son WILLIAM, the plantation I live on called "Shrewsbury."
　　To son JOHN, plantation where Anthony Hadder now lives.
　　Son WILLIAM, to pay unto my dau. MARY, 15 pounds money.
　　Son JOHN, to pay my dau. ELIZABETH, 15 pounds money.
　　To young. dau., MARGARET, 1500 pounds tobacco, she to have
Lott No. 10 in Ogletown.
　　Wife ANNE MEREDITH and Robert Norris Wright exs.
Wit: Joseph Harris and Charles Wiggins.　　　24. 239 - 241

RUTH, THOMAS, Queen Anne's Co.   8 Mar, 1739
                                       14 Nov, 1745
  To son JOHN RUTH, my dwelling plantation.
  To grand-dau. MABLE RUTH
  Son JOHN ex.
Wit: Thomas Baley, Samuel McCosh, Sarah McCosh.
                                       24. 242

EAVINS, John, Queen Anne's Co.   30 Jul, 1745
                                     14 Nov, 1745
  Wife MARY EAVINS, and son JONATHAN, exs.
  Mentioned: Tract "Winfield"
  To dau. RACHEL, stock.
  To dau. MARY EAVINS,
  My 4 child., to have my estate, whose names are ELIZABETH,
WILLIAM, RACHEL and MARY EAVINS.
Wit:Nathaniel Satterfield, Wm. Hurd, Stephen Yoe.
                                       24. 241

JUMPE, WILLIAM, Queen Anne's Co.   30 Dec, 1741
                                     31 Nov, 1745

  To son WILLIAM JUMPE, 100 A. "Jump's Point," lying in
Dorchester Co., north side Little Choptank River.
  To son THOMAS JUMPE, 50 A.
  To son VAUGHAN JUMPE, tract "Pokety Ridge."
  Mentions son BENJAMIN JUMPE
  To son THOMAS JUMPE, plantation where he lives.
  To son ABSOLOM JUMPE, remaining tract "Jump's Chance."
  To son SOLOMON JUMPE, my dwelling plantation.
  My wife SUSANNA JUMPE; my 5 sons and 3 daus.: THOMAS, VAUGHAN,
BENJ., ABSOLOM and SOLOMON JUMPE; SUSANNA LANE, MARY CRONEY and
ESTHER JUMPE.
  Wife, SUSANNA JUMPE, sons, VAUGHAN and BENJ., exs.
Wit:Richard Mason, Benj. Sylvester, James Karton, Wm. Roe and
John Roe.
SUSANNA JUMPE made her election Dec. 10, 1745.   24. 244 - 246

TOOTEL, RICHARD, City of Annapolis, sadler.
                                    22 Feb, 1742
                                    30 Nov, 1745
  Wife HELEN TOOTEL; son RICHARD TOOTEL
  Sons JOHN and RICHARD, the other of my houses and the tan
yard.
  Wife HELLEN, and son RICHARD, exs.
Wit:Wm. Chiselin, Benj. Swinket; Milcah Lusby, probated.
30 Nov, 1745: The names of witnesses also appear as follows:
  Wm. Ghisolin and (who is dec'd at time of probate) and
Benjamin Swinket (the same person now called and known by name of
Benedict Calvert); came 13th Dec, 1745, Benedict Calvert, Esq.
(lately Benj. Swinket)   24. 246 - 248

CLAYWELL, SELBY, Worcester Co., a ship carpenter.
4 Dec, 1744
22 Nov, 1744
To dau. MARY CLAYWELL, some slaves.
To my bro's. son PETER CLAYWELL, in case my dau. MARY should
die without hrs.
To my sister's dau Rachel Porter.
Peter Claywell ex.
Wit:Joshua Mitchell, John Porter, Jemime Whelor.
(Note: This will was omitted being recorded in Liber D.D. No.
2, Folio 459), which is written in the margin.
24. 248

PARRATT, ISAIAH, Talbot Co.   7 Jan, 1745
- - - - -
Deposition of CATHERINE WARDLOWE, age 40, together with SUSANNAH,
the wife of ISAIAH PARRATT, of sd. county were personally present
and heard Thomas Higgs who then lay ill, say that Job Guest
should bury him and take what he had, except his horse, which he
bought of William Parratt, which he desired sd. William to have
(paper torn here and words missing), but the name of "Elijah
Skillington" appears. The affirmation of SUSANNAH PARRATT, wife
of ISAIAH PARRATT, age 38, being a Quaker affirmed, who stated
the same as above witness; and it is plain in this affidavit that
Elijah Skillington owed him ten s., which he had loaned him at
Oxford, all which might be paid to Joab Guest.
24. 249 - 251

LOWE, NICHOLAS, Talbot Co., gentleman.   25 Jan, 1744
7 Dec, 1745
To wife MARGARET LOWE, land now in possession of John Paddison
and 100 A., same tract at upper end of my plantation, which was
purchased of my father, NICHOLAS LOWE of the widow Elizabeth
Wilson, to have and to hold the same land unto the same MARGARET
LOWE, pt. of tract "Anderton" now in possession of afsd. John
Paddison, unto my nephew NICHOLAS LOWE, son of my bro. VINCENT
LOWE.
To nephew HENRY LOWE, son of my sd. bro. VINCENT LOWE.
To nephew BENNETT LOWE, son of my bro. VINCENT LOWE, and if no
hrs., then to my nephew WILLIAM son of the same VINCENT LOWE, and
for default of such issue, of the same WILLIAM LOWE, I give unto
my kinsman, NICHOLAS LOWE GLEN, son of nephew NICHOLAS GLEN and
his hrs.
To nephew HENRY LOWE, son of bro. VINCENT LOWE, 100 A. pt. of
"Anderton."
To NICHOLAS EASON, son of my sister DOROTHY EASON, land.
Nephew SAMUEL EASON, son of sd. sister DOROTHY; niece MARY ANNE
BOZMAN, dau. of sister MARY BOZMAN, dec'd.
To nephew NICHOLAS LOWE, land which my father purchased of
widow Willson
Wife MARGARET LOWE
Mentions: land purchased of Joshua Winters lying in Talbot
Co.; his land called "Squire's Chance" in Dorchester Co.
To VINCENT PADDISON, son of afsd. John Paddison, 200 A.

To niece, ELIZABETH LOWE, dau. of bro. VINCENT LOWE, land purchased of Mary, the heiress of Thomas Earle, dec'd.

To MARY OLDHAM, dau. of Edward Oldham, land called "Jack's Point," lying near Oxford, Talbot Co.

Mentions: Henrietta, Maria, Louise (?), and Mary Lowe, daus. of bro. Vincent.

To nephew, NICHOLAS LOWE, after decease of my wife, piece of silver with the letters "M.R.," which belonged to his grandmother.

Wife extx.

Wit:Anna Prout, Andrew Roberts, Wm. Goldsborough.

24. 251 - 255

WHITE, WILLIAM, Talbot Co.   29 Sep, 1745
                                             14 Dec, 1745

To son HENRY WHITE, 2 tracts bought of Henry Sworder.

To wife CASSANDRA WHITE, slaves.

To dau. CASSANDRA, slaves.

Wife, extx.

Wit:Tristram Thomas, James Chaplin, Edward Bryning.

24. 255

JONES, MARY, Anne Arundel Co.   14 Jun, 1743
                                             15 Feb, 1745/6

To 2 sons JOSHUA JONES and RAY JONES, my land.

Ray Jones, Ex.

Wit:John Merricken, Sr., John Merriken, Jr., Joshua Merrikin.

24. 256

LOCK, RICHARD, Calvert Co.   2 Oct, 1745
                                             19 Nov, 1745

To dau. MARY PEARY, money.

Son RICHARFD LOCK, ex.

Wit:Mary Trouton, Benj. Dixon.   24. 257

FREEMAN, JAMES, Christ's Church Parrish, Calvert Co.
                                              7 Nov, 1739
                                              7 Dec, 1745

To son RICHARD, and my dau. MARY, tract "Smith's Foarg," equally; son RICHARD, to have upper pt, and MARY, the dwelling house.

To dau. MARGARET, tract "Huckellbury Hills."

To son JAMES, 1 s.

James Dotson ex.

Wit:John Freeman, Benj. Deaver, Richard Freeman.

24. 258

FRYER, RICHARD, Calvert Co., weaver.   27 Oct, 1745
                                             14 Dec, 1745

My wife, ELIZABETH FRYER

My 4 child.: WM. FRYER, JOHN FRYER, ELIZABETH NORVOST (?) and ANNE FRYER.

Page 260: My dau. MARY THOMAS; my son GEORGE FRYER, 1 s.

Wife ELIZABETH, extx.

Wit:Richard Stallings, Isaac Taylor, Richard Gibson.
24. 259 -260

WOOD, WILLIAM, Calvert Co.   29 May, 1745
13 Jan, 1745
To son LEONARD WOOD, my dau. REBECCA, 1 slave.
To son WILLIAM, slave.
To son BENJAMIN, 1 slave.
Appoint bro. Edward Wood, ex.
Wit:Wm. Whittington, Elizabeth Stennitt.   24.   261

PRIMROSE, WILLIAM, Queen Anne's Co., blacksmith
18 Sep, 1745
13 Dec, 1745
To dau. CATHRINA RICH, 1 s.
To dau. RACHEL NAVEL, 1 s.
To dau. ESTHER PRIMROSE, stock.
Son JOHN PRIMROSE, leave him under care of my son, GEORGE
PRIMROSE.
Appoint son-in-law, John Navell, ex.
Wit:Edward Colgan, Rachell Primrose, Francis Hood.
(A note at the foot of the probate paragraph as follows: "I sign
over my right to my mother, BRIDGETT NEVILL." signed: John
Nevill)   24. 262

HAWKINS, JOHN, Queen Anne's Co.   12 Sep, 1744
24 Dec, 1745
To eldest son JOHN HAWKINS, JR., money.
To my ERNAULT (?) HAWKINS, 5 pounds money.
To dau. FRANCES SAULSBURY, 10 cattle.
To son JOHN, the plantation where JOHN YARDSLEY now lives.
And at decease of my grand-son ERNAULT HAWKINS, son of my sd.
son JOHN HAWKINS
To son MATTHEW HAWKINS, plantation land, "Quarter," on south
side Heard Creek, east side main road that leads down to
Ogletown, and so by Wm. Merideth's lott.
To son ROBERT HAWKINS, plantation I now live on, and
plantation James Long (or Lang) now lives on, "Tulley's Delight."
Daus.: MERINA (MERUNE?) and DEBORAH BANCKS
Wife extx.
Wit:Edward Brown, Edward Brown, Jr., Mary Walker and Samuel
Milton.   24. 263

WILDE, EDITH, Queen Anne's Co., widow.   5 Aug, 1745
13 Feb, 1745
To son CHARLES MOORE, my corn, growing on my plantation.
To daus.: REBECCA CHAIRES, HANNAH WILCOCKS and DORCAS
STANTON, 1 pewter plate each.
To dau. MARGARAET WILDE, and appoint her extx.
Wit:Henry Webb, Charles Biss, Geo. Bennett.   24. 265 - 266

ARMSTRONG, THOMAS, Talbot Co., planter.   16 Dec, 1745
5 Feb, 1745
To RACHEL BERRY, cattle.
To my dau. ELIZABETH ARMSTRONG, cattle.

To JOHN ROWLESON, son of Richard Rowleson, stock.
My son JOHN and ELIZABETH ARMSTRONG, share and share alike.
John Coward, ex.
Wit:John Robinson, David Robinson, John Mackland.

24. 266

SHERWOOD, JOHN, Talbot Co.   22 Jan, 1744
                                                13 Feb, 1745
    To son JOHN SHERWOOD, land in Dorchester Co., "Skillingstons
Right" and pt. of "Richardson's Folly."
    My 3 daus.: LYDIA SHERWOOD, ELIZABETH SHERWOOD and SARAH
HAMBLETON, wife of Mr. Philimon Hambleton, my friend and
son-in-law.
    To JAMES BERRY, my personal estate, which I have given to my
dau. ELIZABETH SHERWOOD, and to take care of her.
    My dau. MARGARET, now supposed wife of John Pattison, Jr.
    My child.: JOHN, DANIEL, LYDIA and ELIZABETH SHERWOOD; SARAH,
the now wife of Philimon Hambleton.
    Son-in-law, Philimon Hambleton ex.
Wit:James Stuart, John Hudson, Penelope Sherwood.

24. 268

BRADBURN, WILLIAM, St. Mary's Co.   31 Oct, 1745
                                                 7 Nov, 1745
    Child.: JOHN, HENRIETTA, PRISCILLA, APPOLONIA, MONICA REDMAN.
ANNE BRADBURN, wife.
    Francis Spinke, son-in-law, mentioned.
    William Yates, Mary Yates, exs.
Wit: John Baptis Rishwick, William Russell. 24. 270

HOPEWELL, RICHARD, St. Mary's Co.   15 Nov, 1741
                                                 6 Jan, 1745
    Child.: JOSEPH, HUGH, JOHN, THOMAS FRANCIS, ANNA, MARY,
SUSANNA, ELIZABETH.
    To son HUGH, 400 A. in Talbot Co
    To son THOMAS FRANCIS, 350 A. in Talbot Co.
    Elizabeth Hopewell, extx.
Wit: Robert Fenwick, Hugh Hopewell, Stephen Milburn.

24. 272

WALKER, ANNE, Somerset Co.   17 Sep, 1745
                                                11 Dec, 1745
    To son THOMAS WALKER, my estate, and if he die before he
becomes of age, I bequeath to my 3 sisters: ELEANOR WALKER, JANE
LUCAS and REBECCA WALKER, and request Mr. James Lucas of this
county, mariner, to take my son THOMAS.
    Appoint sd. James Lucas, ex.
Wit:Isabella Lynn, Hannah Jackson, William Robison, Thos. Bluett.

24. 276

JONES, WILLIAM, Somerset Co.   14 Jan, 1743/4
                                                 4 Feb, 1745
    To son THOMAS JONES, my dwelling plantation.

That my 5 daus.: MARY, ELIZABETH, REBECKAH, TABITHA and ANN
JONES may have privilege to live on sd. plantation while they are
single
    To grand-son JAMES GLASGOW, 2 silver spoons.
    To dau. MARTHA GLASGOW, 4 head cattle.
    Son Thomas ex.
Wit:John Anderson, James McGrah, Tunstall Hack.   24. 277

BIRD, ARABELLAH, Somerset Co.   19 Jun, 1745
                                             11 Feb, 1745
    To son-in-law THOMAS TYLER and my dau. JEMIMEY, his wife
    Mentions: Henry Culling
    To dau REBECCA TRICE
    Mentions: corn at her son's, whose name was JACOB CULLINS.
    Son-in-law Thomas Tyler ex.
Wit:John Evins, Job. J. Parks, Ansalenor Parks.   24. 277

BARWICK, WILLIAM, Talbot Co.   31 Oct, 1742
                                             17 Feb, 1745
    Wife ROSANNA BARWICK.
    To son WILLIAM BARWICK, the son of Mary Thunderman, base born,
    the other half of my estate.
    At decease of my wife, son WILLIAM BARWICK, shall have the
    half of estate.
    Wife ROSEANNA BARWICK extx.
Wit:Wm. Landergen, John Baynard, Daniel Rundle, Sarah Ogle.
                                                     24. 279

MAYNADIER, DANIEL, Talbot Co.   11 Jan, 1741
                                              7 Mar, 1745
    To dau. JANE FEDDEMAN, now wife of Richard Feddeman
    To grand-son DANIEL FEDDEMAN, slaves now in possession of his
    father, Richard Feddeman.
    To grand-dau. HANNAH JENKINS, slaves.
    To wife HANNAH MAYNADIER, 1/3 of my personal estate.
    Son DANIEL, sons-in-law, JOSEPH PARRETT, FRANCIS PARRETT and
    ABNER PARRETT
Wit:James Troth, John Mackcoon, Frances Pepper.
I, the subscriber was appointed executrix of the within last will
of the Rev. Daniel Maynadier, dec'd; hereby renounce the same,
this 3-3-1745; signed: Hannah Maynadier.   24. 281

WHARTON, HENRY, St. Mary's Co.   26 Nov, 1745
                                              4 Feb, 1745/6
    Child.: ANN, ELEANOR, HENRY, FRANCIS, JESSE, ELIZABETH PILE,
    MARY, JANE.
    Bros.: WILLIAM and EDWARD DIGGS.
    JOSHUA DOYNE, mentioned.
    Josheph Pile, John Parrkam; sons-in-law, exs.
Wit: John Llewellen, Wm. Edly, Wm. Wincet   24. 282

FANNING, JOHN, St. Mary's Co.   1 Dec, 1745
                                              4 Feb, 1745
    Child.: JOSIAH, JOHN, ELIZABETH.
    ELIZABETH WAKEFIELD.

MARY FANNING wife, extx.
Wit: Geo. Mills, Thom., Noble, Jas. Fyffe.   24. 284

THARP, JOHN, Kent Co.   9 Feb, 1743
                                              9 Nov, 1745
   My wife ELIZABETH
   To son JOHN, at decease of my wife
   To son JOHN, and for default of issue to my son JAMES LOUIS
(or LEWIS), die, then to my dau. MARY, and if no issue, then to
my friend, RALPH PAGE (?).
Wit:John Cooper, Jno. Gresham, Jno. Puzey.   24. 286

CROW, WILLIAM, Kent Co.   20 Nov, 1745
                                              7 Jan, 1745
   To son WILLIAM CROW, JR., except to have a home on the land
with either of his bros.
   To son ISAAC CROW, called "Crow's Chance," half middle
plantation.
   To son THOMAS CROW, tract called "Crow's Addition."
   To dau. MARTHA JACKSON, one ring.
   To son ISAAC
   To son WILLIAM, slaves.
Wit:Jno. Smith, Stephen Canady, Amos Adderton.   24. 288

RICE, WILLIAM, Kent Co.   13 Jan, 1745/6
                                              7 Feb, 1745
   Wife REBECKAH RICE
   To son WILLIAM
   That my wife keep all my child. until they arrive at age, and
my little dau. remain with her mother until she arrive at age 16.
   My little dau. REBECKAH RICE
   To HARRY ENLOWS, my clothing.
Wit:Marmad. Tilden, Henry Enlows, Alexander Mackelain.
                                              24. 290

SALLER, WILLIAM, Kent Co.   8 Jan, 1745/6
                                              14 Feb, 1745
   To cousin NATHANIEL RICKETS
   My wife ANN RICKETS
   To my friend, MARGARET GROOM, clothing.
   Appoint friend, Nathaniel Rickets ex.
Wit:Samuel Groome, Wm. Browning, Wm. Breffet.   24. 291

THORNTON, CATHARINE, Kent Co.   21 Sep, 1745
                                              22 Feb, 1745
   To son WM. LUTHER THORNTON, my dwelling plantation. He pay to
my son JEREMIAH BURCHINAL, cattle.
   To dau. MARY CLARK, 1 ring.
   To dau. ELIZABETH FIELDS, 600 pounds good tobacco.
   To son THOMAS
   To dau. CATHARINE PAGE
   To son JOHN THORNTON
   To dau. RACHEL EVERETT
   Son WM. LUTHER THORNTON ex.

56

Wit:John Gleaves, Isaac Redgrave, Richard Bentham.
24. 292

HATCHESON, SARAH, Kent Co.   9 Jan, 1745
                                             22 Feb, 1745
    To son JOHN JONES, one servant.
    To dau. SARAH JONES
    To son GRIFFITH JONES
    To son PHILLIP JONES
    To grand-son WILLIAM JONES (son of my son JOHN JONES)
    To grand-dau. SARAH JONES (dau. of my son JOHN. JR), my
diamond ring
    My 2 sons, GRIFFITH and PHILLIP
    Son Griffith ex.
Wit:Edward Tillard, Elizabeth Tillard, Nicholas Smith.
                                             24. 293

CHAPMAN, RICHARD, Charles Co.   1 Dec, 1745
                                             7 Dec, 1745
    SARAH, WILLIAM, JANE JACKSON.
    ELIZABETH REAGON, dau. of Mathew Reagon.
    MARY CHAPMAN wife, extx.
Wit: James Carell, John Gray.   24. 295

MACKHORN, ROBT., Charles Co.   17 Oct, 1745
                                            20 Dec, 1745
    ELIZABETH MACKHORN wife.
    Child.: ROBERT, ELIZABETH, WILLIAM, MARTHA DUFFEY, JANE WOOD,
ANNE ASH.
    Grand-child., BENNETT WOODSON.
    Sons-in-law, Jacob Wood, Thomas Ash.
    Ex., none mentioned.
Wit: Samuel Amery, James Dyson.   24. 296

KING, RICHARD, Charles Co.   8 Oct, 1745
                                             3 Jan, 1745
    Child.: THOMAS, RICHARD.
    Sisters: ANN GRAY, CATHERINE MONCASTER.
    Jas. Moncaster, bro.-in-law, ex.
Wit: William Cooper, John Grimes.   24. 298

WATHEN, JOHN, Charles Co.   16 Dec, 1745
                                             13 Jan, 1745
    ANN WATHEN, wife.
    Child.: JOHN, JOSEPH, BENNETT, CLEMENT, BARTON, MARY, SUSANNA.
    John Wathen son, Hudson Wathen, bro., exs.
Wit: James Ashby, John Tounton, Justian Williams. 24. 299

BRENT, WILLIAM, Charles Co.   4 Jan, 1745
                                             - - - - - -
    Child.: HENRY BRENT, WALTER CHANDLER BRENT; mentions unborn
child.
    Land called "Goose Creek" to be divided among sons.
    Mentions CHARLES EWILL of Prince George's County, colony of
Virginia.

JANE WATTS, mother.
Mentions Walter Hanson and William Neale, "kinsmen."
JANE BRENT wife, extx.
Wit: Ralph Falkner, Jeremiah Chase, Walter Pye.   24. 301

GOODRICK, FRANCIS, Charles Co.   8 Apr, 1745
                                                 22 Feb, 1745
MARY GOODRICK wife. 300 A.
Child.: EDWARD, FRANCIS, GEORGE, HENRY, ANN VIOLETTA, MARY,
ANN.
    Mary, wife; Edward, Francis, George Goodrich, sons, exs.
    To son EDWARD, pt of tract that I live on, 300 A.; "Goodricks
Addition," 50 A.; Franham Royall, 160 A.
    To son HENRY VINCENT GOODRICK, "Beech Neck," "Addition to May
Day," 120 A.
    To son George Goodrick, "Barbadoes," 552 A.
Wit: Robert Hanson, John Hanson, Ignatius Luckett, William
Luckett.   24. 304

NEALE, BENJAMIN, Charles Co.   15 Nov, 1745
                                                 20 Jan, 1745
    Child.: BENNETT, JOHN, ELIZABETH CURRY, MARY, ANN.
MARY NEALE, extx.
    To son BENNETT, 1/2 tract I live on, "Part of Gills Tract."
    To son JAMES, other half of above tract.
    To son CURRY, given me by Richard Edelin.
    To dau MARY, other half of tract given by Richard Edelin.
Appoint bro. Wm. Neale and bro.-in-law Edward Edelen as trustees.
Wit: John Lancaster, Jos. Lancaster, James Neale.
                                                  24. 307

BARNES, MATHEW, Charles Co.   Jun, 1745
                                                 10 Feb, 1745
    Child.: GODSHALL, MATTHEW, PHILIP, HENRY, JANE HENEFORD,
ELIZABETH COURTS, ANNE HARRISON, FRANCES HARRISON.
    Mentions 1/3 of tract left to his wife by her former husband,
John Theobald.
    MARY wife; Henry son, exs.
Wit: Geo. Godfrey, Geo. Harris.   24. 308

ALLMAN, ABRAHAM, Cecil Co.   1 Apr. 1745
                                                 - - - - - -
    Wife MARGARET ALLMAN
    My friends: BENJ. SLYTER and EDW. RUMSEY
Wit:John Woods, Edw. Rumsey, Jos. Allman   24. 310 - 311

SAVIN, SAMUEL, Cecil Co.   16 May, 1745
                                                 16 Aug, 1745
    To cousin BENJ. RICHARDSON
    To bro. JOHN SAVIN, my personal estate.
Wit:Thomas Savin, Mark McMulling, Sarah Starling.
                                                  24. 311

WATSON, JOHN, Cecil Co. - Fredericks Town   4 Oct, 1745
                                              15 Oct, 1745
                                              16 Jan, 1745
   I justly owe Christopher Marshall, and appoint James Calden,
atty., in Kent Co., and John Drummond, merchant in Cecil Co., my
ex. This statement made before Isaac Freeman, Dr. Benj. Bradford
and Dr. Andrew McKitrick. Signed: John Watson.
Wit:Benj. Bradford, Andrew McKittrick and Isaac Freeman.
                                                     24. 312

PENNINGTON, JOHN, Cecil Co.   29 Apr, 1745
                                              15 Oct, 1745
   To son JOHN PENNINGTON, JR., my dwelling plantation; tract "2
Branches" plantation bet. George Neasey's whereon now Wm. Lovely
lives.
   To son BENJAMIN PENNINGTON, my dwelling plantation and George
Neasey's.
   To sons: SAMUEL PENNINGTON, JOHN, THOMAS, EDWARD, and WILLIAM
BOYER PENNINGTON, land bought from John Lusby and Margarett, his
wife, called "Hazell Branch," 130 A.
   Wife MARY
   Daus.: RACHEL BEEDLE; SARAH PENNINGTON, dau. of MARY.
Wit:Benj. Pearce, Rachel Mainley, John Keye.   24. 313

DUFFEY, SARAH, Cecil Co.   26 Mar, 1745
                                               1 Sep, 1745
   To dau. MARY DILLON, the 3rd pt. of my orchard; during her
husband, Robert Dillan's absence, to have equal pt. with her
sister, MARGARET DUFFEY.
   To dau. SARAH JONES, furniture.
   To dau. MARGARET DUFFEY, my furniture be divided bet. MARY
DILLON and MARGARET DUFFEY.
Wit:James Grady, Moses Jones, Jane McClure or McLure.
                                                     24. 316

HUKILL, DANIEL, Cecil Co.   16 Jan, 1743
                                              13 Aug, 1745
   Wife JOANNA, extx.
Wit:Charles Ford, Mary Forster, Thomas Forster. 24. 317

LARKIN, JEREMIAH, Cecil Co.   30 Aug, 1745
                                              17 Oct, 1745
   Wife RACHEL LARKIN
   Sister MARY MULLEN
Wit:Bartholomew Hukill, Charles Ford, Andrew Crow.
                                                     24. 318

VAN BEBBER, HARMANA, Cecil Co.   11 Sep, 1745
                                               2 Dec, 1745
   To 2 younger sons, MATTHIAS and HENRY VAN BEBBER, my personal
estate.
   To sons JACOB and ADAM VAN BEBBER; daus. REBECCA VAN BEBBER
and HESTER NAUDINE, 10 pounds money.
   By virtue of my dec'd. husband's will, appoint my 2 sons JACOB
and ADAM, guardians of my 2 sons MATTHIAS and HENRY.

Sons JACOB and ADAM, exs.
Wit:James McLocklan, Christopher Pugh.   24. 319 - 320

TOWSON, JOSEPH, Baltimore Co.   17 Jan, 1745
                                            5 Mar, 1745
   Wife ELIZABETH TOWSON, extx.
Mentioned: unborn child; it to be named JOSEPH if a son, and
ELIZABETH, if a dau.
Wit:Wm. Towson, John Bond, Thomas Towson.   24. 321

TAYMAN, SARAH, St. George's Parish, Baltimore Co.
                                            14 Feb, 1739
                                             9 Nov, 1745
   To grandson JOHN HANSON; grand-dau.: SIBYL HANSON and SARAH
MARIARLE (?), slaves.
   To grand-sons: BENJAMIN HANSON, HOLLIS HANSON, THOMAS HANSON
and grand-dau. VARILLAH HANSON, tract called "Jonesale," 150 A.,
and my gun which was Layman's.
   To grand-dau. SIBYL HANSON, my slave, white woman named JANE
BINER, having yet 2-1/2 years to serve.
   To dau-in-law SARAH HANSON
   To grand-son JACOB HANSON
   To my friend JAMES OSBUENARED (or OSBURN), 1 heifer.
   To son JACOB HANSON, and after his death to be divided bet.
his child., which he begat of REBECCA, his first wife.
   Appoint JACOB HANSON ex.
Wit:James Osburn, James Maxwell, John Matthews and Wm. Osburn.
                                            24. 322 - 323

MALE/MAYE/MAYLE, ANTHONY, Talbot Co.   14 Oct, 1689
                                            24 Mar, 1689/90
   Memorandum in pursuance of Order of this Court, Jan. last, to
Mr. Wm. Finney to take depositions and prove the will of Mr.
Anthony Male (?), spelled "Mayle" at the signing of same, and
spelled "Anthony Maye" in the 2nd line of sd. will. Desired his
debts paid by his wife, MARY MAYLE, and to her, 250 A. on Miles
River called "Ashby" and other tracts called "Cabsin Neck" and
"Goose Neck."
   Wife, extx.
   To my friend, ANTHONY RUMBEL, my horse.
Wit:John Worly, John Maymon, Christ. Peppard, John Davis.
                                            24. 323

HOLLAND, MARGARET, Prince George's Co.   5 Mar, 1745
                                            1- Dec, 1745
   To son RICHARD HOLLAND, 25 s.
   To dau. ELIZABETH ENGLAND, son THOMAS HOLLAND, sum of 12
pounds sterl. at decease of my mother, which she has left me by
will.
   To 3 daus.: CASANDRA, MARGARET and ISBALE, remainder of
estate.
   My child.: RICHARD and CASANDRA, exs.
Wit:Elizabeth Moore, Samuel Water, Jr., John Lewis.
                                            24. 325 - 326

WOODHEAD, GEORGE, Prince George's Co.   16/17 Jan, 1745
                                          12 Feb, 1745/6
    DUNCAN FERGUSON, ex., and leave to him all that I am possessed
of either in the Province or in the Kingdom of Great Brittain,
except tobacco due from Benj. Harris, I now leave to him.
Wit:George Scott, Francis Jenkins and Daniel Jenkins.
                                          24. 327

WILSON, JOSHUA, Prince George's Co.   - - - - - -
                                          27 Nov, 1745
    To bro. JAMES WILSON (page 320), pt. of Mt. Calvert Mannor,
which my father purchased of Capt. Ennes, then to my nephew WM.
WILSON SELBY, son of Wm. Magruder Selby.
    To niece MARTHA WILSON, dau. of my bro. JAMES WILSON, slave.
    To nephew WM. WILKINSON WILSON, 1 slave.
    To nephew JOSIAH WILSON, son of bro. JAMES WILSON, 1 slave.
    To bro. JOSEPH WILSON, tract which my father formerly
purchased of John Deakins; also the land he purchased of
Christsopher Beanes.
    To nephew WILLIAM WILSON SELBY
    To my friend THOMAS HODGKIN, 10 pounds sterl.
    To sister, MARTHA SELBY, 20 pounds sterl.
    To nephew SAMUEL SELBY, nephew NATHANIEL SELBY, bro. LINGAN
WILSON
    If it please God to afflict me with sickness in any foreign
country, and take me out of this world, then I will my bro.
JOSEPH an equal pt. with my bro. JAMES.
Wit:Richard Marsham, Waring Henry Hall, Samuel Magruder.
                                          24. 327

PARKER, GABRIEL, JR., Prince George's Co.   27 Nov, 1745
                                             16 Dec, 1745

    Wife SARAH PARKER
    Father GABRIEL PARKER, appoint ex.
Wit:Samuel Taylor, Richard Pile.   24. 330

HELLEN, SUSANNA, Calvert Co.,   18 Apr, 1741
                                            19 Mar, 1745
    To son JAMES HELLEN, my slave man, called Robin.
    To grand-dau. SUSANNA HUNGERFORD, my slaves.
    To grand-son THOMAS HELLEN, son of DAVID HELLEN, dec'd.
    To grand-dau. SUSANNA HELLEN, meaning dau. of RICHARD HELLEN,
my young. son, some furniture.
    To grand-dau. BARBARA HELLEN, money.
    To sons JOHN and PETER HELLEN, and grand-son DAVID HELLEN,
meaning the son of RICHARD HELLEN, desire son nor grand-son,
except those before named, shall have any pt. of my estate.
    PETER HELLEN ex.
Wit:John Greves, Jr., Thomas Dorneby and John Bannester.
                                            24. 331

BILLINGSLY, WM., St. Mary's Co.   11 Aug, 1745
                                            16 Dec, 1745

    Child.: MARY WOOD, ANN HARDESTY, WILLIAM, JAMES, MARGARET,
CLARE, FRANCIS, ELIZABETH.

Wm. Billingsly, son, ex.
Wit: Rachel Billingsly, James Keech.   24. 333

PHIPPARD, WILLIAM, St. Mary's Co.   22 Aug, 1745
                                              4 Apr, 1745
    Dau., SUSANNA.
    Niece, MARY PHIPPARD.
    Sister, URSULA HASKINS.
    MARY PHIPPARD wife, extx.
Wit: Kenelm Boult, Thos. Allston, John Luisforde.
                                                  24. 334

HARDING, HENRY, Talbot Co., planter.   18 Feb,, 1745/6
                                              14 Mar, 1745
    To bro. JOS. HARDING, 400 pounds tobacco.
    To bro. WILLIAM HARDING, stock.
    Wife ELIZABETH extx.
Wit:Even Jones, Samuel Abbot   24. 335

POWELL, JOHN, Talbot Co.   4 Oct, 1745
                                              29 Mar, 1746
    To nephews: DANIEL DICKINSON, son of JOHN DICKINSON; POWELL
COX and DANIEL COX, sons of DANIEL COX, that the guardians of sd.
POWELL and DANIEL COX, pay unto ANN MC CEMMY, wife of Roger
McCemmy, annually, 5 pounds money each.
    Desire my late mother, SUSANNA POWELL'S will, in every
particular, shall take place.
    To nephew DANIEL DICKINSON, my dwelling plantation.
    To nephew POWELL COX, the dwelling plantation where my mother,
SUSANNA POWELL, lived.
    To nephews DANIEL DICKINSON and POWELL COX, all land called
"Boston Clift."
    Appoint friends Daniel Powell, Wm. Richardson, Thomas Bullen
and Abner Parratt.
    Sd. nephews to have land left me by my grandfather PITTS,
lying near the head of Tuckahoe Creek, about 2 miles above the
bridge called "Coldrain," that my nephew ISAAC COX
Wit:James Dickinson, John Dickinson, Michael Nowland, Thomas
Bullen.   24. 336

POWELL, SUSANNAH, TALBOT CO., widow.   9 Jul, 1745
                                              29 Mar, 1746
    To dau. ANN KENNEY, my slaves, and at her death to my
grand-dau. SARAH COX.
    To dau-in-law, SARAH RESSON, 1 silver spoon.
    To grand-son POWELL COX, my clothing consisting of Camblet
coat which was his uncle Thomas', now dec'd.
    To grand-dau. REBECCA COX, slaves.
    To son JOHN POWELL, a slave formerly belonging to my son
THOMAS POWELL, dec'd.
    To son JOHN POWELL, 1/3 pt. of personal estate.
    To 5 grandchild.: DANIEL DICKINSON, POWELL COX, SARAH COX,
DANIEL and ISAAC COX, 2/3 of remainder of estate.
Wit:L. H. Bozman, Thos. Bullen and Merriday Pew (?).
                                                  24. 339

BRAWHAN/BROHON, THOMAS, Dorchester Co.   1 Nov, 1744
14 Nov, 1745
    To young. son PATRICK, 1 slave.
Wit:John Stewart and John Brohon.   245. 340

ECCLESTON, THOMAS, Dorchester Co.   22 May, 1745
19 Nov, 1745
    To sons: HUGH ECCLESTON, THOMAS ECCLESTON, JOHN ECCLESTON and
JOSEPH ECCLESTON, land I now live on bet. Garies Creek and Arthur
Wright's Creek, viz., my dwelling plantation.
    To son HUGH, the plantation where Peter LeCompt now lives.
    To son THOMAS, the plantation where Wm. Proctor formerly lived
at the mouth of Arthur Wright's Creek.
    To son JOHN, plantation I bought of John Davis.
    To 3 sons CHARLES, WILLIAM and JAMES ECCLESTON, land that I
bought of John Tootle and of the child. of John Orrell, called
"Middle Division" and tract adjoining I bought of Joseph Hinton
and Mary, his wife, called "Whittlewood," sd. land being bet.
Branches of Cabin Creek and the north west fork of Nanticoack.
    To JOHN ORRELL, the land he now lives on lying on Ingram's
Creek, upon terms that if the son of JOHN TOLLET and MARY, his
wife, lately dec'd., conveyed and make over to my 3 sons CHARLES,
WILLIAM and JOSEPH, and the title of that pt. of Middle Division
that belonged to his mother and sold by JOHN ORRELL, his uncle to
me as the deed for same approveth, then sd. JOHN ORRELL to have
the land he now lives on, on Ingram's Creek, called "Layton's
Discovery."
    Mentions his bro. JOHN ECCLESTON; dau. SARAH; my 9 child.
    To dau. ELIZABETH ECCLESTON, slave.
    Wife Eleanor Eccleston and son Hugh Eccleston, exs.
Wit:Samuel Lecompt, J. Eccleston, Rachel Stevens, Margaret Noel.
24. 341

PERRY, HUGH, Dorchester Co.   - - - - - -
19 Nov, 1745
    To grand-dau. ELIZABETH JOHNSTON, my cattle.
    To son RICHARD PERRY,
    Son-in-law PERRY JOHNSTON, ex.
Wit:Richard Webster, Thomas Rumball and Wm. Rumball.
24. 343

WILLEY, FRANCIS, Dorchester Co.   - - - - -
13 Dec, 1745
    To son JOHN WILLEY, 32 A. on lower pt. of tract called
"Wiley's Outlet."
    To grand-son JOHN WILLEY, cattle.
    To son ROBERT WILLEY, my dwelling plantation.
    To 3 sons: EZEKIAS WILLEY, EDWARD WILLEY and EZEKIEL WILLEY,
cattle.
    To son FRANCIS WILLEY, cattle; my cooper tools, also.
    To grand-son, ABSOLOM WILLEY, cattle.
    To dau. ELIZABETH INSLEY, cattle.
    To dau. ALICE WILLEY, furniture.
    Wife DIANNA WILLEY
Wit:Job Hammond, Phillip Wingett.   24. 345

MACKEMEE, ROGER, Dorchester Co.   27 Nov, 1742
                                             17 Dec, 1745
    To son JOHN MACKEMEE, 5 s.
    Dau. SARAH MACKEMEE, desire that James Fooks and wife
Elizabeth, may take my dau. SARAH, and bring her up in a
Christian manner, and have her estate, and if she die without
issue, my sister SARAH DUDLEY, to possess same.
    Wife ANN MACKAMEE, extx.
Wit:John Hodson, Rosanna Hodson, Isaac Charles.
                                             24. 346

TAYLOR, ELIZABETH, Dorchester Co.   14 Dec, 1745
                                           29 Dec, ----
    To RAMOND STABLEFORD, my still.
    To PRISE HIGINGS, Negroes: Jem, Peter, Sidney.
    To DORITHY GOLOTHON, Negro men: Jack, Julion.
    To HANSY BYAS, furniture.
    To RAMOND STABLEFORD, Negro Harry.
    To CHARLES STABLEFORD, Negro Robin.
    To THOMAS STABLEFORD, Negroes Vance and Cate.
    To CHARLES STABLEFORD, pt. of "Edmunson's Referee," where
afsd. STABLEFORD now lives.
    To THOMAS STABLEFORD, land where Wm. Golithan now lives.
    Balance to the above-mentioned STABLEFORD and DORITY
LOCKERMAN, DORITY GOLITHON and PRICE HIGGINS.
    That WM. BYAS have estate heretofore given PRICE HIGGINS.
    Appoint RAMON, CHARLES and THOMAS STABLEFORD, exs.
Wit:Jos. Ennalls, William Byas and Mary Greenby.
                                             24. 347

MANNING, MARGARET, Dorchester Co.   20 Apr, 1744
                                           4 Jan, 1745
    To sister, MARIA ROGERS, my clothing.
    To SARAH GUN, my saddle.
    To MARY GUN, silver dishes.
    To ARTHUR PHIPPS, 50 s.
    To JAMES BRIGHT, 10 s.
    To JOHN PHIPPS, my real and personal estate, making him hr. to
all my lands, sd. JOHN PHIPPS, ex.
Wit:Wm. Rowland, James Palmer, George Leigg.   24. 348

VAULX, JAMES, JR, Dorchester Co.   18 Jan, 1745
                                           14 Feb, 1745
    To son JAMES VAULX (illegible).
    To dau. PEGGY, tract "Bolton's Venture," and if she die
without issue, land to fall to my son JOSIAH VAULX (There is
another name, but too illegible to be read.)
    Wife, extx.
Wit:Wm. Smith, Sherman Johnson, Edward Rumbley. 24. 349

VAULX, JAMES, Dorchester Co.   24 Jan, 1745
                                           17 Feb, 1745
    To son EBENEZER VAULX, 50 A. called "Vaulx's Adventure."
    To son JOHN VAULX, remainder of "Vaulx's Adventure."

64

To wife, plantation.
To dau. MARGARET, 20 s.
To dau. HASTEN, 20 s.
Wife, extx.
Wit:Peter Taylor, Pr. Taylor, Jr., Wm. Smith, Jr. and Lemuel
Goodwin.   24. 350

EDMUNDSON, WILLIAM, Dorchester Co., merchant.
                                       10 Dec, 1745
                                       19 Feb, 1745
    To son HENRY EDMUNDSON, my land in Talbot Co., "Wilderness,"
pt. of "Heirdier Loyd," 500 a.
    To sons: KENSEY EDMUNDSON, WM. EDMUNDSON, pt. of tract called
"Edmundson's Purchase," 112 A. and land called "Range," which I
bought of John Harp (Sharp?), of 50 A., give sd. son 200 A.
    To dau. SARAH RAISIN, 1 slave.
    To dau. PRISCILLA, 1 slave
    To dau. ANN, 1 slave.
    That if my 2 sons HENRY and KENSEY, shd. die without issue,
that my land in Talbot Co., called "Wilderness" go to my wife
ELIZABETH EDMUNDSON, during life. At her decease, to son WM., he
to have money to carry on an action in law against Mary Alford,
or her son Wm. Alford, but if Wm. Alford will take the sd. land
called "Shipton" beginning at the bounds, I have proved by Edward
Hardicain.
    Wife Elizabeth, and son Wm., exs.
Wit:John Edmondson, Thos. Edgell, Wm. Edmondson, 3rd, James
Safarson and Richard Safarson.   24. 351

STANDFORD, CHARLES, Dorchester Co.   15 Dec, 1745
                                            20 Feb, 1745
    To son THOMAS, tract on Kanedy Branch, land that Wm. Harvey
rented from me last year. The remainder of my 3 tracts of land
lying on Lovedy (Havedy?) Creek, tract where Thomas Braddis now
lives.
    If my son LEVIN die without issue, my wife to hold his lands.
    Wife ROSANNA STANDFORD
    To dau. BETTY STANDFORD, land on Fowling Creek, "Controventry"
(?), and if BETTY shd. die, desire my dau. SARAH STANDFORD, have
her pt.
    My son THOMAS, dau. BETTY, son LEVIN, dau. SARAH, son CHARLES,
grand-child. called JOHN LYDEN and MARY LYDEN, my wife ROSANNA,
and my son THOMAS
    Appoint friend, Col. Joseph Ennals, Trustee.
Wit:J. Eccleston, Andrew Arnett, John Arnett and Edw. Coffey.
                                            24. 354

STANDFORD, JOHN, Dorchester Co.   11 Dec, 1745
                                            20 Feb, 1745
    To bro. CHARLES STANDFORD, a new coat at Wm. Norton's, and
pair leather breeches.
    Bro. THOMAS STANDFORD, ex.
Wit:Isaac Partridge, Joseph Records.   24. 356

HOOPER, GRACE, Dorchester Co.   13 Aug, 1745
                                     20 Feb, 1745
   Sons: ABRAHAM HOOPER, JOHN HOOPER.
Wit:Ezekiell Keene and Mary Keene.   24. 357

STANFORD, WILLIAM, JR., Dorchester Co.   -- Jan, 1745/6
                                   21 Feb, 1745
   To bro-in-law, ABRAHAM BRODISS, money.
   To sister, MARGARET STANDFORD, my right to land called
"London."
   Bro. SAMUEL STANDFORD, ex.
Wit:Isaac Patridge, Thomas Smith, Elizabeth Meers. 24. 358

STAPLEFORD, CHARLES, Dorchester Co.   26 Feb, 1745
                                    3 Mar, 1745
   To my father, my white horse.
   To LEVIN, the reputed child of REBECCA WALL, of this county,
and if he die without issue, I give my lands to my 2 bros.
RAYMOND STAPLEFORD and THOMAS STAPLEFORD.
   Appoint Rebecca Wall, extx.
Wit:Cha. Goldsborough, Catherine Keyes, Dorothy Loockerman, Mary
Greenby.   24. 359

PRITT/PITT, JOHN, Dorchester Co., mariner. 31 Jan, 1745
                                    12 Mar, 1745
(Name written "Pritt" in first pt. of Will, but he signed his
name "John Pitt" on p. 361)
   To son ROGER PRITT (?), my dwelling plantation, land formerly
called "Nick's Branch" and "Refuge" and "Pitts" and land
belonging to "Mason's Happyyard," which I bought of Wm. Ennals.
   To son THOMAS PITT
   To son WILLIAM PITT
   To son PHILIP PITT
   Dau. Sarah Pitt and son Roger Pitt, exs.
Wit:F. Ennals, Thos. Airey, Henry Hayward, Henry Hayward, Jr.
                                  24. 360 - 361

LANGRELL, SARAH, Dorchester Co.   13 Mar, 1745
                                    23 Mar, 1745
   To son JAMES LANGRELL, furniture.
   To son GEORGE LANGRELL, slaves.
   Son JAMES LANGRELL, ex.
   All my estate desired that it shall be equally divided amongst
all my child., except what is before bequeathed.
Wit: Wm. Adams, Sarah Adams, Mary Creachey, Francis Lee.
                                  24. 362

TURPIN, JOHN, Dorchester Co.   5 Jan, 1745
                                    24 Mar, 1745
   That wife, CLARE TURPIN, shall have my plantation and lands
until my dau. SARAH, comes to age 18.
   Unborn child is mentioned.
   Appoint bro. BEACHES TURPIN and wife, exs.
Wit: Wm. Turpin, Charles LeCompt, Mary Nutterwill.
                                  24. 363

CHILLCUTT, GEORGE, Dorchester Co.   11 Nov, 1745
                                           24 Mar, 1745
   To son JOHN, my plantation, 60 A.
   To son JOSHUA, the other pt. tract "World End."
   To dau. JAMASON
   Wife SARAH, extx.
Wit: John Layton, Benj. Falconer, Anthony Chillcutt.
                                              24. 364

GRIFFITH, LEWIS, Dorchester Co.   4 Oct, 1745
                                         12 Apr, 1746
   To my oldest son LEWIS GRIFFITH, land called "Worlds End" and
"Olfins Increase."
   To son JOHN GRIFFITH, likewise.
   To son EDWARD GRIFFITH, land which I bought of Josias
Moore(?).
   To 2nd son, JOHN GRIFFITH, the dwelling plantation where my
mother Hannah Griffith now lives, bet. Worlds End Creek and
Stablefort's Creek.
   To son JOHN GRIFFITH, 35 A. called "Lewis' Addition," on the
head of a marsh called "Hell Hook Marsh."
   My wife FRANCES GRIFFITH, extx.
Wit: Raymon Staplefort, Joseph Shinton, Robert Griffith.
                                              24. 365

BEACHUMP, TURPIN, Dorchester Co.   19 Mar, 1745
                                         12 Jun, 1745
   To my mother ELIZABETH BEACHUMP, my lands and at her decease
to bro. JOHN TUTTER HORNE, and appoint him ex.
Wit: James Vaulx, Curtis Beachump, Stephen Owens.
John Tull made note that he renounces the admr. "of my dec'd
bro-in-law, Turpin Beachump's, estate who appointed me ex."
                                            24. 367

SIMMONS, ABRAHAM, JR., Anne Arundel Co.   28 Aug, 1745
                                         16 Apr, 1745
   To son ABRAHAM, and dau. BETRIDGE SIMMONS, 2 tracts I had by
my wife, SARAH DRURY, lying in Prince George's Co., called
"Drury's Good Luck" and "Drury's Adventure."
   To dau. BETRIDGE SIMMONS, 1 slave.
   My wife SARAH SIMMONS, my 2 bros-in-law, Charles Drury and Wm.
Tillard, trustees.
Wit: Wm. Coale, Sr., Thomas Sheels and William Tillard.
                                            24. 368

HOWARD, JOHN, Elk Ridge, Anne Arundel Co., gentleman
                                      5 Feb, 1745/6
                                     21 Apr, 1746
   To wife RUTH HOWARD, my dwelling plantation, by name "Valey Of
Owen," and 25 A. called "Little Worth," and at her decease, to
JOHN GRINIFF HOWARD, and hrs.
   To JASSON FRIZELL, tract "Frizell's Chance," land of JASSON
FRIZEEL to fall to JOHN GRINIFF HOWARD.
   To wife's grand-dau. ELIZABETH HAMMOND, 1 slave.

To wife's grand-dau. RUTH TODD, 1 slave girl.
To MARY COOHOON, 5 pounds sterl. money.
Balance estate to wife RUTH HOWARD, and JOHN GRINIFF HOWARD,
and appoint them exs.
Wit: James MacGill, John Dorsey, Jr., Edward Dorsey, Lance Todd.
24. 369-370

YOUNG, JOHN, Anne Arundel Co.   15 Oct, 1742
                                       29 Apr, 1746
     To MARGARET YOUNG, late MARGARET HANDS, my beloved wife, my
dwelling house and plantation.
     Son JOHN YOUNG
     To 3 daus.: JOHANNAH, ELIZABETH and CATHERINE, 5 pounds money.
Wit: Richard Wilkins, John Thompson, Joseph Evits.
                                       24. 371

MAGRUDER, ALEXANDER, Prince George's Co.   4 Feb, 1739/40
                                            20 May, 1746
     To wife SUSANNAH MAGRUDER, the plantation I now dwell upon.
     To dau. ELIZABETH WHITEAKER, 1 slave.
     To ROBERT WHITKER and wife ELIZABETH, the southernmost half of
a lott of land.
     To dau. SARAH BUTLER, 1 slave.
     To son HEZEKIAH MAGRUDER, 180 A. pt. of "Jordan," 80A.
"Quicksale" formerly belonging to William Collins.
     To son ALEXANDER MAGRUDER, remaining pt. of my land, and after
decease of my wife, the plantation that I now live on to him and
hrs. that is divided bet. my bro. NATHANIEL MAGRUDER, late dec'd.
     Mentions bro. Nathaniel Magruder and his 2 sons George and
Alexander Magruder to equally divided bet. the 2 sons.
     To my son ALEXANDER, my surveying instruments. The name of
his 2 daus. were Priscilla and Ann Magruder.
     Appoint my loving wife Susannah Magruder, extx. Wit: Samuel
Taylor, James Truman.   24. 372

HICKS, JAMES, Tuckahoe, Queen Anne's Co., planter.
                                       16 Feb, 1744
                                       25 Feb, 1745
     To wife ANN HICKS, this plantation whereon I live called
"Edmondson's Green," and at her decease, to son GHILES HICKS.
     To son JAMES HICKS, the plantation where he now lives on, with
100 A., the land to be divided equally bet. my 2 sons JAMES and
GHILES HICKS, and if GILES shd. die without issue, my daus.
HENRIETA HICKS and MARGARET WEEDS, shd. have 5 pounds each.
     To grand-son JOHN HICKS, 2 ewes.
     The balance of my personal estate, to my wife ANN HICKS.
     To grand-son JOHN WHEATLEY, 2 sheep.
Wit: Hawkins Downes, John Wheatley, Richard Collings.
                                       24. 374

BOON, MARGARET, Queen Anne's Co., widow   15 Aug, 1745
                                             8 May, 1746
     To son ABRAHM BOON, 50 A. land in Queen Anne's Co. on
Dickason's Branch, which land was taken up in partnership bet.

Richard Purnell, William Purniell (?) and John Boon, called and
named, "Partnership."
    To son ABRAHAM BOON, 100 A. "Tamp's Lain" (?), near main road
and Wm. Jump's fence.
    To son JOSEPH BOON,
Son BENJAMIN BOON, ex.
Grand-dau. ABIGALL BELL
Wit: Wm. Starkey, Nathaniel Clough, Thomas Truet. 24. 376

HAMBLETON, JAMES, Queen Anne's Co.   1 Apr, 1746
                                           19 May, 1746
    My estate divided bet. my 3 child.: HANSE, SARAH and JAMES
HAMBLETON.
    Appoint bro. WILLIAM HAMBLETON, ex.
Wit: Gilbert Reed, John Collines   24. 377

O'NEALE, CHARLES, Queen Anne's Co.   10 Sep, 1744
                                     27 Feb, 1745
    To O'NEIL PRICE, son of Charles Price, 100 A. in Tulley's in
Queen Anne's Co., pt. of tract called "Winfield," that pt. I
purchased of Thomas Thomas.
    To CHARLES PRICE, JR., son of afsd. Charles Price, slaves.
    To WILLIAM PRICE, son of sd. Charles
    To JOHN PRICE, son of sd. Charles
    To Mary Emory, wife of Thomas Emory
    To ELIZABETH PRICE, dau. of Charles Price
    To SARAH PRICE, dau. of Charles Price.
    My son, CHARLES PRICE, ex.
Wit: Henry Costin, Wm. Elbert, James Costin.   24. 378

THOMAS, TRUSTRAM, SR., Tulley's Neck, Queen Anne's Co.
                                   30 Dec, 1745
                                    4 Mar, 1745
    To son STEPHEN THOMAS and MARY, his wife, 80 A. upper corner
of land where he now lives, pt. of tract called "Hawkins'
Pharsalia," and at their decease, to ROBERT THOMAS, son of sd.
STEPHEN and MARY THOMAS.
    To son PHILEMON THOMAS, 60 A. adjoining upon branch of
Tuckahoe Creek, being pt. of tract called "Hawkins' Pharsalia."
    To son BENJAMIN THOMAS (after decease of my wife), my
homestead plantation being remaining pt. of my sd. plantation
called "Hawkins' Pharsalia," together with 30 A. purchased out of
"Alcock's Pharsalia."
    To wife JANE THOMAS
    To sons and daus.: TRUSTRAM, SIMON, THOMAS, PENELOPE JARMAN,
ANN JARMAN and NANCY SANDMAN, widow, 500 pounds tobbacco each.
                                       24. 380

CARMAN, JOHN, Queen Anne's Co.   16 Feb, 1745/6
                                   17 Apr, 1746
    To son WILLIAM BURTON CARMAN, 2 s.
    To son HENRY CULLY CARMAN, near land called "Hawkin's Range."
    Appoint wife RACHELL CARMAN, extx.
Wit: Vincent Vanderford, R. Porter, Jr., Wm. Carman.
                                      24. 382

SOTHORN, BENJAMIN, Charles Co.   21 Jan, 1745
                                          4 Apr, 1745
    To bro. SAMUEL SOTHORN, 125 A., "Two Friends,," then to his
son, LEAVEN SOTHORN.
    To bro. SAMUEL's sons, RICHARD and JOHN JOHNSONS SOTHORN.
personalty.
    MARY CLERK, sister; dau. ELIZABETH.
    To bro. RICHARD SOTHORN; his son JOHN.
    Mother mentioned, but name not given.
    Ex. not mentioned.
Wit: Elizabeth Clerk, John Burch, Mary Swann, Wm. Nation, Leonard
Clark.   24. 383

REED, THOMAS, Charles Co.   18 Dec, 1741
                                           2 Apr, 1746
    To wife ELIZABETH REED, plantation where I now live.
    Child.: SARAH COOKSEY, SUSANNA DULEY, MARY COOKSEY, ELIZABETH
DULEY.
    To eldest dau ELIZABETH DULEY, wife of JAMES DULEY.
Wit: Robt. Yeats, John Harris, Robt. Yeats, Jr.   24. 384

ASTON, ELENOR, St. Mary's Co.   17 Apr, 1730/9
                                          14 Apr, 1746
    Child.: JOHN SMOOT, SARAH SMOOT.
    Grand-child.: THOS. RIGG, WM. NEALE RIGG, SARABELLA RIGG,
WINIFRED RIGG, WILLIAM HARRISON, ASTEN SANFORD SMOOT, SARAH RICE,
ELIZABETH DORSEY, JOHN DORSEY, JOHN THOMAS.
    John Smoot son, ex.
Wit: John Stevens, William Bryan, Sarah Dorsey.   24. 385

JONES, MARY, St. Mary's Co.   4 Apr, 1746
                                          12 May, 1746
    Child.: SUSANNA BISSCOE, JOSEPH, JOHN.
    Joseph Jones, son, ex.
Wit: Thos. Granan, William Thomas.   24. 387

BERRY, JAMES, Talbot Co.   10 Dec, 1739
                                          29 May, 1746
    To wife SARAH BERRY, my dwelling plantation.
    My lands divided bet. my 4 sons: JOHN, JAMES, JOSEPH and
BENJAMIN BERRY.
    That his men friends, members of the people called Quakers in
Talbot Co., choose or appoint by the meetings from time to time
to act in the division of land.
    Wife SARAH, extx.
Wit: Francis Neall, Robert Harwood, James Ratcliff, Thomas
Thompson.   24. 388

SKINNER, RICHARD, Talbot Co., gentleman. 21 Oct, 1745
                                          20 May, 1746
    To my 2 sons ANDREW and RICHARD SKINNER, my land lying bet.
St. Michael's River and a creek called The Bear Point Creek or
Leeds Creek, to be divided bet. sd. sons.
    To son DANIEL SKINNER, land called "Adventure" in Dorchester
Co., on south side of Great Choptank River.

To dau. MARY SKINNER
To dau. ELIZABETH SKINNER, slave and slaves not already
bequeathed KATHERINE SKINNER.
Wife, extx.
Wit: Jo Hopkins, Robert Spencer, Elizabeth Hopkins, Mary Spencer.
24. 390

STUDHAM, JOHN, Talbot Co.   24 Mar, ----
                                             9 May, 1746

To son THOMAS CLEMENT STUDHAM, land "Studham's Chance," on
Island Creek, adjoining "Boon's Hope."
Wife, JANE STUDHAM, extx.   24. 391

SPRY,, THOMAS, SR., Talbot Co.   13 Jan, 1741
                                             18 Apr, 1746

To wife, ELIZABETH, my dau. ELIZABETH, some slaves.
To son THOMAS SPRY, land on Chester River called "Dodington."
Sons CHRISTOPHER SPRY and THOMAS SPRY, exs.   24. 392 - 393

RYAN, MICHAEL, Talbot Co.   14 Mar, 1744/5
                                             14 Apr, 1746

Wife, MARY RYAN
Wit: Benj. Callaghan, John Christian.   24. 394

DASHIELL, WILLIAM, Somerset Co.   8 Dec, 1745
                                             20 Mar, 1745

To son JAMES DASHIELL, my land below Witiponen Creek, bet.
where I live and Thomas Shirman, and in case my son JAMES shd.
die without issue, then the right of my WILLIAM DASHIELL.
To my JOSEPH DASHIELL, upper pt. of tract called "Dashiell
Purchase," and if JOSEPH shd. die without issue, son WM., shd.
inherit.
To my 3 sons, my right of "Great Marsh" which was given me by
my father.
To dau. SARAH DASHIELL, 1 gold ring.
Wife ISABELLA DASHIELL, extx.
Wit: Jos. Dashiell, Jesse Dashiell, Daniel Day.   24. 394

MILES, WILLIAM, Somerset Co.   7 Feb, 1745/6
                                             9 Mar, 1745

To son WILLIAM MILES, land near head of Manakin, provided he
or hrs. pay to his bro. GEORGE MILES, 25 pounds money, and if he
die without issue, then to my son SAMUEL MILES, that neither of
them disturb my son STACY MILES from peaceably possessing the
plantation whereon I live.
Wife MARY MILES
My 3 child.: SAMUEL, MARY and HANNAH
Appoint wife MARY HANNAH MILES, and son STACEY, exs.
Wit: Daniel Maddox, Barnaby Willis, William Fordred. 24. 396

BOYER, ROBERT, Pocomoke, Somerset Co.   27 Mar, 1746
                                             12 Apr, 1746

To my sister MARY BOOTH, cattle.
Son JOHN CLIFTON, that I had of George Clifton

To cousin SAMUEL MATTHEWS, son of my sister HANNAH MATTHEWS,
gun I bought of John Evans.
To wife SARAH BOYER, lands during life.
To my negro man, HARRY, 50 A. after decease of my wife.
To GEORGE DICKESON, son of Abraham Dickeson, remainder of my
lands.
After decease of my wife, my sisters MARY BOOTH and HANNAH
MATTHEWS and JOHN DICKESON and SARAH DICKESON, my personal
estate.
Wife SARAH BOYER, extx.
Wit: James Nairne, Ralph Milbourne, Sr., Wm. Evens, Hannah
Milbourn.   24. 397

YOUNG, ELIZABETH, Christ Church Parish, Calvert Co.
                                             9 Apr, 1746
                                            10 May, 1746
To dau SUSANNAH HOWERTON, 1 slave.
To dau MARY HOWERTON, 1 slave.
To dau. ELIZABETH GILLEY, 10 pounds money.
To grand-son WILLIAM GILLEY, 1 slave.
To son WILLIAM WILLIAMS, SR., slaves.
My 3 child.: WILLILAM WILLIAMS, SR., SUSANNAH HOWERTON and
ELIZABETH GILLIS.
Wit: William Williams, Sr., John Howerton, A. Bower, Aaron
Williams, John Young.   24. 399

WATKINS, GASSAWAY, Anne Arundel Co.   23 May, 1746
                                              9 Jul, 1746
To son JOHN WATKINS and hrs., land on the side of branch
called "Jacob's Branch," where his dwelling house now stands,
bounded with the water of the river.
Remainder of my plantation called "Townhill" to be divided
bet. my son GASSAWAY WATKINS, JR. and son NICHOLAS WATKINS.
To dau. ELIZABETH RAWLING, 1 slave.
To dau. MARY
Son John Gassaway, and Nicholas my son-in-law, Richard Harwood
and son Gassaway Watkins, exs.
Wit: Jno. Jiams, Wm. Jiams, Will Chettin.   24. 400

RIDDLE, JOHN, Prince George's Co.   19 Aug, 1745
                                            20 May, 1746
Wife ELENOR RIDDLE, extx.
To son JOHN RIDDLE, 5 sh.
To dau. ELIZABETH LINTEN, 5 s.
Wife ELINOR, my whole estate.
Wit: John Evans, Sr., John Evans, Jr., Wm. Smith. 24. 402

WARING, SAMUEL, Prince George's Co.   1 Jun, 1744
                                            23 May, 1746
To bro. BASIL WARING, land in sd. county given me by my bro.
THOMAS WARING, being pt. of tract called "Warring's Lott."
Wit: Thos. Waring, John Belt, 3rd, James Waring. 24. 403

BELT, MIDDLETON, Prince George's Co.   25 Feb, 1745
                                     21 May, 1746
   To nephew MIDDLETON BRASHEAR, son of Basil Brashear, at the
decease of my honoured father Benjamin Belt, 1 slave.
   My father, Benjamin Belt, ex.
Wit: George Wells and John Brashears.   24. 403

BURGESS, SAMUEL, Charles Co.   20 Feb, 1745/6
                                     7 May, 1746
   To son JOHN BURGESS, 1 saddle.
   To son THOMAS BURGESS, 1 horse.
   To my wife, unnamed, 1/3 pt. of my estate.
   To my 3 child.: THOMAS, JANE and the unborn child., 1/3 pt. of
my estate.
   My wife, extx.
Wit: John Jones, Matthew Breeding   24. 404

THOMAS, TRUSTRAM, Queen Anne's Co.   24 Apr, 1746
                                   29 May, 1746
   To wife ANN THOMAS, my dwelling plantation, whereon I now
live.
   To son CHRISTOPHER THOMAS, containing 100 A. where he now
lives called "Trustram."
   To son JOHN THOMAS, 100 A.
   To son TRUSTRAM THOMAS, tract called "Trustram."
   To son JOSEPH THOMAS, as remainder of land called "Trustram,"
of 200 A.
   To son JOHN THOMAS, furniture.
   To son JOSEPH THOMAS, furniture.
   To dau. RACHELL THOMAS, furniture.
   To dau. ELIZABETH PRYER
   Wife, extx.
Wit: John Emory, Jr., Edmund Thomas, John Emory. 24. 405

COUNTISS, PETER, Queen Anne's Co.   7 May, 1746
                                   30 May, 1746
   To son JAMES COUNTISS, tract "Hawkins Farm," whereon I now
live, on tract which my father bought of Robert Smith, Esq., of
70 A., which 2 tracts I give son JAMES.
   Remaining pt. to wife and my other child.
   Wife, extx.
Wit: Thos Wilkinson, Wm. Rench, Jr., Henry Rench.
                                    24. 407

DISHAROON, LEVIN, Worcester Co.   15 Mar, 1745/6
                                   4 Jun, 1746
   Wife REBECCA DISHAROON.
   To loving son, LEVIN DISHAROON, 2 tracts, "Holdar's Folly,"
the plantation I now live on.
   To daus.: MARY, SARAH, REBECCA, JANE, ELIZABETH and EUNICE
DISHAROON, land called "Wilson," 200 A., equally.
   Wife REBECCA, extx.
Wit: Benjamin Handy, George Smith, Robt. Hand.   24. 408

MURRAY, DAVID, Worcester Co.   15 Sep, 1745
                                       25 Jun, 1746
   To dau. ESTHER MURRAY, son WILLIAM MURRAY, lot in town, No.
29, on west side of courthouse lots, which I bought of John
Martin, after his mother's decease, that is she to have during
her life.
   That Isaac Morris shall have my son WILLIAM, until he is age
21.
   To son NATHANIEL HOPKINS MURRAY, sixty feet square of land in
Snow Hill Town, being pt. of lot No. 16, purchased of Patrick
Gootey, his mother to have during life, then to NATHANIEL HOPKINS
MURRAY.
   To son SAMUEL MURRAY, young horse; land I bought of Matthias
Nicholson in Indian Town, be sold by my extx. to pay my debts.
   Son NATHANIEL HOPKINS MURRAY be bound as an apprentice as soon
as he is capable to any trade his mother shall think proper.
   Wife extx.
Wit: Henry Lowe, John Scarborough, Temperance Round, Elizabeth
Stevenson.   24. 409

CLARKSON/CLERKSON, ROBERT, Dorchester Co.   2 Mar, 1745/6
                                     25 Apr, 1746
   To eldest son ROBERT CLERKSON, JR., land called "Poplar Neck."

   To son JOSEPH CLERKSON, 2 tracts, "Clarkson's Industry,"
"Clerkson's Folly."
   Wife, PHILLIS CLARKSON.
Wit: Wm. Carman, Jr., John Neal, Joshua Carman.   24. 410

SMITH, HENRY, Dorchester Co.   20 Apr, 1745/6
                                     10 Jun, 1746
   To daus.: RACHEL SMITH, MARY SMITH and MAGER SMITH, the land
which I now lilve on.
   To wife MARY, my furniture.
   To dau. RACHEL, cattle.
   To dau. MARY, cattle.
   To dau. MAJOR SMITH, cattle.
   To ELIZABETH BUCKWORTH, cattle.
Wit: John Woodgate, James Hall, David Williams.   24. 412

PHILLIPS, CATHERINE, Dorchester Co.   22 Mar, 1745/6
                                     29 May, 1746
   To son WILLIAM PHILLIPS, 1 slave.
   To dau. MARY FERGUSON, furniture and my clothing.
   To grand-son CHARLES FERGUSON, 1 cow.
   My estate shall be divided bet. my son WILLIAM PHILLIPS, and
my dau. MARY FERGUSON, except 1 s., which I give my grand-son
LEVIN PHILLIPS.
Wit: Joseph Shinton and Mary Shinton.   24. 413

WHEELER, CHARLES, Dorchester Co.   17 Sep, 1742
                                     21 May, 1746
   To son JOHN WHEELER, land "Rights Lot."
   To son THOMAS WHEELER, tract "York and York's Addition."
   Son SAMUEL WHEELER

To dau. MARY FURGUSON, 1 s.
To dau. ELIZABETH SOWARD, 1 chest.
To dau. ALICE THOMAS, furniture.
To grand-sons: JOSEPH WHEELER, JOHN WHEELER, PATRICK HUGHS,
JOHN HUGHS, 10 s. each.
My friends, William Ross, Sr., and Stewart of sd. county to
see that my will is fulfilled.
Wit: John Stewart, Edward White, Thomas Young.   24. 414

HUGHS, JOHN, Dorchester Co.   2 Jun, 1746
                                                     -- Jul, 1746

To son PATRICK HUGHS, 1 horse.
To son JOHN HUGHS, stock.
To dau. ANN HUGHS, cattle.
Wife CATHERINE HUGHS, extx.
Wit: Josias Mace, Wm. Trego, John Stevens, Philemon Trego.
                                                     24. 415

ROGERS, DAVID, Dorchester Co.   8 Feb, 1745/6
                                                     21 May, 1746

To wife ELCE, land "Espasia," bet. Tedious Creek and Goose
Creek, 40 A.
To sons WILLIAM RODGERS and DAVID RODGERS (OR ROGERS), my
lands near mouth of Slater Creek and "Meekings Horecon," 390 A.
Personals divided bet. child.: WILLIAM, DAVID, MARY, JOHN,
ELIZABETH and BORDINE.
Wife, extx. Wit: John McKnamar, Hue Cannon, Rachel Spicer.
                                                     24. 416

WILLEY, JOHN, Dorchester Co.   5 Nov, 1743
                                                     11 Jun, 1746

Son FRANCIS WILLEY
Dau. ELSE RODGERS
To dau. ROSANNA, 1 s.
To dau. SARAH INSLEY, 1 s. sterl.
Dau. CATHERINE WILLEY
My son Wm. Willey, I constitute ex.
Wit: John McNamara, Hue Cannon, Wm. Carson, John Willin.
                                                     24. 418

WROUGHTON, WILLIAM, Dorchester Co.   29 Jan, 1745
                                                     21 May, 1746

Son THOMAS WROUGHTON
Dau. RACHEL (RACHELL) PRITCHETT
Wife RACHEL, my estate.
My wife RACHEL, half the orchard.
Wit: Thomas Adams, Thomas Wroughton, Sr., Henry Johnson.
                                                     24. 419

PHILLIPS, JAMES, of Blackwater, Dorchester Co. 9 Feb, 1745
                                                     11 Jun, 1746

To bro. ANDREW SALSBURY, land which my father, PHILL PHILLIPS,
gave me in his will, called "Phillips' Adventure."
To father-in-law, JOHN SALSBURY, personal estate, and appoint
him ex.

Wit: Matthew Wright, Patrick Carraum, Richard North.   24. 420

GOLDSMITH, THOS. NOTLEY, St. Mary's Co.   14 Apr, 1746
                                              3 Jun, 1746
     To sons JOHN, MICHAEL and NOTELY, all my tract in Bashfor
Manner.
     To son JOHN, where I now live, then to his son John.
     To son NOTELY, that pt where son JOHN now lives.
     To son MICHAEL, that pt where son BENONI now dwells.
     To son WILLIAM, tract in Chaptico Hundred.
     To son BENONI, tract called "Nichols's Hope."
     To daus: TRUMAN GOLDSMITH, MARY TAYLER, JUDITH SHANKS, SUSANNA
ROBERTS, personalty.
     John, Michael and William Goldsmith, exs.
Wit: Justian Jordan, Justian Jordan, Jun., Sarah Smith.
                                                        24. 421

ALVEY, MARGARET, St. Mary's Co.   16 May, 1736
                                              3 Jun, 1746
     Child.: LEONARD, JOSEPH, ARTHUR, MARY, MARGARET GRAVES,
ELENDER.
     Joseph Alvey son, ex.
Wit: John Alvey, George Greeves.   24. 422

EDWARDS, JOSEPH, St. Mary's Co.   3 May, 1746
                                              3 Jun, 1746
     Child.: JOSEPH, BENJAMIN, STOURTON, JOHN, JOSIAS.
     MARY EDWARDS wife, Stourton Edwards son, exs.
     To wife MARY, "Dimonds Venture."
     To son JOHN, "Edwards Back Land."
     Sons JOSEPH and BENJAMIN to receive land after decease of wife
MARY.
     To son STOURTON EDWARDS, "Taunton Deen," 164 A.
Wit: Melvill Lock, John Edwards, Roberts Edwards.
                                                        24. 423

GRASON, RICHARD, St. Michael's Parish, Talbot Co.
                                              17 Jun, 1746
                                              19 Jul, 1746
     To my 2 sons, RICHARD GRASON and THOMAS GRAYSON, land "Tanners
Help" and "Grason's Discovery."
     Wife, SARAH, extx.
Wit: Meshack Boffield, Nt. Wright, Wm. Fairbank, Thomas Price.
                                                        24. 424 - 425

HOPKINS, ROBERT, Talbot Co.   28 Apr, 1746
                                              5 Aug, 1746
     To wife ELIZABETH HOPKINS, my houses and lot at Talbot County
Court House.
Wit: Joshua Hopkins, Sarah Hopkins, Phillemon Armstrong.
                                                        24. 426

EDWARDS, THOMAS, Talbot Co.   22 Sep, 1745
                                              17 Aug, 1746
     To son ISAAC, my desk and printing books.

Daus. MARY, RACHEL
Son SAMUEL
Appoint Mr. Phillip Martin and Thomas Martin, exs.
Wit: Cornelius Brady, James Akers.
Renounce the will, Aug. 7, 1746. Signed: Phillip and Thomas
Martin.   24. 427

MATTINGLY, WILLIAM, Talbot Co.   11 Feb, 1745
                                        25 Aug, 1746
    To CONSTANT PELLY, my tracts in Baltimore Co., near Garrison
Ridge, known by "Logston's Addition," but now called "Pleasant
Green," 97 A., also land in Anne Arundel Co. and land and estates
in England; appoint her extx.
Wit: William Macclan, Hugh Roberton, Mary Macclan.
                                                      24. 428

HALL, CHRISTOPHER, Kent Co, gentleman.   13 Mar, 1745/6
                                         7 Apr, 1746
    To dau. ELIZABETH GRAY, wife of James Gray, pt. of tract where
she now lives, as it is divided bet. her sister, SARAH WOODLAND,
and herself.
    To dau. SARAH WOODLAND, wife of James Woodland, that pt. of
tract where she lives, as it has been divided bet. her sister,
ELIZABETH GRAY, and herself.
    To dau. MARY HALL, my mannor land, being upon "His Lordship's
Manner" in Kent Co.
    To dau. RACHELL HALL, my plantation with the land thereunto
belonging.
    To dau. ELIZABETH GRAY, wife of James Gray, 2 slaves.
    To dau. MARY HALL, 4 slaves.
    To dau. RACHELL, 5 slaves.
    To dau. MARGARET WILSON, 4 slaves.
    To dau. SARAH WOOD, land slaves.
    To dau. RACHELL HALL, all my money due to me in England.
    To dau. MARY HALL, my money.
    My movable estate, divided bet. my daus.: ELIZABETH GRAY,
SARAH WOODLAND, MARGARET WILSON, MARY HALL and RACHEL HALL.
    Appoint son GEORGE WILSON and daus. MARY HALL and RACHEL HALL,
exs.
Wit: Edward Piner, Richard Guarnap, Richard Bentham.
                                            24. 429 - 430

WORRELL, EDWARD, Kent Co.   4 May, 1746
                                         17 Jun, 1746
    To son EDWARD WORRELL, tract I now live on called "Hillstone"
300 A., another tract called "Switnam's Addition" 100 A.
    Wife MARY WORRELL
    Son EDWARD, and he will not convey tract called "Witness
Farm" to his 2 bros. WILLIAM and SIMON WORRELL.
    To son JOSEPH WORRELL, land called "Bristow."
    To dau. SUSANNAH WORRELL, 30 pounds money.
    Dau. FRANCES COLEY
    To dau. HANNAH WORRELL, money.
    To dau. ANN, 30 pounds.

To son EDWARD and hrs., my pt. of the pew in the old pt. of the church, which I have with Mr. Miller.
To son JOSEPH, my pt. of the pew I hold with Mr. Tovey.
To sons WM. and SIMON, that which I have in the new pt. of the church with Vincent Hatcheson.
Wit: Thos. Ringgold, Martha Hynson, Elizabeth Ringgold.
24. 431

HICKS, ROGER, Kent Co., blacksmith.　　　2 Aug, 1737
　　　　　　　　　　　　　　　　　　　　19 Apr, 1740
To my bro's. son, which is in England, my dwelling plantation. Give 100 A. called "Hick's Intention" to be sold to pay my debts.
But if my bro's. son does not come into this country in 3 years time, then I give same to WORLDLY SMITH, Queen Anne's Co.
Ex., Christopher Williams.
Wit: Wm. Cove, Susnna McKey, Samuel Beck.　　　24. 433

NEALE, NICHOLAS, Kent Co.　　　　　30 Apr, 1746
　　　　　　　　　　　　　　　　　 7 Jun, 1746
My wife and my bro., Charles Neale, exs.
To my 5 child., personal estate to be divided equally amongst them as follows: CHARLES NEAL, JAMES NEAL, DANIEL NEAL, REBECCA NEAL, and an unborn child. REBECCA NEAL, my dau., to be brought up by Benj. Green.
Leave son DANIEL NEAL, in care of his unkle EDMUND DILLHUNT, to learn his trade of a sadler.
Wit: Thomas Goodman, Daniel Dillihunt, Malcum Stewart.
24. 434

MILLER, MARTHA, Kent Co.　　　　　27 Nov, 1744
　　　　　　　　　　　　　　　　　 5 Apr, 1746
Desires to pay debts contracted since death of her husband, by her son SAMUEL MILLER.
To son MICHAEL MILLER, my great Bible and common prayer book.
To son NATHANIEL MILLER, Negro Bob.
To dau. MARTHA, now wife of Pridor Blakeston, 10 s.
To dau. MARY, wife of Stephen Glanvill, 1 s. sterl.
To dau. ELIZABETH, wife of Ralph Page, Negro Little Jane.
To dau. REBECCA, wife of Jacob Glenn (or Glann), Jr.
To grand-son SAMUEL MILLER, son of my son SAMUEL, Jeffrey.
To grand-dau. REBECCA WICKS, 1 silver nutmeg grater.
To grand-sons MICHAEL THOMAS and JAMES, and my grand-dau. ANNE MILLER, child. of my son MICHAEL, some sheep.
To grand-son RICHARD MILLER, son of my son SAMUEL, Negro Venus.
To son SAMUEL, 1 slave.
Son SAMUEL, to have fashionable tombstone to cover his father's tomb.
Also SAMUEL, her son, ex.
Wit: Isaac Francis, William Newton, Thomas Stinton, John Goodwin.
24. 435

GREENWOOD, JAMES, Kent Co., planter.　　26 Feb, 1745/6
　　　　　　　　　　　　　　　　　　　　 7 Apr, 1746

To son JAMES GREENWOOD, my wife, JOHANNA GREENWOOD, my
plantation.
Wife, JOHANNA, extx.
Wit: James Kelly, James Berry, Richard Benham (or Bentham).
24. 436

MACKDANNAN, JAMES, Anne Arundel Co.   2 Jun, 1746
                                          21 Jul, 1746
My wife SOPHIA.
To grand-dau. MARY SCRIVENOR, 1 slave.
Son-in-law, Charles Connant, ex.
That what is left of my estate after the decease of my wife,
be and remain in hands of my beloved son-in-law, CHARLES CONNANT,
to be divided equally bet. his 3 daus. viz. HENRIETTA CONNANT,
ELIZABETH CONNANT and SARAH CONNANT, when they are age 16.
Wit: Richard Camden, Wm. Tillard.   24. 438

TROTT, THOMAS, Anne Arundel Co., planter   3 Mar, 1739
                                           16 Jul, 1746
My wife, SARAH, the care of my eldest son THOMAS, and to take
care of all my other child.
To son JOHN TROTT, my sword and guns.
To son THOMASON TROTT, land where WM. and ELIZABETH LUDWICK
now live, called "Trent."
To dau. MARY, wife of Thomas Scott, 1 s. sterl.
To dau. ELIZABETH, wife of William Parrot, 1 s.
Wit: John Powell, Richard Scrivener, Jr., James Pickering.
                                                24. 439

PACA, RACHEL, Baltimore Co.   27 Jan, 1745
                                           26 Mar, 1746
Son PERRIGRINE BROWN
To dau. MARTHA PACA, 1 slave.
Col. John Hall receive my dau. MARTHA PACA, with her portion
left her by her father.
To son PERREGRINE BROWN, 10,000 nails now in his possession
and etc.
If both above child. die without issue, then to my six
cousins: namely, JOHN TILDEN, CATHERINE TILDEN, WM. BLAY TILDEN,
WM. WEATHERSHEAD, SAMUEL WEATHERSHEAD and JOHN WEATHERSHEAD.
My friends John Hall and Jacob Giles
Wit: Mary Clerk, Michael Webster, Wm. Smith.
Codicil date, 27 Jan, 1745.
Wit: Elizabeth Bradford, Mary Clerk, Michael Webster.
                                                24. 440

STOKES, SUSANNAH, Baltimore Co.   25 Aug, 1745
                                           26 Mar, 1746
Son JOHN STOKES, 3 grand-child., ROBERT STOKES, CORDELLIA
STOKES and FRANCIS STOKES.
To grand-son JOHN PACA, stock.
To grand-son ROBERT STOKEY, slaves.
To grand-dau. CORDELLIA STOKES, slaves.
To grand-dau. FRANCES STOKES, 1 slave.

Mr. Perrigine Frisbey give up to my son, JOHN STOKES, the lease that was assigned over to me by Mr. Samuel Howell and my son.
My kinsman, Mr. Perrigrine Frisby, ex.
Wit: Rachel Paca, Peregrine Brown, Mary Clerk.   24. 441

BUTLER, HENRY, Baltimore Co.   8 Jun, 1745
                                                2 May, 1746
    Son ABSOLOM, son HAMAN, dau. ELIZABETH and daus.: SUSANNAH KEITH (?), SOPHIA and TEMPERANCE.
Wit: T. Sheredine, Robert North, Wm. Hammond.   24. 442

COLE, CASSANDRA, Baltimore Co.   19 Jun, 1745
                                                13 May, 1746
    To son SKIPWITH COALE, my slaves.
    To son WILLIAM COALE, my slaves.
    To WILLIAM'S child.,
    To dau. CASSANDRA RIGBIE, a chair.
    To dau. ANN JONES,
    To grand-son, SKIPWITH, slaves.
    To son WM. COALE'S child., my grand-dau. CASSANDRA JOHNS, slaves.
    To grand-dau. SUSANNAH RIGBIE, 1 slave.
    Son SKIPWITH COLE, and son-in-law, Nathan Rigbie exs.
Wit: Joseph Jones, Charles Williams, Daniel Kenley. (Joseph Jones, being one of the people called Quakers.)
                                                24. 444

PARISH, JOHN, Baltimore Co.   4 Oct, 1745
                                                2- Jun, 1746
    To son ROBERT PARISH, 1 slave.
    To dau. MARY PARISH, 1 slave.
    To dau, ELIZABETH,
    My wife ELIZABETH PARRISH, 1/3 of my estate, and appoint her as extx.
Wit: Joseph Taylor, John Wooden (one of the people called Quakers).   24. 445

RATTENBURY, JOHN, Baltimore Co., gentleman.   3 Mar, 1745
                                                4 Jun, 1746
    To nephew JOHN CROMWELL, and nephew RATTENBURY JONES, my lands in Baltimore and Anne Arundel Counties.
    To RICHARD IRELAND, my clothing and 10 pounds money to buy him a suit of mourning.
    To CAPTAIN PHILLIP JONES, JR., my stallion.
    To GEORGE BRAMWELL, schoolmaster, a mourning gold ring.
    My wife MARGARET RATTENBURY.
    To nephews RATTENBURY JONES and NICHOLAS JONES   Appoint wife Margaret Rattenbury, and Capt. Phillip Jones, Jr., exs.
Wit: Richard Richardson, Wm. Lynch, Geo. Bramwell.   24. 446

SMITH, WILLIAM, Baltimore Co.   18 Mar, 1746
                                                10 Jun, 1746
    To my wife JOHANNA SMITH, son JOHN SMITH and son THOMAS SMITH, 1 s.

80

To son WILLIAM SMITH, my plantation where I live, my mill and buildings, and only he shall pay to his sister, CHISTEN, 10 pounds money, and sister ESTHER, at expiration of 4 years. All remains to be equally divided among my daus. My wife and son THOMAS SMITH, exs. Son WM. SMITH, and daus. CHRISTIAN SMITH and ESTHER SMITH, is to be educated with pt. of benefit of the mill. Joseph Crockett and Alexander Hill, guardians over his child. Wit: Samuel Crockett, Samuel Tencher, Joseph Crockett.

24. 447

WRIGHT, ISAAC, Baltimore Co.   17 May, 1746
                                                5 Aug, 2746
    Appoint MARY, my wife.
    To son ISAAC, my dwelling plantation.
    Tract "Wright's Range" be sold to maintain wife and child.
Wit: Mary McGill, John Brown, William Murphy. Came William
Winchester and probated the will.   24. 448

UNDERWOOD, SAMUEL, Baltimore Co.   27 Mar, 1745/6
                                                7 Aug, 1746
    To dau ELIZABETH, 50 A.
    Son SAMUEL
    Wife MARY UNDERWOOD
Wit: Aquilla Carr (Quaker), John Hust, Charles Gorsuch.
                                                24. 449

NUTTER, JOHN HEWETT, Somerset Co.   14 Dec, 1745
                                                18 Jun, 1746
    To son HEWETT NUTTER, land I bought of my bro. MATTHEW NUTTER,
as will appear by deed from Robert Jones, atty. for Mr. John
Nutter, of Pennsylvania, by records of Somerset Co.
    That lands where James Dunkin formerly lived to be the right
of my son CHARLES NUTTER.
    To sons, HEWETT, CHARLES and JOHN, my land down the bottom of
Nutter Neck.
    To my 2 child., SARAH and NANCY, slaves.
    Gives his child. his estate in Great Brittain.
    To wife, ANN NUTTER, her choice of slaves.
    Friends Col. Geo. Dashiell, Capt. Day Scott, Capt. Isaac
Handy, trustees.
Wit: Charles Rawlins, Elizabeth Rawlins, Robert Price.
                                                24. 450

HARPER, WILLIAM, Somerset Co.   4 Aug, 1746
                                                20 Aug, 1746
    My bro. JOHN HARPER, when he is 21
    Cousin JOHN HARPER, furniture.
    To JOHN PITCHER, my crop.
    To my unkle, EDWARD HARPER, stock, he to be ex.
Wit: Wm. Revill, James Hayman, John Hayman.   24. 452

EARLE, John, Queen Anne's Co.   19 Mar, 1745
                                                17 Jul, 1746
    To my 4 sons: JAMES, JOHN, WILLIAM and BENJAMIN, my 2 tracts.

To son John, Grist Mill on tract "Heathworth."
To wife, HANNAH, my horse and furniture.
To dau. MARGARET EARLE, slaves.
My son, JOHN, and his estate in care of my friend, James
Ringold, son of William Ringold, until 21.
Leave son, JAMES EARLE, with his unkle, Thomas Ringold, during
minority, desiring the same THOMAS RINGOLD, to deal kindly by
him.
Sons WM. and BENJAMIN EARLE, in care of their unkle, John
Ringold.
Wife, Hannah, extx.
Wit: John Collins, Jr., Wm. Powell, Wealthy Ann Collins.
24. 453

PRICE, HENRY, Queen Anne's Co.   23 May, 1746
                                              31 Jul, 1746
To wife ELIZABETH PRICE; at her decease, to son WM. PRICE, the
land whereon I live, but if he marry against her will, then land
to fall to my son, THOMAS.
To grand-dau, ELIZABETH NOBLE, cattle.
Wife, extx.
Wit: James Swan, Rebecca Swan, Sarah Swan, Wm. Stoneman.
24. 454

FOURMIN, JOHN, Queen Anne's Co.   29 Aug, 1746
                                               9 Sep, 1746
To widow REBECCA WILLIAMS, my personal estate and appoint her
extx. I have no land.
Wit: Thomas Cloak, John Morris.   24. 455

HEATH, CHARLES, Cecil Co., gentleman.   25 Apr, 1746
                                              12 Jun, 1746
400 A. conveyed by my unkle, James Heath, deceased, to me.
Same to be in possession of my wife, REBECCA. At her decease,
son CHARLES, shall have same.
To son JAMES HEATH, other 100 A. devised me by my unkle JAMES,
and a lot in the town of Warwick.
To my dau. REBECCA, and her hrs., my other lot in Warwick.
My kinsman, James Paul Heath, ex.
Wit: John Jackson, Daniel Bryan, John Rice.
Probated by Dr. John Jackson and Daniel Bryant. 24. 457

NOLLAND, HENRY, Cecil Co.   29 May, 1739
                                              13 Jun, 1746
To bro. RICHARD NOLLAND, 5 s. sterl.
To bro. JAMES NOLLAND, 5 s. sterl.
To sister, MARY, now wife of Matthew Hodgson of Cecil Co.
To sister, SARAH, 5 s. sterl.
Sister Mary, and Matthew Hodgson, exs.
Wit: John Herbert, Michael Wallace, William Crage.
24. 458

WRIGHT, JAMES, Cecil Co., cooper.   30 Sep, 1745
                                              20 Aug, 1746
To wife, the 2 pts. of my estate.

To son JOHN, the other third pt., and if my wife dies, the
one-half of her share is to be divided bet. my 2 bros., WILLIAM
and DAVID; but if son, JOHN, shd. die, his pt. is to be divided
bet. my 2 bros. likewise, WM. and DAVID.
She is to bring up the child and school it until it is fit to
put to a trade (probably means unborn child, name not given).
Wife and James Evans, exs.
Wit: Thomas Thompson, Richard Giddens, John Smyth.
24. 459

LAWSON, DAVID, Cecil Co.   19 Feb, 1741/2
                                            24 Aug, 1746
Son JOHN LAWSON, and dau. SUSANNAH.
To son PETER, 1 s. to be paid by my ex., hereafter nominated.
To dau. ELIZABETH, 1 s.
To son JOHN
Wit: Walter Diven, Catharine Diven, Nicholas Wood.   24. 460

WILSON, ALEXANDER, Charles Co.   12 Aug, 1745
                                            20 Aug, 1746
MARY WILSON, wife.
Grandchild.: MARY BUCHANAN, WM. BUCHANAN, CHLOE OWEN, ANN
WILSON, ALEX. WILSON.
Mentions his children, unnamed.
Ex., no name given.
Wit: Geo. Tarvine, Charles Vermilian.   24. 461

TRUITT, GEORGE, Mulberry Grove, Worcester Co.
                                            5 Jun, 1746
                                            9 Jul, 1746
     To eldest son JOHN TRUITT, after decease of his mother,
ELIZABETH TRUITT, land on the northwest side of the county road,
until it comes to the division bet. me and my cousin, Phillip, it
being the tract whereon I live, called "Mulberry Grove."
     To son GEORGE TRUITT, 140 A., after decease of his mother,
ELIZABETH TRUITT, lying on the southeast side of the county road,
and being pt. of "Mulberry Grove."
     To son JOE TRUITT, 100 A. called "Truitt Harbour."
     To son OUTEN TRUITT, 1 slave.
     To son SAMUEL TRUITT, 1 slave, after decease of his mother,
ELIZABETH TRUITT.
     To dau. ESTHER TURNER, cattle.
     To dau. ELIZABETH TRUITT, and my wife, use of plantation where
I now live.
     To 2 young. daus., after decease of their sd. mother,
ELIZABETH, which is my dau. MARY TRUITT and TABITHA TRUITT,
     Wife Elizabeth, extx.
Wit: Walter Evens, Wm. Jarman, Joseph Carter.   24. 462

TINGELL, ELIZABETH of Somerset Co. [Recorded in Worcester Co.]
                                            18 May, 1740
                                            19 Jul, 1746
     To son DANNELL, tract known as "Hillard's Discovery," 75 A.,
and "Powell Inclosion," 128 A.
     Son DANIEL, ex.

To CALIP TINGELL, pot and pot hangers.
To MARY TINGELL, dau. of DANNIELL TANGELL, 1 chest.
To son DANIEL TINGELL, cattle.
To CALLIP TINGELL, horse colt.
To dau. MARY, dishes.
To MARY COD, JR, 1 wheel.
Wit: Benj. Davis, Richard Biddard.   24. 464

ENNISS, WILLIAM, SR., Worcester Co.   20 Apr, 1746
                                              5 Aug, 1746
     To son WILLIAM ENNISS, 300 A. "Cannarnee," and 5 A. bought of
Nathaniel Enniss, being pt. of tract called "Cannarnee."
     Mentions son NATHANIEL ENNISS
     To son JOHN ENNISS, tract "Enniss Addition," 100 A. and 100 A.
that I bought of my bro. Charles Enniss, it being pt. of tract
called "Cannarnee."
     To son NATHANIEL ENNISS, land bought of Wm. Robertson, lying
in Snow Hill Town.
     Wife to have land where he now lives.
     To son WM. ENNISS, cattle.
     To son NATHANIELL ENNISS, slaves.
     To dau. MARY BRITTINGHAM
     To dau. REBECCA ENNISS, cattle.
     To wife, furniture.
     To dau. REBECCA ENNISS, pasture on the land of her bro. JOHN.
     Mentions his 5 child.
     My wife REBECCA ENNIS, and son WM. ENNIS, exs.
Wit: John Fossitt (or Fassitt), Hannah Davis, Thomas Robins
                                              24. 465

LANGSDON, JOHN, Somerset Co.   18 Aug, 1735
                                             28 Aug, 1746
     Wife, extx.
     I desire that my son-in-law, JAMES SMITH, have education.
Wit: John Short, Samuel Griffith.
Codicil: My son-in-law, JAMES SMITH, may be peaceably possessed
with my principle estate to him and hrs. at his mother's decease.
     To sons-in-law, DAVID SMITH, eldest son, 1 cow; SPEER
LANGSDON, 1 s. sterl.
     To WILLIAM LANGSDON, 1 s. sterl.
     To PRISCILLA BAKER, who was the dau. of Wm. Langsdon, dec'd.,
1 s. sterl.
     The within JOHN LANGSDON, acknowledge right of 3 cattle, which
was left him by his dec'd. father JAMES SMITH, to belong to my
son-in-law, JAMES SMITH, by a lawful inheritance from his father.
     To wife MARY LANGSDON, the land and plantation I live upon,
called "Woodstock," and at her decease to her son, JAMES SMITH.
28 Aug, 1746, came John Short and Samuel Griffith and made oath
that they saw John Langsdon sign his will; that they saw Molten
Ubanks, the other witness sign his name.   24. 467

TURVILL, WILLIAM, Worcester Co.   1 Sep, 1746
                                             6 Oct, 1746
     To JOHN TURVILL, tract "Royall Oak," being pt. of tract in
possession of Walton Purnell.

To cousin RHODAH KENNET, 1 pair gold bobs.
To cousin RACHEL KENNET, same.
To cousin RHODY COLLINGS, same.
To cousin ELIZABETH EVANES, the dau. of Ebenezer Evanes, same.
To RACHEL TURVILL, gold ring.
To cousin WILLIAM COLLINGS, son to JOHN, some cattle.
To cousin MARTIN KENNETT, gold ring.
To sister BRIDGIT KENNETT, stock.
To cousin JOHN WHALL (?), stock.
To sister MARGERY TURVILL, my personal estate.
Wit: Wm. Gault, Wm. Evans, Obed. Gault.   24. 469

CHANCE, WARNER, planter, of Beufort Co., NC. This will was
probated in Queen Anne's Co., MD.   24 May, 1746
                                           18 Sep, 1746
     To dau. ABIGAL CHANCE, 85 A. on south side of Bare (?) River,
head of Moses Creek, being my first purchase of land, 170 A.
     To dau. NEOMI CHANCE, 85 A., remaining pt. of the afsd., to
their hrs.; if both of my sd. daus. shd. die, having no child or
child., then I desire my bro. ELIJAH CHANCE, shd. have both pts.
of afsd. tract.
     My wife's last child JONATHAN CHANCE, 1 s. sterl.
     To my daus. ABIGAL and NEOMI CHANCE, personal estate, and if
they die without issue, then my bro. ELIJAH CHANCE, shd. have
same.
Wit: Thomas Priest, James Andrew, Martha Priest. 24. 470

TUNSTALL, JOHN, Somerset Co.   7 Aug, 1746
                                           22 Sep, 1746
     To grand-son, TUNSTALL HACK, out of my personal estate to full
value of what was left.
     To grand-son PETER SPENCER HACK, the will of his grandfather,
Col. Peter Hack, of Virginia.
     My friends, COL. GEORGE GALE and DAVID WILSON, shall be judges
of the value of afsd. legacy's.
     My friends, above mentioned, and SAMUEL WILSON, the sum of 15
pounds paper money.
     To grand-sons, PETER SPENCER HACK and TUNSTALL HACK, lands in
"Rawley's Neck."
     To the visitors of Public School of Somerset Co., land lying
opposite to THOMAS JONES, about 9 or 10 A., which is called "Mill
Lott."
     To grand-sons TUNSTALL HACK and PETER SPENCER, land lying near
Princess Ann Town, which I bought of John Finch, to be equally
divided bet. them, or to be sold as they shall think it.
     Exs., his 2 grand-sons, mentioned above.
Wit: Ja Robertson, David Wilson, John Holt.   24. 471

COCKEY, JOHN, Baltimore Co.   22 May, 1740
                                           11 May, 1746
     To eldest son WILLIAM COCKEY, land called "Cockey's Folly,"
200 A. on north side of Jones Falls in Baltimore Co.
     To son JOHN COCKEY, slaves.
     To son JOSHUA COCKEY, 1 tract "Antony's Delight" and 1 tract
"Tyes Delight" 100 A, and "Cow Hill" 100 A.

To son EDWARD COCKEY,
To son PETER COCKEY, slaves.
My son JOHN,
To son THOMAS COCKEY, gold watch.
To dau. SARAH COCKEY, slaves.
To sons, WM., JOHN, JOSHUA, EDW. and PETER COCKEY and daus.
SUSANNA GIST, MARY OWINGS and SARAH COCKEY, my personal estate.
Son-in-law Joshua Owings, ex.
Wit: Michael Diskin, Wm. Harvey, Alex Tonzey (or Tenzey), a
quaker affirmed 4 Apr, 1747.   24. 473

TOWNSEND, JAMES, Queen Anne's Co., planter
                                          13 Apr, 1745
                                           9 Oct, 1746
    To wife JANE TOWNSEND, my estate, and at her decease, to my
child.: THOMAS, SOLOMON, JAMES, AARON, MARY, SARAH and JANE.
Wife, extx.
Wit: Henry Price, Thomas Soden, Rachel Roe.   24. 475

CLOUDS, ELIZABETH, Queen Anne's Co.   19 Apr, 1744
                                           16 Oct, 1746
    To son NICHOLAS CLOUDS, tract "Cloud's Chance," provided that
my sd. son NICHOLAS, lives on this island, but if my sd. son shd.
remove off this island, then my will is that my sd. son deliver
possession with all his rights to my son BENJAMIN KERBY, and in
case my son BENJ. KERBY, die without hrs., then I give the same
land to my grand-dau. MARY EVANS and her hrs.
    To son NICHOLAS CLOUDS, 50 pounds paper currency and 10
guineas, and also 1 of my boats.
    Bequeath to SARAH CLOUDS,
    To dau. SARAH PRICE,
    Inasmuch as my husband BENJAMIN CLOUDS, left at his decease,
10 slaves, I now desire that they be divided bet. my 2 sons
NICHOLAS and BENJAMIN.
    I give my grand-dau. MARY EVANS, slaves.
Wit: Mary Griffith, George Benham, John Emory.   24. 476

PEIRPOINT, FRANCES.   23 Feb, 1737/8
                                           13 Oct, 1746
    My wife ELIZABETH PEIRPOINT, extx.
Wit: Thos. Worthington, Charles Yealdhall, Hannah Sewell, Francis
Rawlings, Wm. Rogers.   24. 478

SHERWOOD, MARY, Talbot Co., widow   21 Sep, 1738
                                            7 Nov, 1746
    To son DANIEL SHERWOOD, my estate.
Wit: Wm. Hambleton, Robert Rolle, Phill Hambleton.
                                                 24. 479

ARMSTRONG, FRANCIS, Talbot Co.   9 Jul, 1740
                                            7 Nov, 1746
    To son FRANCIS ARMSTRONG, my now dwelling plantation, tract
"London Derry."

To son FRANCIS, 6 months after my decease, make over to my son RUSSEL ARMSTRONG, all of his estate called "Huntington Grange" lying on St. Michael's River in Talbot Co., 100 A.

My 4 sons, RUSSEL, HENRY, PHILEMON and SOLOMON ARMSTRONG, provided they pay to my dau. MARY ARMSTRONG, 1,000 pounds tobacco when she is 16.

Son FRANCIS ARMSTRONG, ex.

Wit: Geo. Prouse, John Guy Williams, Zadock Betfield, John Guy Williams, Jr. 24. 480

PARR, JOHN, Prince George's Co. 27 Apr, 1745
13 Nov, 1746

To son MARK PARR, 1 s.
To son JOHN PARR, 1 s.
To dau THAME WARD, 1 s.
To dau. ELIZABETH PARR, 1 s.
To son ARTHUR PARR, land near Prince George's Co., called "Parr's Range," 100 A.
To son MATTHEW PARR, land in Prince George's Co., called "Bush Creek Hill," for 100 A.
If both ARTHUR and MATTHEW die without issue, then to dau. ELIZABETH PARR.
To wife MARY PARR, the plantation and land whereon I live.
Wit: John Hobbs, Benj. Clarey, Wm. Brown.
On the back of the foregoing will was written, viz; Nov. 13, 1746. Mr. Robert Brown of Anne Arundel Co. being a person of full age, says that he wrote the foregoing will, at the request and direction of JOHN PARR. Wm. Brown, one of the witnesses, declares upon oath that he saw testator deliver the foregoing will, but did not see him sign it. 24. 482

EUBANKS, RICHARD, Talbot Co. 15 Oct, 1746
13 Nov, 1746

To wife TAMSON EUBANKS, my personal estate in Talbot Co., and if it should so happen that my son HENRY shd. die, then I give my wife TAMSON EUBANKS, my real estate in Talbot Co.
Wife TAMSON EUBANKS, extx.
Wit: R. Porter, Alice Porter, James Porter. 24. 483

MILES, MARGARET, St. Mary's Co. 12 Dec, 1745
11 Aug, 1746

ENOCH FENWICK, friend.
CHILD. of Michael Burn, dec'd., and wife Priscilla, mentioned.
Enoch Fenwick, ex.
Wit: Joseph Stone, John Thompson. 24. 484

HOPEWELL, HUGH, St. Mary's Co. 14 Aug, 1746
13 Oct, 1746

To Mother ELIZABETH HOPEWELL, "Hogpen Neck."
Bros.: JOSEPH, JOHN HOPEWELL.
"Bloomsberry" in Talbot Co. to be sold.
Ex. Joseph Hopewell
Wit: Nicholas Lewise Sewel, Richard Milburn, Richard King. 24. 485

GOODSON, WILLIAM, Kent Co.   18 Aug, 1746
                13 Sep, 1746
 Give sons JOHN GOODSON, WM. GOODSON, THOMAS GOODSON, and dau.
CATHARINE GOODSON, to the care of my son JOHN GOODSON.
Wit: Thomas Atkinson, Thomas Richfield, Abraham B. Porter.
                  24. 486

GREENWOOD, JOHANNA, Kent Co.   3 Sep, 1746
                4 Oct, 1746
 To dau. MARY GREENWOOD, my dau. SARAH TURNER, my gown.
 My third of estate belonging to my husband, JAMES GREENWOOD,
late dec'd., bet. my son JACOB GREENWOOD, and my daus. RACHEL
GREENWOOD and JENNY GREENWOOD, to be equally divided bet. them.
 My will and desire is that my son JOHN MARCH, may have the
management of it until my sd. 3 child., JACOB, RACHEL and JENNY
GREENWOOD, comes to age.
 Appoint my 2 sons JOHN MARCH and JONATHAN TURNER, exs.
Wit: Robert R. Elliott, Patrick McBride, Richard Bentham.
                  24. 487

JAMES, JOHN, Kent Co.   15 Sep, 1746
                11 Oct, 1746
 Wife MARTHA, "Heaths Long Land."
 To young. sons, JAMES and JERVES, son JOHN JAMES, land "Good
Hope" near Church Creek.
 To son SEADNEY JAMES, land "Simsco Prime Choyce," near Farley
Creek.
 To sons JOHN and SEADNY, a gold ring.
 To sons JAMES and JERVIS, 20 s.
 Wife MARTHA, extx.
Wit: J. Bordley, Anthony Knowlman, Mariah White (or Martha
White).   24. 488

TILDEN, JOHN, Kent Co.   5 Aug, 1746
                13 Oct, 1746
 To son JOHN TILDEN, my dwelling plantation called "Bishford
Resurvey."
 To dau. CATHARINE TILDEN, the other half of my lot at
Chestertown.
 To son WM. BLAY TILDEN, tract and plantation called "Blay's
Range" and "Blay's Addition," 200 A. and 75 A.
 To son WM. BLAY TILDEN, my lot in Georgetown, which I bought
of Mr. Giden Pearce.
 To dau. CATHRINE TILDEN, cattle.
 To cousin JOHN THOMAS, stock.
 To sister ANN WILLSON, a suit of mourning.
 To my sons JOHN and WM. BLAY TILDEN, land called "Blay's
Range."
 My good friend, Wm. Hynson
 My dau. CATHARINE TILDEN, leave her
 Cousin Mrs. SARAH KENNARD, and to pay due regard to her aunt
WETHERED.
 Appoint son JOHN TILDEN, ex.
Wit: Henry Hart, John Read, Cornelius Hurt.   24. 489

JONES, ELIZABETH, Kent Co.   9 Apr, 1746
                                       1 Nov, 1746
    To my sister MARGARET JONES, slaves.
    To my bro. DAVID JONES, slaves.
    If my sister MARGARET JONES shd. die before of age, my bro.
THOMAS RASIN JONES, shd. have slaves.
Wit: Abraham Raisin, Margaret Hall, John Raisin.   24. 491

JAMES, MARTHA, Kent Co.   2 Nov, 1746
                                  18 Nov, 1746
    To my friend JAMES CLAYPOOL, my 2 sons JAMES JAMES of JERVIS
JAMES. If James Claypool refuses to take care of his 2 sons,
that Mr. Essaw Watkins shd. have rearing of them; if sd. Esaw
Watkins refuses to raise my sons, then James McClean, Jr. to do
so.
    To ANN LYNCH, an orphan girl, now in the house, clothing.
    Appoint my trusty friend JAMES CLAYPOOL, ex.
Wit: Martha White, James Whight, I. Borsley.   24. 492

MACLINAHAN (or MACLANAHAN), NATHANIEL, Kent Co.
                                  28 Aug, 1746
                                  20 Nov, 1746
    To son JOHN WYAT MACLINAHAN, stock.
    To dau. ELIZABETH, personal estate.
    Wife MARY MACLANAHAN, extx.
Wit: Wm. Carmichael, John Dixon.   24. 493

THOMAS, DAVID, Baltimore Co.   15 Jun, 1746
                                  20 Sep, 1746
    To wife ELIZABETH THOMAS, slaves.
    To son DAVID THOMAS, slaves.
    To dau. ELIZABETH THOMAS, slaves.
    Equal share with the rest of my child., HANNAH THOMAS, slaves.
    To dau. MARY THOMAS, slaves.
    And my unborn child.
    Wife ELIZABETH THOMAS and Thomas Wheeler, exs.
Wit: Ignatius Wheeler, William Few, Patt Conner.
                                            24. 494

COLE, JOHN, Gun Powder, Baltimore Co.   12 Nov, 1745
                                  5 Nov, 1746
    Wife DINAH COLE, extx.
    To son CHARLES COLE, my land, 100 A. called "Cole's Chance."
    To son CHARLES COLE
    To son JOSEPH COLE, land where he now lives called "Cole
Chance" 200 A.
    To son MATTHEW COLE, the land I have constranted by virtue of
assignment from Solomon Cross, with fork of the falls, after
decease of his mother.
Wit: Dennis Garret Cole, Matthew Hale, Wm. Cole.   24. 495

PACA, MARTHA, Baltimore Co.   27 Oct, 1746
                                  17 Nov, 1746
    To son JOHN PACA, slaves.
    To dau. MARY CHEW, slaves.

To my correspondent, JOSEPH ADAMS, merchant in London, my money, sterl. money in his hands.
To friend, ELIZABETH BRADFORD, and her husband,
To grand-son JOHN PACA, son of my dec'd. son AQUILA PACA,
To grand-son, SAMUEL CHEW, slaves.
To grand-dau. PRISCILLA SMITH, 1 slave.
To grand-dau. PHELOPTA CHEW,
To grand-dau. MARY PACA,
To grand-dau. MARTHA PACA, dau. of my son JOHN PACA
To grand-son AQUILA PACA
To grand-dau. SUSANNAH GALLOWAY.
To grand-son WILLIAM PACA, slaves.
To grand-dau. ELIZABETH PACA, slaves.
To MARY BRADFORD, dau of Wm. Bradford, and MARTHA BRADFORD, dau of Wm. Bradford
To friend, ELISABETH BRADFORD, wife of Wm. Bradford
Son JOHN, ex.
Wit: Jos. Middleman, Frances Middleman   24. 496

HOPKINS, HAMPTON, Worcester Co.   15 Feb, 1745
                                               18 Oct, 1746
To son SAMUEL HOPKINS,
To HAMPTON HOPKINS, son of MATTHEW HOPKINS, land at Indian River.
The money due me from the estate of Harvey Wilks be put in the hands of Isaac Morris, for sd. Wilks.
Desire Isaac Morris to act as trustee to my wife.
Wife extx.
Wit: James Martin, Isaac Morris, Samuel Wise.   24. 499

RAIN, MATHEW, Somerset Co.   30 Jan, 1736/37
                                               6 Nov, 1746
To wife ARROCADA, the plantation and 100 A. where she now lives and appoint her extx.
To son MATTHEW, the plantation and 100 A. tract "Greenland," at decease of her mother.
To son JOHN, the other 100 A., and if son JOHN, dies without hrs., my son PHILIP to him.
My estate to be equally divided among my child.
Wit: Wm. Davis, Ishmael Davis, Benjamin Davis.
Signed by and before Benton Harris, Deputy Commissioner of
Worcester Co.   24. 499 - 500

THOMAS, ANN, Prince George's Co.   9 Jul, 1746
                                               21 Jul, 1746
To grand-sons, WILLIAM TENALY and PHILLIP TENALY, JR., slaves.
To 2 grand-daus. SARAH BERRY and ANN BERRY, cattle.
WILLIAM FENDLY (?) (The names of Wm. and Phillip Tenaly, probably may be meant for Fendly).
To dau. WENEFRED LOIS, my wearing apparel.
To son WILLIAM, 1 s. sterl.
To son DANIEL, same.
To dau. ELIZABETH CLENSEY, same.
To son JOHN, same.
Wit: Henry Humphrey, Hugh Humphrey.   24. 501

WEAVER, ANN, Prince George's Co.   15 Jul, 1746
                                       27 Aug, 1746
   To son JAMES VEATCH, 1 slave.
   To dau. ANN DAVIS, 1 slave.
   To dau. MARY MASTERS,
   To son RICHARD WEAVER, 2 leather chairs.
   To son JOHN VEATCH, 1 slave.
   Son John Veatch, ex.
Wit: Charles Hayes, Ephram Gold, John Norris.   24. 501

QUATERMUS, JOHN, Dorchester Co.   4 Jun, 1746
                                       8 Aug, 1746
   To wife SARAH, my whole estate.
Wit: Patrick Quartermus, Geo. Andrew, Geo. Hutton.
                                          24. 502

ROBINSON, WILLIAM, Dorchester Co., planter.
                                  23 Nov, 1745
                                  15 Sep, 1746
   To grand-dau, ELIZABETH ROBINSON, my grand-dau. ELIZABETH
GOULD, my wife RUTH ROBINSON, my now dwelling plantation.
   To son ANDREW ROBINSON, the plantation where he lives, being
pt. of tract of land called "Joseph Lane," the other called
"William's Prevention"
   Sons WILLIAM and ANDREW, exs.   24. 503

HUBBERT, DANIEL, Dorchester Co.   10 Apr, 1741
                                    25 Sep, 1746
   To son HUMPHREY HUBBERT, and NEHEMIAH HUBBERT, tract
"Aclantiss."
   My dau. ELIZABETH.
Wit: Wm. Gray, Henry Ellot.
                                        24. 505

GRIFFITH, LEWIS, Dorchester Co.   1 Jul, 1743
                                  12 Nov, 1746
   My wife ELIZABETH GRIFFIN (2 different spellings appear on the
records).
   To dau. MARY KEENE, 1/3 of all my personal estate.
   To God-dau. ELIZABETH MESSIX, cattle.
   To son LEWIS GRIFFIN, remainder of estate.
The will was signed "Lewis Griffin," first written in the first
paragraph of sd. will.
Wit: Lewis Griffith, Susanna Edgar.   24. 506

MOCKBEE, JANE, Prince George's Co.   2 Mar, 1743/4
                                    27 Nov, 1746
   To son JOHN JOICE, my now dwelling plantation, 104 A., pt. of
"Taylor's Discovery."
   To the child. of my dec'd husband, MATTHEW MOCKBEE, 7 s. and 6
pence sterl.
   To dau. JANE DOULL, my clothing.
   To dau.-in-law SARAH JOICE, my brown Holland gown.

To my 2 child., THOMAS JOICE and JANE DOULL, my personal estate.
Son-in-law Dr. James Doull, ex.
Wit: Lewis Lee, James Elliot, George Maccanlie.   24. 507

CHAMPHIN or CRAMPHIN -- He signed his will "HENRY C. CRAMPHIN")
Prince George's Co.   4 Jul, 1741
                                              27 Nov, 1746
My wife MARY CHAMPHIN
My son JOHN CRAMPHIN
To my sons, JOHN, HENRY, THOMAS AND BAZIL CRAMPHIN, my slaves.
To grand-son WALKINS CRAMPHIN,
To grand-son DENMAN CRAMPHIN, son of JOHN CRAMPHIN,
To grand-dau. MARY CRAMPHIN, dau. of JCHN CRAMPHIN,
Wife MARY, extx.
Wit: Edward Willett, Jr., Walter Davis, John Johnston.
                                                   24. 508

FARRELL, WILLIAM, Queen Anne's Co.   18 Jun, 1746
                                              27 Nov, 1746
To son EDMOND FARRELL, my now dwelling plantation, land in sd.
county called "Plain Dealing."
To wife MARY, use of sd. land and slaves during life, until
EDMUND arrives to age 21.
To 2 eldest sons, JOHN and WILLIAM FARRELL, pt. of tract
"Wright Reserve."
To dau. ELIZABETH FARRELL, 1 slave.
To dau. MARY FARRELL,
He mentioned a debt due Thos. Hynson Wright;
My 5 child.: JOHN, WM. EDMOND, ELIZABETH and MARY FARRELL.
My wife MARY FARRELL, and my bro. JOHN FARRELL, exs.
Wit: Jas. Newnan, Edmd. Farrell, Elizabeth Prier.
                                                   24. 510

SPEAKE, MARY, Charles Co.   25 Sep, 1746
                                              31 Oct, 1746
Child.: MARMADUKE SEMMES, JAMES SEMMES, JOSEPH MILBURN SEMMES,
MARY CAVANAUGH, ANN WARD, SUSANNA JOHNSON, ELIZABETH SPEAKE, ANN
WARD.
Grand-child.: IGNATIUS SEMMES, MONICA JOHNSON, JULIANA WARD.
Cousin WILLLIAM GOODRICH.
Marmaduke Semmes, Jos. Milburn Semmes, exs.
Wit: Betty Jenefer, Robert Hanson, Betty Hanson.
                                                   24. 512

TURNER, SAMUEL, Charles Co.
                                              29 Oct, 1746
Child.: EDWARD, JOHN, SAMUEL, RUTH, MICHA.
LYDIA TURNER wife; Edward son, exs.
Wit: Jos. Glaze, Samuel Glaze, Timothy Dement.
                                                   24. 513

WRIGHT, HENRY, JR., Anne Arundel Co.   31 Mar, 1745(?)
                                              14 Feb, 1746
To son PERSON (?) WRIGHT, land in Anne Arundel Co.

To son REASON WRIGHT, 4 slaves.
To dau. AUSTINCOMB, my slave.
My son-in-law LEWIS LENCOM (STENCOM?), ex.
Wit: Henry Wright, Jr., Wm. Kitley, Wm. Hacraft.

24. 515

WHEATLEY, JOHN, JR., Queen Anne's Co.   14 Sep, 1746
                                      3 Dec, 1746
To my bro. WM. WHEATLEY,
To my sister ELEANOR WHEATLY,
My father JOHN WHEATLEY, and my 2 bros., WM. WHEATLY and
DANIEL WHEATLY, whom I appoint exs.
Wit: Wm. Stoneman, John Cooper, Margaret Kanen. 24. 517

WRIGHT, ROBERT NORRIS, Queen Anne's Co.   14 Nov, 1746
                                      8 Jan, 1746
To my sister, MARY GOODWIN, land called "White Marsh
Addition," lying to the eastward of tract called "Tooley."
To my bro. NATHAN WRIGHT, as ex.
Wit: Wm. Clayton, Thomas Meridith, W. Wright.   24. 518

PERSONS, THOMAS, Queen Anne's Co.   17 Feb, 1741
                                   24 Jan, 1746
To wife TABITHY PERSONS, 1/2 my estate.
The other 1/2 to my 4 grand-child.: THOMAS TAYLOR, JOHN
TAYLOR, JOSEPH TAYLOR and ELIZABETH TAYLOR, sons and dau. of my
dau. ELIZABETH DODD, to be equally divided bet. my sd. 4
grand-child.
To dau. ELIZABETH DODD, cattle.
To grand-son JOHN TAYLOR, son of my dau. ELIZABETH DODD, tract
called "Neglect." If grand-son JOHN TAYLOR, die, then to my
grand-son THOMAS TAYLOR, and if he die, then to his grand-son
JOSEPH TAYLOR.
Wife Tabithy Persons and John Dowes, Jr. exs.
Wit: Thomas Hammond, John Dodd, Wm. Hammond.   24. 519

SPENCE, PATRICK, Talbot Co.   16 Feb, 1745/6
                                   13 Jan, 1746
To dau. HANNAH, cattle.
Wife REBECCA, extx.
To son PATRICK SPENCE,
Wit: Job Guest, John Davidson, James Cook.   24. 520

GOLDSBOROUGH, ROBERT, Talbot Co.   28 Jun, 1744
                                    2 Feb, 1746
To son ROBERT, I give the plantation which I bought of
Griffith J. Jones, and also land called "Fox Harbour."
To sons, CHARLES, WILLIAM, ROBERT, NICHOLAS, my land in "Plain
Dealing Creek," land called "Wyate's Fortune," "Grundy's
Addition" and pt. of "Hall's Neck."
To son JOHN, land called "Four Square," the triangle "Woodland
Neck."
To son HOWES, land called "Cottenham," land "Benjamin's Lott."
To 2 grand-sons, viz; ROBERT, the son of my son ROBERT and to
ROBERT, son of my son JOHN, 500 A. in Queen Anne's Co.

As it has pleased God to bless my 2 sons with handsome
estates, whose names are CHARLES and WILLIAM, all the money I now
have in the hands of John Hanbury, merchant, to be equally
divided bet. them, except 60 pounds money to be paid to my exs.
for use of my grand-dau, MARY MONEY.
Exs., sons Robert and Nicholas
Wit: James Cockayne, Samuel Kininmont, Thomas Ray, Daniel
Shehane.   24. 521

CLARK, THOMAS, Talbot Co.   6 Dec, 1746
                                               4 Feb, 1746
    To wife SARAH, slaves, land and houses that I bought of James
Tilghman, and at her decease, to my bro. JOSHUA CLARK, and if he
shd. die without issue, then to my bro. ISAAC CLARK, my bro.
JOHN.
    To bro. ISAAC, land in Dorchester Co. called "Clark Fortune"
Wife SARAH, extx.
Wit: George Parise (or Pairise), John Jones, John Booker,
Jonathan Shanahan.   24. 522

WATSON, ABRAHAM, Cecil Co.   20 Mar, 1743/4
                                               29 Sep, 1746
    Son WM. WATSON
    To wife, ELIZABETH WATSON, to have the estate to raise and
educate our child.; my 2 sons ABRAHAM WATSON and ISAAC DECORD
WATSON, come of age 21.
    To dau. CHARITY, slaves.
    Son WM., ex.
Wit: Richard Harrison, Henry Jackson, Edward Jackson.
                                                        24. 524

BLAKE, WILLIAM, Cecil Co.   31 Jul, 1746
                                               18 Nov, 1746
    To son WILLIAM BLAKE, some slaves.
    Wife MARY BLAKE.
    Friend, Capt. Nicholas, ex.
Wit: Nathan Baker, James Baxter, Elizabeth Cummings.
                                                        24. 525

ABELL, JOHN, St. Mary's Co., yeoman.   25 Sep, 1746
                                               8 Nov, 1746
To be buried at the chapple by my former wife.
    2nd wife, name not given.
    Child.: ENOCH, CUDBURD, JOHN HOWELL (son of wife).
    Mentions dau-in-law, CACTRAN HUCHINGS.
    To son ENOCH, tract where he now lived, 53 A., called
"Saturdans Conclusion."
    Wife extx.
Wit: Nathan Hickman, John Walker.   24. 527

DEAVOUR, RICHARD, St. Mary's Co.   25 Jul, 1746
                                               7 Nov, 1746
    Child.: RICHARD, ELIZABETH, SARAH, PETER.
    APPELLA (ASSILLA?) DEVOUR wife, extx.
Wit: Chas. King, Hugh Hopewell.   24. 528

HARBERT, MATHEW, St. Mary's Co.   16 Oct,1746
                               20 Jan, 1746
  Child.: WILLIAM, MATHEW, FRANCIS.
  To son William, my dwlg. plantation after mother's decease and
tract, "Herberts Swamp."
  To son Mathew, water mill and land of mill, "Herberts Rest,"
and pt of "Herberts Swamp."
  GRACE HARBERT wife, extx.
Wit: Richard Cooper, Thos. Mattingly, Roger Dugrings.
                                       24. 530

HEARD, JOHN, St. Mary's Co.   23 Dec, 1746
                              20 Jan, 1746/7
  Child.: JOHN, JONAH, WILLIAM, JAMES, JOHN BASIL, SUSANNA
NORRIS, MARK PEAKE.
  To son John, 160 A., "Well Found."
  To son William, rest of "Well Found."
  To son James, "Heard Harship."
  Mentionioned Luke Heard.
  To son John Basil. dwlg. plantation.
  To dau Susanna Norris, 1 sh.
  James and John Basil Heard, sons, exs.
Wit: Mathew Heard, Ignatius Jarboe, Peter Peaks. 24. 531

HAMMOND, MORDACAI, Anne Arundel Co.. Gent.   9 Jan, 1746
                                   30 Jan, 1746
  To JEMINA ROBERSON, 3 year possession which I have reserved in
the deed.
  To SAMUEL HYDE of London, merchant for land and moveables of
personal estate and my silver plate, and nominate her as ex.
Wit: Geo. Lengan, Isiah Wilson, Frances Wolf.   24. 532

EVANS, JONATHAN, Kent Co.   28 Nov, 1746
                              28 Nov, 1746
Catharine Wood and Elizabeth Devine came before me, B. Hands, one
of the Lordships for the county of Kent, made oath that 27th of
Nov., Elizabeth Devine did hear JONATHAN EVANS, who was then
approaching death, say that if he shd. die, it was his will that
his child shd. be by him left to Catharine Wood, to be brought up
by her, and if the sd. child shd. die, that 1/2 of his estate
shd. pass to his father, and the other half to Catharine Wood.
Received the above noncupative will, Nov 28, 1746, at 8 of the
clock. Signed: Cs. Hynson, Deputy Commissioner of Kent Co.
                                     24. 533

CROW, WM., Kent Co.   8 Oct, 1746
                              19 Nov, 1746
  To my 2 bros. ISAAC CROW and THOMAS CROW, my estate.
Wit: John Smith and James Smith.   24. 533

GLEN, JACOB, Kent Co.   22 Apr, 1746
                              5 Dec, 1746
  To wife RACHEL GLEN, third pt. of my estate.

To 2 sons EPHRIAM GLENN and SANDER GLENN, stock and lot in Chestertown.
To dau. CHRISTIANA, 1 slave.
To dau. CATHARINE, slaves.
To dau. ANN BLAKISTONE, slaves now in possession of her husband, William Blakistone.
To dau. CATHARINE, and at decease of all my afsd. daus.; to son JACOB GLENN, my 3 youngest sons: SAMUEL, JOHANNES and NATHANIEL GLENN, 3 slaves.
My grand-dau. ANN MORE shall be educated out of residue of my estate.
My 2 daus. CATHARINE and CHRISTIANA GLENN
To 3 sons, SAMUEL, JOHANNES and NATHANIEL GLENN, 10,000 pounds tobacco.
To 3 sons, JACOB, SANDER and EPHRAIM GLENN, remainder of slaves.
Mentions dau. ANN BLAKISTONE.
Sons JACOB and SANDER GLENN, exs.
Wit: John Grant, John Smithers.   24. 534

GREY, JAMES, Kent Co., planter.   23 Nov, 1746
                                           7 Feb, 1746
To son JAMES GRAY, JR., my dwelling plantation.
To dau. ELINOR GRAY, after she arrives age 16, 1 slave.
Dau., ELIZABETH GRAY,
To dau. SARAH GRAY,
My wife ELIZABETH GRAY, extx.
Wit: Thomas Slater, Wm. Mullett (?), Catharine Davis.
                                                24. 536

HARATY, PATRICK, Kent Co.   May, 1746
                                           17 Feb, 1746
Name of wife not mentioned.
The name of NEALL MC CLEAN and several others, in the form of an account, but not relationship stated.
Wit: James Bady, Daniel Bryan, Matthew Deadman. 24. 538

REVILL, CHARLES, Somerset Co.   16 Aug, 1746
                                           6 Dec, 1746
To son RANDALL REVILL, personal estate.
To son WM. REVILL, slaves.
To dau. SENAT REVILL, slaves.
To my 6 young. child.: JOHN, CHARLES, DAVID, SAMUEL, SARAH and STEPHEN, my slave.
To sons, RANDALL and WILLIAM REVILL, the plantation whereon Wm. Roack (Ruark?) now lives.
My 2 friends, David and Samuel Wilson.
Wit: Esker Turpin, David Wilson, Samuel Wilson. 24. 539

BAILY, GEORGE, Stepney Parish, Somerset Co. 11 Nov, 1742
                                           21 Feb, 1746
To wife MARY BAILY, plantation.
To son GEORGE, providing he pay his bro. BENJAMIN BAILEY, 5 pounds money and give to BAILY MAGLACKLINE, a young heifer.
My wife, extx.

Wit: Wm. Knowles, Robert Mullone, Clement Christopher.

24. 539

PRESBURY, JAMES, Baltimore Co.   3 Dec, 1744
                                              2 Jan, 1746
   To son GEORGE PRESBURY, a warrant due to me from the land
office for 130 A. land called "Elk Neck" on Gunpowder River.
   To dau. MARTHA GARRETSONE, 1 gold ring, marked "M. G.," which
was her mother's.
   To son THOMAS BURNEY, alias PRESBURY, land called "Oxford" on
the east side of Elk Creek, in sd. county.
   My son WILLIAM PRESBURY,
   My son THOMAS,
   My eldest dau. by my second wife, viz; SARAH PRESBURY.
   My dau. HANNAH PRESBURY.
   My dau. ELIZABETH PRESBURY,
   To my dau. SUSANNAH PRESBURY, dau. MARY PRESBURY, son JOHN
PRESBURY; my 7 child. by my last wife; viz; THOMAS BURNY, alias
PRESBURY, SARAH PRESBURY, HANNAH PRESBURY, WM. PRESBURY,
ELIZABETH PRESBURY, SUSANNAH PRESBURY and MARY PRESBURY, my son
GEORGE to allow sd. child. to live on plantation for 1 year after
my decease.
   Son THOMAS BURNEY, alias PRESBURY, ex.
Wit: Wm. Bradford, Petger Golding, Daniel Howell.

24. 542

FELL, WILLIAM, Baltimore Co.   12 Jan, 1746
                                             29 Jan, 1746
   To son EDWARD FELL, land called "Long Island," "Point Copes
Harbour," "Tankett Field" and "Carter's Delight."
   To son EDWARD, 12 A. lying on "Jones' Folly," whereon my mills
are; also lot #5 in Baltimore Town, formerly called Jones's Town.
   To dau. ANN FELL, my interest in 296 A. pt. of tract
"Freeburn's Progress" on Elkridge in Anne Arundel Co., formerly
belonging to Robt. Ridgley.
   To daus. JENNETT FELL and MARGARET FELL, my interest in
"Fell's Forrest" in Balto. Co.
   That Norton Grover Baker pay back the just sum of money, with
interest, which he sold me 100 A.
   Mentions bond given Oct. 8, 1744.
   To dau. CATHARINE FELL, land called "Stone's Adventure."
   To my cousin WILLILAM HOLMS, slaves.
   Wife SARAH FELL, and friend Joseph Taylor, exs.
Wit: Richard Hopkins, John Metcalfe, John Randall, Thomas Davis.

24. 544

RUTTER, THOMAS, Baltimore Co.   26 Sep, 1744
                                             29 Jan, 1746
   My wife ESTHER RUTTER,
   To son RICHARD RUTTER, tract of land called "Edward's
Enlargment" where his dwelling houses stand.
   To son HENRY THOMPSON RUTTER, land called "Saulsbury Plains"
in the fork bet. Stoney Run and John Bearings' Spring Branch, and

the widow of HENRY THOMPSON RUTTER, but if in case of her death
or re-marriage, then the land to descend to my son THOMAS.
To son SOLOMON RUTTER, land called "Edward's Enlargement."
To son MOSES RUTTER
To grand-daus. SUSANNAH and ANN GOODWIN, each, stock.
To dau. ESTER RUTTER, slaves.
Wife ESTER, extx.
My 2 grand-daus., SUSANNAH and ANN GOODWIN, that my son HENRY
THOMPSON RUTTER, take care of them and their estate.
Wit: Jonathan Hanson, James Morray, Sarah Hanson. 24. 547-8

BREREWOOD, THOMAS, Baltimore Co.   8 Aug, 1741
                                         10 Feb, 1746
     Whereas, my dau. THE HONORABLE CHARLOTTE BREREWOOD, did by
deed of settlement, dated Aug. 30, 1730, convey to me land in
Baltimore Co., called "Lord Baltimore's Gift," or more commonly,
"My Lady's Mannor," consisting of 10,000 A., I appoint my sd.
dau., extx., in England to this my last will, and give up the
whole of sd. estate to her, and appoint my grand-son, WILLIAM
BREREWOOD, ESQ., ex., here in MD.
     I request both my dau., THE HON. CHARLOTTE BREREWOOD, and my
grand-son, WILLIAM BREREWOOD, not to molest Mrs. Elinor Turner in
a settlement I made to her dated 4/4/1740. As for my estate at
Chester in Old England, which was chiefly leased out upon lives
with small quit rents, which I suppose several of them are now
drop'd. and that my grand-son WILLIAM BREREWOOD, transmit the
deeds with copy of this will afsd. to England. If I shd. not
live long enough to build a burying place or vaults upon the
hill, I desire to be laid in one of my houses.
Codicil: Feb. 10, 1746, states that his grand-son is now dec'd.,
and he appoints Mr. William Dullan, merchant in Joppa, to supply
the place of sd. grand-son.
Wit: George Buchanan, N. Rigbe, Jr., Wm. R. Caswell.
The will probated says "Thomas Brerewood, Senior, late of
Baltimore" - signed: Colls. Thos. White, Deputy Comry of
Baltimore Co.   25. 1 - 4

DAY, EDWARD, Baltimore Co.   8 Jan, 1746
                                         12 Feb, 1746
     Wife, unnamed.
     To son JOHN, 20 s. sterl.
     To sons NICHOLAS, and EDWARD, my lands, equally, and shd. the
2 sons die without issue, their estate to be divided among my 3
young. daus.: AVARILA, JANE and ANNA.
     To son-in-law VINCENT DORSEY, all that he now possesses.
     To dau SARAH DORSEY, 2 lots, Nos. 29 and 30 in the town of
Joppa, and if she die without issue, the sd. lots return to my
dau. JANE.
     John son, ex.
Wit: Hugh Deans, Roderick Cheyne, James Lemix.   25. 4

BUTTERWORTH, ISAAC, Baltimore Co., planter. 14 Jan, 1746
                                         13 Feb, 1746
     To wife, 200 A., called "Isaac and Johns Lott," with my

plantation I now live on of 180 A., being pt. of tract called
"Unkle's Good Will," to be laid out at the discretion of Thomas
Wheeler and Leonard Wheeler, and after her decease, to fall to my
son BENJAMIN BUTTERWORTH.
    To son ISAAC BUTTERWORTH, land called "Unkle's Good Will,"
lying bet. Thomas Run and the main road.
    To 2 daus. MARY and ELIZABETH, remainder of tract called
"Unkle's Good Will."
    To dau CHARITY BUTTERWORTH, pt. of sd. land.
    To son BENJAMIN, my sword.
    Wife JANE BUTTERWORTH, and ISAAC BUTTERWORTH, exs.
Wit: Samuel Gilbert, Edw. Flanagan, Samuel Webster.
    25. 7

VINE, ROWLAND, Baltimore Co.   29 Dec, 1746
                           27 Feb, 1746
    To son THOMAS VINE, tract "Brown's Lot," after decease of his
mother.
    Balance to my 4 child.: THOMAS, MARY, SARAH, RACHEL VINE.
    Wife SARAH VINE, extx.
Wit: Isabella Summer, Wm. Wadlow, Thos. Dulany.   25. 9

MAC QUAIN, DUGAL, Baltimore Co.   26 Mar, 1746
                            4 Mar, 1746
    To sons WILLIAM and FRANCIS, lands which I now live on.
    To son THOMAS, my clothing.
    To son-in-law JOHN BROWN, clothing.
    That the bond which I have of John Kees shall be signed over
to Mr. Alexander Lawson for security for the money which I owe
him.
    Wife GRACE MAC QUAINE, extx.
Wit: Wm. Hall, Edward Logsdon, Richard Stevens.   25. 10

DAWKINS, WILLIAM, Calvert Co.   19 Sep, 1740
                           20 Jan, 1746
    To my dau. ELIZABETH,
    To my 2 daus., ANN and DORCAS, all the 2 tracts I bought of
Col. Gale, called "Ashten Chance" and "Ashten's Addition," to be
divided equally.
    To 2 young. daus., REBECCA and BARBARA, the plantation whereon
I live, by Island Creek, called "Smith's Purchase," equally.
    To 4 daus., ANN, DORCAS, REBECCA and BARBARA, my land on
Eastern Shore, called "Blinkhorne's Desire," which I purchased of
my bro. JAMES DAWKINS.
    To wife DORCAS DAWKINS, the whole plantation whereon I live
called "Smith's Purchase," during her life, if she remain single;
otherwise, to take her 1/3.
    Wife, extx.
Wit: Robert Sollers, James Mackall, Wm. Allistra.
    25. 11 - 12

WILLIAMS, JOSEPH, Prince George's Co.   26 Nov, 1746
                                 13 Feb, 1746
    To son JOSEPH WILLIAMS, a gun called "Machabee," a horse and
desk.

To son WILLIAM WILLIAMS, all the Smith tools and old iron in
my shop.
To dau. SARAH WILLIAMS, cattle.
To grand-son JOSEPH WILLIAMS, cattle.
To wife CATHARINE WILLIAMS, the 1/3 pt. of crop.
To sons JOSEPH and WILLIAM WILLIAMS, and daus. SARAH and MARY
WILLIAMS,, the other 2/3 of crop.
Wife and son Joseph, exs.
Wit: John Stoddard (who was a captain), John Vermillion, Richard
Owen.   25. 12

WATSON, ROBERT, Worcester Co.   24 Feb, 1746
                                            6 Mar, 1746
     To son CHARLES WATSON, the plantation, 225 A. with my water
mill,, during life, and then to grand-son ROBERT WATTSON, son of
CHARLES.
     To grand-son JOHN WATSON, son of JOHN, when he arrives age 18,
and ELIZABETH WATTSON, dau. of JOHN, a slave and her increase.
     To son ROBERT WATSON, 100 A., where he now lives and slaves.
     To dau. MARY WHARTON, 1 s. sterl.
     To dau. RHODA WALKER, slaves, but the increase of slaves, to
grand-child., namely, DANIEL WALKER, and his sister MARY WALKER,
to be divided equally.
     To grand-son ROBERT WATTSON, son of CHARLES, my plantation
with my two stills.
     To grand-sons NATHAN WATSON and ROBERT WATSON, sons of
CHARLES, my plantation with 2 stills.
     To grand-son CHARLES WATSON, son of CHARLES, slaves.
     To dau. HANNAH FISHER, 1 s. sterl.
Wit: Wm. Aydelott, Jr., Wm. Veasey, Solomon Webb.
                                                    25. 14 - 15

NELSON, JOSHUA, Northumberland Co. (state not given)
                                    13 Apr, 1744
                                     9 Jul, 1744
     To wife ELIZABETH, use of 2 slaves, and at her decease, to my
3 child., CHLOE, MARY ANN and SENECA.
     To son LANCELOT, 45 pounds sterl. to be paid out of my estate.
5 slaves to be divided bet. my 3 above-mentioned child.
Wit: George Mills, Robert Boyd.
On the back of the will was thus written: I give to VIRGILIA
BARTLIGHT, 21 s., to be paid to my exc., and that my sd. son
LANCELOT requires any payment of a legacy left him by his grand
mother in England, that I do exclude him from every pt. of the
afsd. legacy. May 11, 1944; signed: JOSHUA NELSON.
Wit: George Mills.
     To son LANCELOT, my gold ring, desires him to ingraciate
himself with some skillful person that useth the sea and endeavor
to get him to go with him to some ship master to Edward Dixon by
name and to be bound as they can agree. My son paying to become a
seaman.
Codicil signed: JOSHUA NELSON (REVEREND) .
Wit: George Mills in Northumberland County.
James Fountain Clerk of court. Copy test by Billy Claiborne,
clerk.   25. 16 - 17

CHESIRE, JOHN, St. Mary's Co.   19 Jan, 1746
                                        6 Mar, 1746
  PRISCILLA CHESIRE wife.
  Child.: JONATHAN, JOHN, TENESAN, PHILEMON, MARY NOBLE.
  Ex., not mentioned.
Wit: Baptist Barber, Elizabeth Hendley.   25. 17

JOHNSON, PETER, St. Mary's Co.   2 Jan, 1747
                                        8 Apr, 1747
  GRACE JOHNSON (2nd wife; formerly wife of John Mattenly).
  Child.: JAMES, JOSEPH, LUKE MATTENLY.
      1st marriage: JOHN, THOS., LEONARD, JESS, MARY, SUSANNA
JOHNSON.
  Grace Johnson wife, John Johnson, bro., exs.
Wit: John Tyson, Wm. Howard, Sarah Howard.   25. 18

WATERS, ELIZABETH, Prince George's Co.   7 Jan, 1745
                                     15 Apr, 1747
  To son JOSEPH WATERS, my plantation, 113 A.
  To son JOHN WATERS, 1 s. money.
  To hrs. of son WILLIAM WATERS, dec'd, 1 s., each.
  To dau. MARY WEBSTER, 1 s.
  To grand-son THOMAS HOLLAND, 11 pounds sterl. money, being the
sum I formerly willed to my dec'd dau. MARGARET HOLLAND, in
consideration of a small balance due her out of her dec'd.
father's estate.
  To hrs. of my dec'd. dau. MARGARET HOLLAND, each of them 1 s.
  Son Joseph, ex.
Wit: Samuel Waters, Jr. (Quaker), John Moore, Sr., Thomas Moore.
                                        25. 20

SMITH, JAMES, Dorchester Co., carpenter.   2 Nov, 1745
                                     17 Feb, 1746
  To son JAMES SMITH, JR., my dwelling plantation called, "Wolf
Neck," 50 A.
  To eld. son, tract called "The Addition To Wolf Neck," 14 A.,
and tract "Smithrange."
  To young. son JOSEPH SMITH, remainder of tract called "Smith
Range."
  If my son JOSEPH, die without issue, then to my dau NELLY, and
hrs.
  Ex. Joseph Brown.
Wit: John Marrett, Darby Barrood, Wm. Clifton.   25. 21

ENNALLS, THOMAS, Great Choptank, Dorchester Co.
                                        7 Nov, 1746
                                     11 Feb, 1746
  To dau. MARY, wife of Thomas Martin, 1 slave.
  To dau ELIZABETH, 1 slave.
  To dau. SARAH, 1 slave.
  To son JOSEPH, tract called "Bartholomew's Neck," which my
father, HENRY ENNALLS, gave me upon Transquakin River.

To son THOMAS, tract which I have at Blackwater, "Ennalls's Discovery," and a tract in Great Marsh of Transquakin, called "Trippes Delight"; several slaves.
To son ANDREW SKINNER ENNALLS, tract called "Ennalls' Resurvey," upon the north division.
To son WILLIAM, tract "Buchrange" bet. northeast and northwest forks of Nanticoke.
To son HENRY, slaves.
To wife ANNE ENNALLS, slaves.
To sons JOSEPH, WILLIAM, and ANDREW SKINNER ENNALLS, several slaves.
Balance of estate to be divided bet. wife, ANN, and 5 sons, HENRY, THOMAS, JOSEPH, ANDREW SKINNER and WILLIAM ENNALLS.
Wife Ann; sons, Henry and Thomas, exs.
Wit: Wm. Murray, Thomas Graham, Philemon Graham, Edward Haile.
25. 23 - 26

BROWN, JOHN, Dorchester Co., merchant, traveller and pedler.
26 Dec, 1746
10 Mar, 1746
To ROBERT BROWN, my lawful son, of Chester County, PA, carpenter, 1 s. sterl.
Wife MARY BROWN, extx.
Wit: John Young, Edward Rumbley.   25. 26

WILLIAMS, PHILADELPHIA, Dorchester Co.   6 Dec, 1745
10 Mar, 1746
To son JOHN WILLIAMS, my dwelling plantation where I now live, and 60 A. thereunto belonging, called "Hogsteallers Prevention"; after his decease, to grand-son ROLLENS WILLIAMS.
Son John, ex.
Wit: John Pritchett, Fisher, Wm. Kirkham, John Hopkins.
25. 27 - 28

SHERWIN (SHAW), ROBERT, Dorchester Co.   4 Feb, 1745
11 Mar, 1746
To son STEPHEN SHERWIN, 160 A., pt. of "Sherwin Chance"; as it also being the mannor plantation where I now dwell.
To son JAMES SHERWIN, 4 A. being the remaining pt. of "Sherwin's Chance"; as that pt. of "Sherwin Chance" where my son JAMES now dwells.
To dau. SARAH TYLER, wife of Jonathan Tyler, 2 s. current money.
To wife MARY SHERWIN, my personal estate; wife MARY, to have my dwelling house.
Wife and son Stephen, exs.
Wit: Cha. Dickinson, Dennis Rilley, Richard Sisarson.
25. 28 - 30

BRAMOCK, JOHN, Dorchester Co.   27 Nov, 1745
11 Mar, 1746
To my bro. EDMOND BRAMOCK, and hrs., my land lying northward of a southeast line, "Bramock's Adventure."
To bro. HENRY BRAMOCK, land I own lying southward of the southeast line given to my bro. EDMOND; that my bro. HENRY,

surrender my deeds to bro. EDMOND.
Mentions: my bro. EDMOND'S son whose name was also EDMOND, to
have land devised to my bro. HENRY.
To bro. PHILIMON BRANNOCK (or BRAMOCK), the land my father
bequeathed.
Bro. Henry, ex.
Wit: Wm. Grantham, Peter Stokes, Thomas Stokes.   25. 30

CLIFTON, WILLIAM, Dorchester Co.   20 Sep, 1746
                                             12 Mar, 1746
    To son JOHN, 20 s. sterl. money of England.
    To son JONATHAN, my manner dwelling plantation.
    To son WEIGHTMAN, 77 A. called "Clifton's Lot."
    To son WILLIAM, land "Venture," "Addition To Venture."
    To son JOHN, 1 slave.
    To dau. SARAH ROBINSON, 1 s. sterl.
    Wife SARAH CLIFTON and son JOHN, exs.
Wit: John Marrett, James Story, James Bary, John Ellitt.
                                                  25. 32

DEAN, HENRY, Dorchester Co., blacksmith.   25 Nov, 1746
                                             13 Mar, 1746
    To son JOHN, 91 A. called "Broad Ridge," pt. of Peaknull, pt.
of "Dean's Prevention," that lieth on the same side of the swamp
of my son JOHN.
    To son HENRY, my dwelling plantation land "Peaknull," also pt
of tract called "Little Brittain," on south side of the marsh.
    To son THOMAS, land called "Rainy Point" on Slaughter Creek.
    Mentions tract called "Dean's Prevention" given to THOMAS
DEAN.
    To son JOHN, dau. MARY TARGINSON, 8 pounds of my estate.
    To wife ELIZABETH DEAN, my slaves.
    Son JOHN, ex.
Wit: Wm. Robinson, John Brohom, James Bright.
Probated by Wm. Robinson and James Bright.   25. 33

MELONEY, JAMES, Dorchester Co.   1 May, 1745
                                             14 Mar, 1746
    To ELIZABETH KEMPER, cattle.
    Daus. MARY and HONOR MELONEY, shd. stay with Ezekiel Keene and
Mary Keene at the intuition until 16 years of age.
    Friend Ezekiel Keene, ex.
Wit: Isaac Patridge, Thomas Smith   25. 35

VICKERS, JOHN, on Little Choptank River, Dorchester Co.
                                             21 Jan, 1743/4
                                             31 Mar, 1746
    To son JOHN, stock, during the stay with his mother.
    To son WILLIAM, stock.
    Son JAMES, son NEHEMIAH, wife SARAH.
    THOMAS and JOHN VICKERS to be guardians over my small child.,
after decease of my wife and dau. ELIZABETH.
Wit: John Cox, John Robinson, Elizabeth Gray.   25. 36

SCANDRETT, WILLIAM, Queen Anne's Co.   13 Jan, 1746
                                           6 Mar, 1746
    To 4 cousins: JAMES, THOMAS, WILLIAM and (A YOUNG CHILD, the
name or sex to be unknown), child. of Thomas Carridine and
Eliner, his wife, 200 pounds money of Maryland, equally.
    To nephew EDWARD GRAY, son of LEON GRAY, late of Queen Anne's
Co., remainder of my estate.
    Appoint my father WILLIAM SCANDRETT, and my bro-in-law THOMAS
CARRIDINE, exs.
Wit: Thomas Hill, W. Govan, E. and Ann Govane.   25. 38

LONG, JOHN, Queen Anne's Co.   Oct, 1746
                                           16 Feb, 1746
    To son DAVID LONG, s. sterl.
    To dau. MARY FLOWERS, same.
    Dau. ELIZABETH ROBERTS.
    Son JOHN LONG, ex.
Wit: Robert Davis, Thomas Gorden, Jonathan Jolley.
                                           25. 39 - 40

SCOTTEN, THOMAS, Queen Anne's Co.   7 Mar, 1746
                                           16 Feb, 1746
    To wife SARAH SCOTTEN, 50 A., and at her decease, to sons:
THOMAS, WILLIAM and RICHARD SCOTTEN.
    To dau. MARY JONES, cattle.
    To dau. HANNAH SCOTTEN,
    To grand-son JOHN SCOTTEN,
    Wife SARAH, extx.
Wit: David Harinton, Thomas Bostick, Wm. Bostick.
                                           25. 40

OSBURN, JNO., Kent Island, Queen Anne's Co. 1 Jan, 1746/7
                                           19 Mar, 1746
    To wife RACHEL OSBURN, extx., my whole estate as long as she
lives; at her decease, to be divided amongst my 4 nephews and
nieces: REBECCA DEROCHBURN, SAMUEL OSBURN, SUSANNA LEGG and
WILLIAM OSBURN, son of my bro. SAMUEL OSBURN.
    Will that Marmaduke Goodhand let my wife live on the
plantation we now live on until the day of death rent free; then
said Goodhand to have an equal share along with my afsd. nephews
and nieces.
Wit: Richard Goodman, Alexander Walters.   25. 42

BAGGS, JOHN, Queen Anne's Co.   7 Jun, 1746
                                           26 Mar, 1747
    To wife MARY, my estate, and at her decease to my child., 4
sons and a dau: NATHAN BAGGS, WM. BAGGS, ISAAC BAGGS, WILSON
BAGGS and REBECCA BAGGS.
    For as much as I have heretofore given something to my 2 sons
and 3 daus.: THOMAS BAGGS, JOHN BAGGS, SARAH JACKSON, MARY BANNY
(or BENNY), and RACHAL FISHER, I now give my sd. 2 sons and 3
daus., 1 s. sterl.
    To son WM. BAGGS, one tract called "Hazard," in forest of
Choptank in Queen Anne's Co., 50 A., and if he die without issue,
same to my son WILSON BAGGS, and if WILSON BAGGS die without

issue, same to ISAAC BAGGS.
    Wife Mary, extx.
Wit: Redmond Fallin, Wm. Hubanks, Mary Cox.   25. 43 - 44

SCOTTEN, RICHARD, Queen Anne's Co.   6 Jan, 1746/7
                                              26 Mar, 1747
    To wife MARY SCOTTEN, my dwelling plantation called "Scotten's
Outlett."
    To son RICHARD SCOTTEN, 100 A., "Scotten Addition."
    To son RICHARD SCOTTEN, 1 smooth bord gun.
    To son NATHANIEL SCOTTEN, 1 plantation with 50 A.to be taken
out of tract, "Alsbury Plains."
    Mentions debt due Richard Bennet, esq.
    To dau. CATHARINE SCOTTEN, cattle.
    Wife MARY, extx.
Wit: Powell, W. David Harington, Richard Smith.   25. 45

CHAMBERS, JOHN, Talbot Co., planter.   18 Feb, 1746
                                               3 Apr, 1747
    To wife REBECCA CHAMBERS, tract called "Bedsteads Adventure,"
and my pt. of tract called "Chambers' Adventure," after John
Goldsborough and Isaac Cox, has their parts laid out.
    I give the afsd. lands and premises to my wife, during her
life, and at her decease, to son ISAAC CHAMBERS.
    To wife REBECCA CHAMBERS, for the bringing up of my child., my
personal estate.
    To ISAAC COX, pt. to be laid out in the long point, up bet.
his land and Isaac Dobsons of 14 A.
    Wife REBECCA, extx.
Wit: Joseph Newman, Wm. Griffin, Wm. Goodsy, John Newman.
                                                    25. 46

CRAWFORD, JAMES, Calvert Co.   7 Nov, 1746
                                     11 Apr, 1747
    To my 2 child., DARKEY and CLEMENT CRAWFORD, 1 s. sterl.
    My sons WM. CRAWFORD, NATHANIEL CRAWFORD, exs.
Wit: James Dorsey (Quaker), Martha Ellte, Elizabeth Crawford.
                                                    25. 48

TULL, GEORGE, Somerset Co.   - - - - - -
                                     4 Apr, 1747
    To young. son GEORGE, all my 3 tracts of land: "Coleman's
Adventure," "Beales" and "Chance," being 700 A.
    To son GEORGE, 1 slave.
    To daus. HANNALL and LEAH, 1 slave.
    To young. dau. MARY, 1 slave.
    I gave son NOBLE and son JONATHAN, some land.
    To 4 young. child., to be equally divided amongst them.
    To 3 young. daus., have 1 year schooling.
    Wife ELIZABETH, extx.
Wit: Wm. Mills, Matthias Costin, Jonathan Mills.   25. 49

WILSON, MARY, SR., Somerset Co.   8 Sep, 1743
                                        23 Apr, 1747
    To grand-dau., MARY WILSON, JR., dau. of ANDREW WILSON,

Appoint Thomas Gilliss, ex.
Wit: John Hayman, James Pope.   25. 51

WILSON, GEORGE, Somerset Co., planter.   26 Apr, 1743
                                               23 Apr, 1747
   To son ANDREW WILSON, my large iron pot.
   To son ANDREW WILSON, my cain, and at his decease to his son
GEORGE WILSON.
   To grand-son GEORGE WILSON, at decease of my wife, my plough
and harrow.
   To grand-dau. MARY WILSON, cattle, at decease of my son ANDREW
WILSON.
   To dau. ANN DUBBINS, 20 s. money.
   To grand-dau. MARGARET LAYFIELD, 2 s.
   To dau-in-law MARY WILSON, 20 s. in paper money.
   To wife MARY WILSON, remainder of my estate.
   Thomas Fillis, ex.
Wit: James Hayman, Abraham Heath, Isaac Hayman.   25. 52

GRAY, JOHN, SR., Anne Arundel Co.   16 Mar, 1746/7
                                               15 May, 1747
   To son SAMUEL GRAY, half pt. of tract called "Plain," and 80
A. "Proctor's Park."
   To son ROBERT GRAY, 250 A. called "Proctor's Park."
   To son JOHN GRAY, 180 A., "Proctor's Park," adjoining.
   To wife BRIDGET GRAY, slaves.
   Wife and son Samuel Gray, exs.
Wit: Godfrey Watters, Lanee Todd, John Todd.   25. 53

JOHNSON, ARCHIBALD, Charles Co., planter   5 Feb, 1746
                                                4 Apr, 1747
   To wife Elenor, land and plantatin whereon we now dwelt,
namely, hald of "Pomfreit Severn," 5 A., and 62 A. called
Johnsons Hazard," and after her deceases to son DUNCAN JOHNSON.
   To son JOS. JOHNSON, tract called "Johnstone," 136 A.
   To son ARCHIBALD JOHNSON, tract calld "Leitchfields
nlargement," 150 A.
   To dau ELIZABETH JOHNSON, slave Lucy.
   To son DUNCAN, slave Massey.
   To Mary Machey, wife of Hugh Machey, 2 ewes.
   To son WILLIAM JOHNSON, corn.
   To son CHARLES JOHNSON, , heifer.
   Wife Elenor, extx.
Test: Alexr. Mepherson, Jr., John Mepherson, Richard Mepherson.
                                                25. 55

ARNEY, WILLIAM, Baltimore Co.   20 Feb, 1746/7
                                               19 Mar, 1746
   To eld. son WILLIAM BARNEY, 6 pounds sterl., which I have
lready paid Henry Morgan on his account.
   To eld. dau., the wife of Richard Hooker, slaves.
   To son ABSOLOM BARNEY, land he now lives on.
   To son BENJAMIN BARNEY, 1 tract of land called "Absolom's
hance."
   To 2nd son, by my wife MARY, 1 tract called "Chilcoald

Hazard."
    To son MOSES BARNEY, at decease of my wife, tract bought of
John Board called "Timber Ridge."
    To dau. MARY BARNEY, 1 slave.
    To dau. RUTH BARNEY, 1 slave.
    To wife MARY BARNEY, 4 slaves.
    My child.: ABSOLOM, BENJ., WM., MOESES, MARY, RUTH, they all
being by my wife MARY.
    Wife, extx.
Wit: Job Evans, John Evans, Jabed Morrey.   25. 56

HOLLAND, FRANCIS, Baltimore Co., gentleman.   Dec, 1746
                                                  20 Mar, 1746
    An unborn child is mentioned; same to have his land in Anne
Arundel Co.; is entitled and not at my disposal, therefore, will
that if my eld. son can and so make and execute a deed of release
to his bro., in such manner that no one can claim under him by
virtue of the afsd. intale, then my will is that son FRANCIS,
shall have Specutie Island, and if he cannot make sd. deed, then
my young. son shall have Specutie Island, and my eld. son lands
in Anne Arundel Co.
    Appoint wife CORDELIA HOLLAND, extx.
Wit: John Hall, Hugh Carlisle, John Hall, Jr.   25. 58

DEAVOR (or DEAVOUR), RICHARD, Baltimore Co.
                                        15 Oct, 1746
                                        4 Mar, 1746
    To wife MARY DEAVOR, after my debts are paid, my whole estate.
Wit: Jacob Giles (Quaker), Winstone Smith, William Smith.
                                          25. 59

SHAW, CHRISTOPHER DURBIN, Baltimore Co.   23 Nov, 1746
                                        21 May, 1747
    To son THOMAS SHAW, my gun.
    To dau. MARY SHAW, stock.
    To dau. ELIZABETH SHAW, cattle.
    To dau. SUSANNAH SHAW,cattle.
    To dau. SARAH SHAW, cattle.
    To son THOMAS SHAW, 71 A., tract "Shaw Privilege."
    Wife SUSANNAH SHAW, extx.
Wit: Thomas Denbow, Abraham Poteet, Thomas Dulany.
                                          25. 60

WELLS, ISAAC, Prince George's Co.   10 Mar, 1746
                                          10 Apr, 1747
    To wife, dwelling plantation and 100 A. called "Low Lands"; at
her decease, to son JOHN WELLS, with that pt. of "Children's
Chance," that is now enclosed, and when he becomes age 21, shd.
pay to his sisters MARY, ELIZABETH and ANN WELLS, 10 pounds
money, and if John die without issue, then sd. land to ISAAC
EDWARDS WELLS, and he to perform unto the 3 sisters afsd.
    To son ISAAC EDWARDS WELLS, land "Wells' Invention."
    To son SAMUEL WELLS, tract "Children's Chance."
    To son BENJAMIN WELLS, remaining pt. of tract "Children's
Chance," on southside of sd. branch.

To wife, personal estate.
George Matthews, friend, ex.
Wit: Charles Davis, Alexander Tanzey, Daniel Matthews.
25. 61

HEATH, JAMES PAUL, Cecil Co.   5 Sep, 1745
                                      3 Jul, 1746
    Wife REBECCA HEATH, and in case she marry until my 2nd son
JAMES HEATH, becomes age 21 and in case of death, until my son
DANIEL, arrives at age; and mentions a "probably unborn child or
should there happen to be an unborn child at the time of my death
and it shd. arrive at age 21," the following lands, viz: my
present plantation, 300 A., all the lands I hold in Sassafras
Neck, below St. Stephens Church, with the lands under lease to
Bernard Van Horn, John Mercer, John Samson and Susanna Vaunsaunt,
if my wife accepts same as her thirds of my lands.
    I would have my cousin HEATH, live on my late dwelling
plantation until my son JAMES HEATH is age 21, until my son
DANIEL arrives at age, the sd. CHARLES to have liberty to get
timber, to keep up the plantation (it would be inferred that in
the paragraph where he gives right for his cousin, HEATH, to live
on plantation and to have timber, that this name was meant to
have been CHARLES HEATH.).
    My exs. to make over to Wm. Nuersborough, John Ward, Patrick
Creagh, John Ruth and John Curry, the several tracts I have
agreed to see them and impower any 2 of my exs. to sell the
following lands: my lands on western shore.
    To niece MARY GRAFTON, a mourning ring.
    To nephew JOHN WARD,
    To my friends hereafter named, I give each a mourning ring:
DANIEL, WALTER, DENNIS, MARGARET and MARY DULANY.
    To WILLIAM and RACHEL KNIGHT, JOS. GEORGE, JAMES CALDER and
PREGRINE FRISBY, son of PERGRINE FRISBY, dec'd.
    To son DANIEL HEATH, the land near Charles Town, I have leased
of the Lord Baltimore with my lands called "Sorrell Manner
Addition," and that pt. of "Heath's Range," always excepting 500
A. that is laid out for Warwick; and give sd. son lots in
Warwick, maraked "J.C.'O."
    To son JAMES, plantation, not already disposed of by me.
    If any aforementioned child. shd. die, then I give my estate
to JAMES HEATH, son of CHARLES HEATH.
    In case of death of my child., then I also give DENNIS DULANY,
land near Charles Town.
    To my nephews and nieces hereafter named, each of them a lot
in Warwick: JAMES CHETHAM, JAMES and MARY WARD, SUSANNAH CHETHAM.
    To my god-son, WM. JACKSON, a lot in Warwick.
    To HENRY NEALE, on the residing priest at Bohemia, the same
sum.
    Friends RICHARD BENNETT, ESQ., DANIEL DULANY, ESQ., CHARLES
CARROLL, ESQ.
    James Calden and my wife REBECCA HEATH, exs., that they will
have my sons sent to St. Omers for their education and have them
brought up in the Roman Catholic religion.
Wit: John Rice, Archibald Douglass, Timothy Breman.
                                      25. 63 - 68

25. 63 - 68

DAVIS, DANIEL, Worcester Co.   7 May, 1747
                                                3 Jun, 1747
    To son WILLIAM DAVIS, 50 A. of land called "Battle Ridge."
    To son JOHN DAVIS, my dwelling plantation, except my wife's
thirds.
    5 young. child.: ISAAC, DENIEL, JAMES, LEVINE and JUDAH DAVIS.

    Wife, extx. (Wife's name not given, but she made her election
June 3, 1747.)
Wit: John Davis, James Smith, Mayor Dorman.   25. 68

COFFAN (or COFFIN), THOMAS, SR., Somerset Co.
                                            14 Oct, 1741/2
                                            3 Jun, 1747
    To eld. son JOSEPH COFFAN, my church Bible.
    To 2nd son JOHN COFFAN, book "Young Man's Companion."
    To 3rd son THOMAS COFFEN, my lands.
    To eld. dau. RACHEL COFFAN, furniture.
    To young. dau. ANNEY COFFAN (her name appears as AMY COFFEN
and AMEY COFFAN), furniture.
    To young. son WM. COFFAN, furniture.
    Nephew SAMUEL COBB.
    To 4 young. child.: THOMAS COFFAN, RACHEL COFFAN, WM. COFFAN
and AMEY COFFAN, and appoint the former ex.
Wit: Alexander Linch, Absolom Bessix, Daniel Coe.
                                                       25. 69

JACKSON, EDWARD, Cecil Co., yoeman.   1 Apr, 1747
                                              19 May, 1747
    To wife SARAH JACKSONk 1/3 pt. of my plantation called
"Jackson Outlet," in Susquehanna Hundred, Cecil County.
    To son JOHN JACKSON, son EDWARD JACKSON, dau. ELIZABETH
JACKSON.
    Wife, SARAH, extx.
Wit: Richard Sedgwick, Henry Jackson, Robert Callender.
                                                       25. 72

MEDFORD, BULMAN, Kent Co.   12 Feb, 1746/7
                                               6 Mar, 1746
    To son MICHEALL BEDFORD, tracts called "Semses Form," "Gals
Addition."
    To son THOMAS MEDFORD, "Hobsons (Heburns?) Choice."
    To son ONATT MEDFORD, sterling money in hands of Mr. Philpott
and Anderson, merchants, in London.
    To son JOSEPH MEDFORD, 100 pounds money, and my will is that
the money be put to interest.
    Wife SARAH MEDFORD, extx.
Wit: George Medford, John Dunn, Richard Kennard.   25. 73

SANDERS, THOMAS, Kent Co.   21 Oct, 1746
                                               6 Mar, 1746
    To wife MARY, and my 5 child.: EBENEZER, TEMPERANCE, JOSEPH,
THOMAS and CLOANNA, lands to be equal; bet. my 3 sons, as to

quantity, to my son EBENEZER, the uppermost pt.; JOSEPH the middle pt.; THOMAS, and in case either son die before of remainder bet. the other 2.
Wife MARY, extx. Wit: Crispin Butler, John Chamell (?), Jacob Caulk.
25. 75

MILLER, MICHAEL, Kent Co.   7 Jan, 1746
                                   6 Mar, 1746
To son MICHAEL, pt. of tract "Miller's Purchase," near Tavern Bridge and Swan Creek Bridge, boundary here given: adjoining land of Ebenezer Blackistone.
To son THOMAS, "Miller's Purchase."
My son MICHAEL, his land which intersects land of Samuel Miller.
To son JAMES, my lands of Samuel Miller.
To wife ELIZABETH, her choice of my horses, and her thirds of my estate.
Wife Elizabeth, and Ralph Page, exs.
Wit: Samuel Miller, Thomas Hinton, Edmund Byrne, Rachel Davis.
25. 77

DOUGLASS, GEORGE, Kent Co.   28 Jul, 1745
                                     9 Mar, 1746
To wife SUSANNA DOUGLASS, my real and personal estate.
Wit: Joseph Douglass, James Frisby, Archibald Douglass.
25. 78

INCH, BENJAMIN, Steele Pone, Kent Co.   15 Dec, 1746
                                          28 Mar, 1747
50 A. to BENJAMIN WOODLAND and _____ CLARK one slave, and one slave shall serve my bro. one year, and one slave to my bro. WILLIAM JONES, 13 sheep to WM. in Quaker Neck.
To bro. BATHIEDG, four cattle.
John Thomas is mentioned.
William Jones, ex.
Wit: Andrew Devine, Ann Planilen (or Flanghin), Michael Bryan.
25. 79

BEAN, JOHN, Kent Co., ship carpenter.   26 Apr, 1744
                                          6 Jun, 1747
To wife JEAN (or JOAN), my whole estate, real and personal.
To dau. ELIZABETH BEAN, 1 s. sterl.
Wife Joan or Jean (?), extx.
Wit: Elemas Cowper, Elizabeth Nowland, Ann Morgan.
25. 80

BARKER, SAMUEL, Prince George'e Co.   13 Oct, 1746
                                        12 Jun, 1747
To son NATHANIEL BARKER and SAMUEL BARKER,
To dau. ELIZABETH HOLLY, MARY DAVIS, SARAH ATHEY, ELENOR BARKER, and ANN BARKER, 1 s. each.
To wife MARY BARKER, to possess remaining pt. of my estate, but if she remarries, then to take her thirds, and the estate to my child., mentioned above.
JOHN BALLARD BARKER and his bro. WILLIAM BARKER, if their

mother die before they are of age, shall be in the care of their
sister MARY DAVIES.
Wife Mary Barker, extx.
Wit: Wm.. Hawkins, Jos. Hatton, Jr.   25. 81

MOORE, CHARLES, Queen Anne's Co.   19 Dec, 1746
                                             27 Mar, 1747
   To wife SARAH MOORE, land called "Smith's Forrest," during her
life, then to THOMAS CHAIRS, the son of JOSEPH CHAIRS, the
above-mentioned land.
   Further, give to THOMAS CHAIRS, stock.
   Wife, extx.
Wit: John Jackson, John Davis, George Smith.   25. 82

WILLIAMS, MATHEW, Queen Anne's Co.   15 May, 1747
                                             27 May, 1747
   To dau. RACHEL WILLIAMS, furniture.
   Wife REBECCA WILLIAMS,
   Son MATHEW WILLIAMS, cut him off from any further claim to my
estate.
   To dau. ESTHER
   To son HENRY WILLIAMS, 100 A. called "Salsbury Plains" in
Queen Anne's County.
   My 4 child. hereafter mentioned: HENRY, RACHEL, ELIZABETH and
JACOB WILLIAMS, share alike after my wife has her 1/3.
Wit: John Baker, Christopher Cross Ruth, Daniel Baker.
                                             25. 83

BAYNARD, JOHN, Queen Anne's Co.   3 Feb, 1746
                                             9 Apr, 1747
   To wife ELIZABETH BAYARD, use of my dwelling plantation,
exclusive of land rented to Alexander Chalmer and The Rowling
House, until my son THOMAS BAYNARD, arrives at age 21.
   To HENRY CASSON, 83 A. laying in "Baynard's Large Range
Addition."
   To dau. MARGARET, the wife of John Casson, my land in
Dorchester Co. (exclusive of land left by John Bramock bet.
Robert Spading and me. Sd. land to be held by her, her hrs. and
assigns forever.).
   To dau. RACHEL BAYNARD, my land in Talbot Co.
   To dau. RACHEL, as all that my exs. or either of them shall
receive for my water mill, sitated on Dilladvanghens (?) Branch
in Tuckahoe Neck, and for 20 A. adjoining sd. mill.
   To wife, ELIZABETH BAYNARAD, 1/3 pt. of my personal estate,
after the child. of Joshua Clark dec'd., have their portion fully
paid.
   To son-in-law, JOHN CASSON, the negro boy I gave and delivered
before to my dau. MARGARET.
   Bro. Thomas Baynard, and John Casson.
Wit: Alexander Chalmer, Robert Caide, John Cocke. 25. 85

NEVIL, JOHN, St. Luke's Parish, Queen Anne's Co.
                                             17 Nov, 1746
                                             9 Apr, 1747
   To son JOSEPH, lands called "Warton," "Pender" and "Outrange"

on the head of Little Red Lyon Branch of 75 A., and land called
"Sewell Fork" at 500 A, and tract "Solomon's Lott" and
"Tilighman's Discovery," which several tracts I give my son
JOSEPH.
. To son JOHN, my remaining lands.
Sd. son JOHN, shall be under care of his mother until age 21.
Son JOSEPH, to be under care of his bro. JOHN.
Wife Ann Nevil, and son John, exs.
Wit: Jno. H. Hambleton, Wm. Carmichael, Joanna Hambleton.
25. 88

BLAKE, RICHARD, Calvert Co.   17 Nov, 1746
                                             31 Mar, 1747
   To dau. MARY BLAKE, 4 slaves, land on eastern shore in
Dorchester County, called "Cammell Hill" or "Shore Ditch," and
one Morgan, a gunsmith, has all the papers relating to it.
   To son THOMAS BLAKE, all the southernmost pt. of my land,
where I now live, bound the main road which leads to All Saint's
Church, and if he shd. die without issue, same to my sons RICHARD
and JOSEPH.
   To son JOSEPH, 1 tract formerly belonging to Richard Dallam,
being pt. of "Upper Bennett," and 50 A. I bought of Thomas
Hinton, called "His Lordship's Favour," and tract I bought of
Richard Dullam, called "Lordship's Favour" adjoining Jeremiah
Johnson and a piece of land on Eastern Shore, called "The
Tuccarora (?) Plains."
   Trustees, son THOMAS and friends, JOSEPH WILSON and JAMES
HEIGHE, to take care of my sons, JOSEPH and RICHARD.
   Wife SUSANNAH BLAKE,
Wit: Priscilla Rhodes (Quaker), Jacob Deal (or Deall or Deale),
Hillean Wilson.   25. 90 - 91

PACE, John, St. Mary's Co.   23 Mar, 1746
                                             11 May, 1747
   To son JONATHAN, dau MILDRED, slave Jack.
   To son JONATHAN, fiddle, gun and pair of money scales, other
personalty.
   To make their unkle Benjamin Williams guaridan over my two
children, Jonathan and Mildred.
   To wife ANN PERCE and my two youngest children, 3 Negroes,
Ben, Frank and Sarah.
   To son STEPHEN, 3 years schooling.
   To wife and my four children, rest of my estate.
   Wife and Benjamin Williams, exs.
Wit: James Egerton, James Granan, James FitzJefferys.
25. 92

FOREST, Patrick, St. Mary's Co.   31 Mar, 1746
                                             25 May, 1747
   To wife FRANCES FOREST, extx.
   To son RICHARD FORREST, uppermost pt of land from wild cherry
tree to Cool spring branch, called "North East."
   to dau SARAH FORREST, remaing pt of said plantation.
   To dau ELIZABETH FOREST, mullata child Esther.
   To dau BETHELEM FORREST, mullata child, Rose.

To wife FRANCES slaves.
300 A. in Baltimore Co., called "Forest Lodge," to pay debts
and residue to my children and wife.
Wit: John Stevens, Bridget Dorsey, Hannah Chiverell.
25. 93

CLOCKER, Daniel, Sr., St. Mary's Co.　　14 Apr, 1747
　　　　　　　　　　　　　　　　　　　8 Jun, 1747
　　To dau ELIZABETH CLOCKER, tract adj plantation whereon I live
called "Clockers Fancy," 56 A. by certificate dated 18 Jan
1741/2; tract adj aforementioned tract, called "Sisters
Freehold," 50 A.
　　To son DANIEL CLOCKER, ex.
Wit: Jno. Hicks, Joseph Taylor, John Taylor.　　25. 94

BIGGS, John, St. Mary's Co.　　　　　　4 Jun, 1747
　　　　　　　　　　　　　　　　　　7 Jul, 1747
　　To wife ANN BIGGS, all my estate.
Wit: Kenelm Truman Greenfield, Samuel Keech.

PELLEY, JAMES (or PILLEY), Mt. Calvert, Prince George's Co.
　　　　　　　　　　　　　　　　19 Mar, 1746/7
　　　　　　　　　　　　　　　　25 Jun, 1747
　　To son JAMES PELLEY, JR., land which I now live on, bought
from John Stoddart; land lying near Upper Marlborough, called
"Bells Wiln," I order to be sold and the money divided bet. my
sons: RICHARD, CALVETT and HARRISON PILLEY.
　　To dau. SARAH LEITCH, some cattle.
　　To dau. ELIZABETH MILLS, cattle.
　　To dau. MARGARET LAUNGE, cattle.
　　To dau. JEMIMA PILLEY, stock.
　　To dau. KEZIE PILLEY,
　　My 4 sons: JAMES, RICHARD, HARRISON and CALVERT PILLEYS.
　　Wife, JANE PILLEY, extx.
Wit: James Harvey, John Orme, Thomas Hamilton.　　25. 96

ECELESTON, HUGH, Dorchester Co.　　29 Jan, 1746
　　　　　　　　　　　　　　　　　27 Jul, 1747
　　To wife LUCRETIA ECCLESTON, mulato woman, called Jane Price
and her child.
　　To son THOMAS ECCLESTON, when he is age 18, the increase of
sd. slave.
　　To wife, some cattle.
　　To son THOMAS ECELESTON, my dwelling plantation; only my
mother ELENOR ECCLESTON, to have use of sd. plantation until my
son is age 18.
　　Mentions the fact that shd. there yet be a child born, it shd.
share an equal pt.
　　Appoint my uncle JOHN ECCLESTON, to take care of my son's
estate, until son is of age.
　　Wife, extx.
Wit: Septimus Noell, Samuel LeCompt, David Peterkin, John
LeCompt.　　　　　　　　　　　　　　　　　　25. 97

REASLING, MATHIAS, Prince George's Co.   25 Mar, 1747
                                           13 Jun, 1747
   Wife, BARBARA REASLING.
   To son JOHN REASLING, 20 pounds money.
   To dau. RACHEL, 1 spinning wheel.
   Wife and Capt. Johannas Middan, exs.
Wit: John Beatty, Elias Brock, Catharine Divilplease,
Arideze...(?)
                                                25. 98

SHIRLEY, RICHARD, St. Mary's Co.   16 Apr, 1747
                                           15 Jul, 1747
   100 A. of tract I now live on should be sold by my wife with
advice of Robert Greenwell, to pay debts.
   To son ROBERT SHIRLEY, tract I live on that lies on E. side of
Westones Branch that leads into the head of St. Mary's River.
   To wife remainder of land.
Wit: Robert Greenwell, Thomas Norris, John Brion.
The widow stands to the will.   25. 100

WALLER, ISAAC, St. Mary's Co.   7 Apr, 1747
                                           27 Jul, 1747
   Desire that my wife MARY WALLER keep my son EDMUND WALLER
until he arrives at age 20 and that Ann Robertson keep my dau
MARGARET WALLER until age 16.
   Mentions all that was left to his children by their
grandfather, THOS. EDMUNDS.
Wife MARY, extx.   25. 100

ALLEN, JOHN, Talbot Co.   25 Jun, 1740
                                           3 Jun, 1747
   Leave my 2 child., named HUGH and PHILEMON, to John Kinnamont
of Talbot Co.
   Wife MARY, extx.
Wit: Francis Jones, P. Benson.   25. 101

HIGGS, AARON, Talbot Co.   6 Dec, 1746
                                           5 Jun, 1746
   Wife AGNESS HIGGS, to keep all my land until my son, MOSES
HIGGS, comes of age 21; and at decease of my wife, to son AARON
HIGGS.
   To dau. SUFFIA HIGGS, a mullatoe girl called "Judah," as a
legacy.
   My 3 child.: MOSES, AARON and SUFFIA HIGGS.
   Wife extx.
Wit: Henry Mill, Richard Start, Wm. Lundegin.   25. 102

RICE, ROBERT, Somerset Co.   17 Sep, 1746
                                           17 Jun, 1747
   My child.: BETTY, WILLIAM, MARY, ROBERT and JOHN PRICE.
   Wife MARY PRICE, extx.
Wit: Robert Given, Ann Hardy, Joseph Husk.   25. 103

HEARN, EDWARD Somerset Co.   26 Feb 1744/5
                                              11 Jul, 1747
   Wife DEBORAH.
   Sons: JAMES, JACOB, ISAAC.
   Dau. Anne.
Wit: Southy Wittington, John White, John Pusey.   25. 104

RICKARDS, JOHN, Somerset Co.   13 May, 1747
                                              18 Aug, 1747
   To wife ANN, slaves
   To son JOHN RICKARDS, tract of land called "Rickards' Delight"
in Somerset Co.
   To son JOSIAH RICKARDS, and to his unborn child, and my dau.
ELIZABETH RICKORDS, the remainder of sd. tract.
   To dau. NICE RICKARDS, my land in Worcester Co., tract
"Turkell Ridge."
   To dau. SARAH RICKORDS, 10 A. in Worcester Co., out of land
called "Shipping Crook."
   To dau. SUSAN RICKORDS, tract in Worcester Co., on branch of
Broad Creek, 75 A.
   To bro. THOMAS RICKORDS, 10 A. called "Goodluck."
   To THOMAS CALLOWAY, land in Worcester Co., land called "John's
Venture," that is if sd. Callaway (or Calloway) discharges rents
due my hrs.
   I likewise leave in care of my wife, 2 pieces of land
adjoining together the one willed to me by Phillip Carater, 100
A., out of tract of land called "Whetstones"; the other 30 A. of
tract called "Goodluck."
   I do empower her, the sd. Ann Rickords to sell,
   Wife, extx.
Wit: Joseph Callaway, Thomas Relph, Solomon Right.   25. 106

HOWARD, RUTH, Anne Arundel Co.   3 Aug, 1747
                                               12 Aug, 1747
   To grand-dau. ELIZABETH HAMMOND, my saddle horse.
   To MARY COHOON, the other half of my clothing.
   To sons JOHN DORSEY and EDWARD DORSEY, my personal estate.
   Sons JOHN and EDWARD, exs.
Wit: James Mac Gill, Edward Dorsey, son of Edward Dorsey, Ely
Dorsey.   25. 108

CHAIRES, BENJAMIN, Queen Anne's Co.   17 Apr, 1747
                                               28 May, 1747
   Wife MARY CHAIRES,
   To eld. son BENJAMIN CHAIRES, JR., land called "Warplesdon
Addition," and 50 A. pt. of "His Lordship's Mannor."
   To dau. MARY CHAIRES, 1 slave.
   To dau. ELIZABETH, 1 slave.
   Wife, extx.
Wit: Edward Godwin, Thomas Wright, Robert Smith.
                                               25. 109

OUTTEN, ABRAHAM, Worcester Co.   22 Apr, 1747
                                                5 Jun, 1747
   To son WILLIAM OUTTEN, 50 pounds money.

My balance of my child., son MATHEW OUTTEN, a plantation
whereon I live, all land I bought of John Nelson, except that I
have alinated out of sd. 2 tracts to Capt. Robert King.
To son ABRAHAM OUTTEN, tract I bought of Whittington Johnson,
with land I bought of Joshua Killen, and land I laid a warrant on
except 25 A., I allotted for Joseph Davis and Joseph Niccelson.
To son MATTHEW OUTTEN, 1 slave called Sampson, at his mother's
decease.
To dau. SARAH OUTTEN, 1 slave.
To son JOHN OUTTEN, 1 slave.
To son THOMAS OUTTEN, 1 slave girl.
To son JOHN OUTTEN, my son THOMAS, to have my land and houses
in Snow Hill.
To dau. SARAH OUTTEN,
Wife, extx.
Wit: Wm. Kitchin, Wm. Nelson, A. Dennis.
Name "ALLENAR" and "ELIONER DENNIS," spelled both ways. RHODA
OUTTEN, widow and relict of ABRAHAM OUTTEN, electeth relinquished
the gifts and bequests made by her husband; electeth to take her
1/3 pt. of deceased's estate.   25. 110

CARLISLE, JOHN, Baltimore Co.   23 Jul, 1747
    The affirmation of RICHARD JONES, age 42, being a Quaker,
affirmed as follows: That JOHN CARLISLE, late of Baltimore Co.,
dec'd., did give in his last illness to his bro. GEORGE CARLISLE,
1 horse, with fold. The fold the sd. mare goes with to his
cousin NANCY CARLISLE; a yearling colt to his cousin RICHARD
DEAVER, son of DANIEL DEAVER, 20 s. due from Robert Scott, to him
the sd. dec'd. to DANIEL DEAVER; 1 shirt to him; bros. ROBERT
CARLISLE, GEORGE CARLISLE, and 2 to his bros. DANIEL DEAVOR.
JOHN CARLISLE did appoint his bro. DANIEL DEAVER to execute the
above will and bury him, the sd. dec'd., at his, the sd. DANIEL'S
discretion and that he, the sd. JOHN CARLISLE at the time of his
pronouncing the above will, was in sound mind and memory to the
best of the affiant's knowledge.
    Deposition of Ford Barnes, Baltimore Co., age 45, who states
tht John CARLISLE of Baltimore Co., dec'd., in his last illness
gave his bro. GEORGE CARLISLE, 1 horse, and the colt to his
cousin NANCY CARLISLE, and to his cousin RICHARD DEAVOR, son of
DANIEL DEAVOR, 20 s. Due from Robt. Scott, and 1 shirt to his
bro. ROBERT CARLISLE, 2 shirts to his bro. DANIEL DEAVOR.
                                                       25. 113

HANSON, HOLLIS, Baltimore Co.   14 Aug, 1747
                                                 15 Aug, 1747
    After my expenses, then my bro. BENJ. HANSON, my slaves, now
in custoday, JAMES OSBURN, and 200 pounds tobacco in hands of WM.
DALLAM; ERICK ERICKSON to make his coffin.
    To my bro. JOHN HANSON.
    To my 2 sisters, names not mentioned.
Wit: Thos. Baker, Wm. Osborn, Jr.   25. 114

ROLLS, ARCHABALD, Baltimore Co.   28 Jul, 1747
                                                 27 Aug, 1747
    To dau. MARY ANN STANDEFOR, land called "Temporance Lott."

To dau. REBECCA ROLLS, 100 A. tract "Rollors Adventure."
To dau. TEMPERANCE ROBERSON, 100 A. tract called "Turkey Hills."
To JAMES HICKS, son of Henry Hicks, 49 A. tract "Archabald Addition."
To the love and affection which I have for his mother, 52 A. remaining pt. of "Rolles Adventure"; at decease of my wife.
Wm. Robertson and my wife REBECCA ROLLS, exs.
Wit: John Bond, Thomas Bond (both Quakers), Pheabe Jackson.
25. 114

YOE, NICHOLAS, Queen Anne's Co.   2 Apr, 1747
                                        16 Jul, 1747
Wife JANE YOE.
To my 3 child.: BENJAMIN, JOHN and ANNE YOE, my personal estate after my wife's 1/3 is taken out.
Wit: Wm. Prior, Wales Egate, Jr., Mary Esgite, or Caleb Esqite, Jr. (or Esgate).   25. 115 - 116

BIRMINGHAM, JOHN, Queen Anne's Co.   10 Apr, 1747
                                        14 May, 1747
To wife ELIZABETH, cattle.
To son CHARLES BIRMINGHAM, my dwelling plantation, 50 A. called "Birmingham Fortune."
To son CHARLES, an orphan by name, Nathan, cattle.
To dau. MARGARET, the plantation she now lives upon, 50 A. pt. of tract "Birmingham Fortune."
To daus.: ELIZABETH THORP, SARAH TEAT, MARY WICKS, ELIZABETH, RACHEL and ANNA BIRMINGHAM, some cattle.
Son Charles Birmingham, ex.
Wit: Elizabth Martin, Chas. Murphy, John Holt. 25. 116 - 118

CHAIRES, JOHN, Queen Anne's Co.   13 Apr, 1747
                                        23 Jul, 1747
To my unborn child., part of tract I now live on called "Macklin Borough," and if sd. child shd. die without heirs, to my bro. CHARLES CLAYTON.
To my afsd. child, that tract that my father lived on called "Cantley" (or "Lantley?)"; and if sd. child die without hrs., to my bro. SOLOMON CLAYTON.
Wife MARGARET CHAIRES, extx.
Wit: Edward Brown, John Brown, Hannah Haden, Elizabeth Tarr.
25. 118

EARECKSON, JOHN, Kent Island, Queen Anne's Co. 16 Apr, 1747
                                        23 Jul, 1747
To wife ELIZABETH EARECHSON, my dwelling house and 100 A.
At her decease, to son JOHN EARECKSON, and if no hrs., to son MATTHEW EARECKSON, and if no hrs., to son JACOB EARECKSON, and if no hrs., to son JOHNSON EARECHSON, and if no hrs., to son CHARLES EARECHSON, and if no hrs., to be divided bet. my 7 child.; 4 sons and 3 daus.: MATHEW, JACOB, JOHN, CHARLES EARECHSON, SARAH, SUSANNA and ELIZABETH EARCHSON.
Wife ELIZABETH EARECHSON, extx.
Wit: Robert Small, Joseph Tolson, Jacob Carter.   25. 120

MILNER, ISAAC, late of London, merchant.   8 Aug, 1729
                                      1 Jul, 1743
   To GODFRY MILNER, ESQ., bro. of dec'd. and the ex.
Brian Philpot of Parish of St. Martin, London, merchant, and
Isaac Rayner of the same parish, bookkeeper, and being sworn,
state were well acquainted with ISAAC MILNER.   25. 121

MILNER, GODFRY, late of Richmond, Surry Co., merchant.
                                 2 Aug, 1744
                           2nd, 8th, 1744
   Before Edward Kynaistor, doctor of laws, surrogate, testament
of GODFRY MILNER, dec'd., was registered. His will was granted
to BRIAN PHILPOT and JOHN PHILPOT, exs.; in trust to my friends
BRIAN PHILPOT and JOHN PHILPOT, both of London, merchants, for
benefit of my much honored mother, MRS. ANN COLMORE, wife of
Thomas Colmore.
   Sd. friends BRIAN and JOHN PHILPOT, exs., 2nd, 8th 1744, on
which appeared personally DANIEL MACKENZIE of the Parish of St.
Clement, East Cheape London, gentleman, and Isaac Raynor of
Parish, bookkeeper, and states they were acquainted with GODFRY
MILNER, late of Richmond in Surry Co., dec'd. and with his
handwriting.   25. 123

GALLAWAY, JOHN, Anne Arundel Co.   9 Oct, 1747
                               2 Oct, 1747
   Land in Baltimore Co. (page 126), called "Forest" and
"Adventure"; that sd. land be sold, and I have contracted with
Jacob Franklin to convey unto him tract called "Gordon," which a
certain Benj. Harrison, land called "Beaver."
   To wife JANE GALLAWAY, sum of 1000 pounds money or the
Province of Pennsylvania to be paid to her at Philadelphia by my
ex. At decease of my wife, to my young. dau.
   As soon as my decease, that my wife, with my young. dau., be
removed to Philadelphia by my exs.
   To son JOSEPH GALLOWAY, several tracts called "Cambustone"
devised unto me by my father, SAMUEL GALLOWAY, and land I
purchased of John Gills called "Cambustone," and tract "Beaver
Dam" and tract "Cumberstone," and 2 tracts formerly belonging to
John Blackmore.
   Appoint son SAMUEL GALLOWAY, to be guardian to my son JOSEPH,
until of age.
   To young. dau. JENNY GALLOWAY, 1/4 pt. of clear residue of my
estate.
   Wife, JANE GALLOWAY, to educate my dau. ANA.
   My trusty friends John Dillwyn and Wm. Coleman, both of the
city of Philadelphia.
   To my 3 child.: SAMUEL GALLOWAY, MARY CHEW and JOSEPH
GALLOWAY.
   Bro. JOSEPH GALLOWAY, and JOSEPH COREMAN, exs.
Wit: Jol. A. Milton, Wm. Coale,, Wm. Coal, Jr., Samuel Coale, Dr.
John Hamilton.   25. 125 - 129

PURDDUM, JOHN, Anne Arundel Co.   10 Aug, 1747
                              19 Aug, 1747
                              14 Sep, 1747

To son BENJAMIN PURDUM, tract whereon I live called "Purdoum's Choice," 100 A.
To wife MARY PURDDUM, my personal estate, to be divided amongst my child.
To my grand-son JOHN PURDUM, son of JAMES, sum of 50 pounds money, when he is age 21, to be paid by my 3 sons.
To JOHN, JEREMIAH and BENJAMIN PURDDUM, 5 pounds, each.
To RICHARD SNOWDEN, SR., 2 tracts addition to Purdum.
Wife MARYH PURDDUM, and son JOHN PURDDUM, exs.
Wit: Matthias Gray, Wm. Hanks, Thomas Hutchcraft.

25. 129

CALDWELL, JOHN, Somerset Co.   11 Jul, 1747
                                    19 Aug, 1747
    That what money is due me from Captain George Parris and Dr. Jackson, with what pt. of the cargo now sent by Capt. Parris, and my will is that my quarter pt. of the sloop be sold and money applied to my just debts.
To son JOSHUA CALDWELL, 1 s. sterl.
To son JOHN CALDWELL.
To sons-in-law, WM. VENABLE and JOSEPH SCROGGEN, liberty and use of saw mill, in full of their wives MARY VENABLE'S and SARAH SCROGGEN'S portions.
To wife MARY CALDWELL.
To young. son SAMUEL CALDWELL, to be paid him when he is free from his Master Robert Mills.
To grand-son JOHN CALDWELL, my landing house and the lot whereon it stands called "MACCOUGHS HOUSE," and also 40 feet square, fronting the main street bet. Longes house, so called, and the quarter where Ammey now lives, to build him a house.
To young. son SAMUEL CALDWELL, at decease of my wife, my lands where I now live, with all my slaves, and my right in the town of Salsberry, houses, mills, stock, etc.
To pay JOHN and MARY HANDY their portions.
Wm. Venables and Joseph Scroggen, exs., with advice of Col. Robert King and Capt. Henry Ballard.
Wit: Joshua Porter, Nick Sountain, Jonathan Shockley.

25. 131

PHEBUSS, George, Sr., Somerset Co.   28 Nov, 1744
                                        1 Sep, 1747
To wife MARY PHEBUS, my slave.
To sons SAMUEL and JOHN PHEBUS, to be equally divided.
To dau ALICE SPICER, personalty.
To 2 grand-daus., MARY and ANN SPICER, slaves.
To eld. son GEORGE PHEBUSS, 1 s. sterl.
To 2 grand-sons, GEORGE and JOHN PHEBUS, the plantation whereon my son GEORGE PHEBUS now lives.
    Land adjoining John Rigsby, before my 2 sons SAMUEL and JOHN PHEBUS, have offer of it and refuse to give as much as any other person shall for same and be in possession of my 2 sons; SAMUEL and JOHN, until my grand-sons GEORGE and JOHN PHEBUS, arrive to age 21, and if they die without issue, then to fall to my 2 sons SAMUEL and JOHN PHEBUS, 10 pounds.
To grand-dau. MARY PHEBUS, 10 pounds money.

To grand-dau. ELIZABETH PHEBUS, 10 pounds money.
To grand-dau. EUNICE PHEBUS, 10 pounds money.
Son SAMUEL, ex.
Wit: Wm. Jones, Wm. Ballard, Henry Wright.   25. 133

BEDFORD, SAMUEL, Dorchester Co.   14 Jul, 1746
                                         19 Jun, 1747
     To wife REBECCA BEDFORD, plantation where I live, to have bet.
my son and she during her life.
     To son-in-law PHILIP FRENCH, 3 pounds.
     To son THOMAS BEDFORD, remainder of estate.
Wit: Jos. Ennalls, Henry Ennalls, Jr., --? Wheland.
                                                   25. 135

SMITH, THOMAS, Great Choptank Parish, Dorchester Co.
                                         28 Apr, 1747
                                         10 Jun, 1747
     To son WILLIAM SMITH, my 2nd best chest of drawers.
     To son JOHN STEVEN SMITH, stock.
     To dau. ANN, wife of Joseph Griffith, my 3rd best chest.
     My 2 sons WILLIAM and JOHN STEVEN SMITH.
Wit: Wm. Murry, George Griffith.   25. 136

WALLIS, RICHARD, Dorchester Co., planter.   22 Jan, 1746
                                              10 Jun, 1747
     My sons: THOMAS WALLIS, CHARLES WALLIS, MATTHEW WALLACE,
STAPLEFORT WALLIS, RICHARD WALLACE, JOSEPH WALLIS.
     Wife BETHULE WALLIS, remainder pt. of estate and appoint her
extx.
Wit: Raymond Stapleford, Wm. Stanford, Henry Fisher.
                                                   25. 137

WRIGHT, EDWARD, Dorchester Co.   1 Mar, 1747
                                        12 Aug, - -
     To son JOSHUA WRIGHT, tract called "Chapmans Fellowship" in
Baltimore Co.
     To wife MARTHA, my lands in Dorchester Co., and at her
decease, give sd. land to my 5 sons: WILLIAM, EDWARD, LEVIN,
JACOB and LEMUEL.
     To 3 daus. at their mother's decease, slaves.
     To wife MARTHA, personal estate, appoint wife, extx.
Wit: Wm. Corsey (Cowsey?), Sr., Wm. Wright, John Finch.
                                                   25. 138

WINGATE, JOHN, Dorchester Co., planter.   15 Jul, 1747
                                            12 Aug, 1747
     To son THOMAS WINGATE, one tract "Joseph Stanaway Lott" and
tract "Fox Point"; "Wingate's Design" and "Southampton" dividing
tree bet. the sd. THOMAS WINGATE and his sister.
     To dau. RACHEL SCOTT, remainder of tract called "Southampton,"
also remainder of tract called "Wingate's Design."
     To son JOHN WINGATE, one tract called "Head of Farham" on
Farham Creek, also tract called "Hants Content."
     To dau. LUCY PARKS, 2 tracts "Muscetor Neck" and "Colliers
Forest."

To son THOMAS WINGATE, furniture.
To dau. PRISCILLA SANDERS, furniture.
To dau. REBECCA WINGATE, slaves.
To dau. MARY WINGATE, slaves.
To dau. COMFORT WINGATE, furniture and slaves.
To dau. LUCY PARCKS, stock.
To dau.: MARY RITCHETT (?), ELIZABETH HARPER and HANNER
MERIDITH, furniture.
To dau. ANN PRITCHETT, cattle.
To my little boy JAMES, my horse.
To wife RACHEL WINGATE, my dwelling plantation.
Wit: Benj. Todd Wm. Wingate, John Mesick.   25. 139

RUSSAM, EDWARD, Dorchester Co., planter.   3 Jun, 1747
                                             27 Aug, 1747
     To wife ANN RUSSAM
My friend and neighbor, EDWARD TRIPPE, care of my 3 sons:
WINLOCK, EDWARD and JAMES RUSAM, until they arrive to age 21.
Edward Trippe, ex.
Wit: Wm. Murray, John and Mary Dean.   25. 142

SMITH, SARAH, Calvert Co., widow.   7 Apr, 1747
                                             13 Oct, 1747
     To son-in-law JOSEPH HALL, slaves.
     To nephew PARKER YOUNG, 1 slave.
     To son JOHN SMITH, slaves.
     Joseph Hall and Parker Young, exs.
Wit: F. Sheredine, Wm. Holland, Jr.   25. 143

YOUNG, JOHN, Cecil Co., blacksmith.   29 Mar, 1747
                                             10 Oct, 1747
     To sons: JOSEPH, SAMUEL and JOHN YOUNG, my plantation, to be
equally divided among them.
     Joseph, the eldest son, a minor.
     Wife MARY YOUNG, extx.
Wit: Amos Fogg, Samuel Watt, John Gibson.   25. 144

WARD, MARGARET, Talbot Co.   2 Jun, 1746
                                               6 Oct, 1747
     To nephew WILLIAM TILGHMAN, 100 pounds sterl., to be paid each
of my relations on the Western Shore, as my bro. RICHARD BENNET,
shall direct.
     If my sd. bro. shd. happen to die before payment of same, then
my nephew EDWARD LLOYD direct.
     To cousins: ANNA MARIA, wife of Thomas Ringold, ANNA MARIA,
dau. of George Robins, HENRIETTA MARIA, dau. of Samuel
Chamberlain, ANNA MARIA, dau. of William Tilghman, and ELIZABETH,
dau. of Jeremiah Nichols, 20 pounds sterl.
     To cousins ANNA MARIA and MARY HEMSLEY, 10 pounds sterl.
     To cousin ANN, dau. of Samuel Chamberlain, 12 pounds sterl.
     To cousins: THOS., JAMES, SAMUEL and ROBERT CHAMBERLAIN, 5
pounds sterl.
     To cousins: RICHARD, JAMES and MARGARET, sons and dau. of
William Tilghman, 12 pounds current money.
     To cousin HENRIETTA MARIA EARLE, 12 pounds money.

To niece ANN, wife of Matthew Tilghman, my gold watch.
To nephew MATTHEW STILGHMAN, 100 pounds money.
To cousin MARGARET, dau. of Matthew Tilghman, 1 slave.
To MARY, dau. of John Wright, 40 pounds money, for the
affection that I have for her, some furniture; also, cattle, left
as a legacy by her grandmother, which I have received.
To cousin ELIZABETH, dau. of Edward Lloyd, my lands in Queen
Anne's Co. called "Neneveth" and "Neneveh's Addition" and "Mill
Range," but if she die without issue, same to cousin EDWARD
LLOYD, son of the afsd. Edward.
To the use of St. Michael's Parish Church, a pulpit cloth and
cushion, a communion table cloath and a prayer book.
To FRANCES BOZMAN, my black satin gown and etc.
To sister ANNA MARIA TILGHMAN, clothing.
To sister and my nieces HENRIETTA CHAMBERLAIN and DEBORAH
NICHOLS, each a suit of cloths.
To niece MARGARET, wife of Wm. Tilghman, my dark suit.
To niece DEBORAH, wife of Jeremiah Nichols, my clothing.
To niece ANN, wife of Matthew Tilghman, clothing.
To nieces MARGARET, wife of Wm. Tilghman, and ANN, wife of
Mathew Tilghman, residue of my wearing apparel, equally.
To niece ANN, wife of Mathew Tilghman and to MATHEW and
MARGARET, son and dau. of the sd. Matthew and Ann, my gold ring.
To 2 cousins, MATTHEW WARD TILGHMAN and MARGARET TILGHMAN, son
and dau. of my nephew MATTHEW TILGHMAN and ANN, his wife, my
plate and negroes, except my negro, Harry, and negro girl, Eve,
and all residues of estate not mentioned be equally divided, but
if MATTHEW WARD TILGHMAN or MARGARET die before of age, then my
nephew MATTHEW TILGHMAN, have sd. estate.
Appoint nephew MATTHEW TILGHMAN, ex.
Wit: Edward Knott, Jo Leeds, George Porter, Sarah Jarman, Mary
Stains.   25. 145

GIBB, JOHN, Queen Anne's Co.   26 Aug, 1747
                                      22 Oct, 1747
He had 19 slaves and gave all of them their freedom.
To his freed slaves (named), land and plantation called
Kelmans Plains Addition," situate on n. side of Unicorn Branch;
also other tract of land known as "Knowlss Range."
To bro. WILLIAM GIBB, and to his son JOHN GIBB, inhabitants in
the Kingdom of Great Brittain, 1 s.
To my kinswoman JANNET CLEITAND, 1 s. sterl.
To godson JOHN THOMPSON, son of Mr. Dowdall Thomson, my riding
horse, all my plate and a gun in possession of his father.
James Massey Sr., and John Hadley, Sr., exs.
Wit: James Massey, Jr., John Sprig, Thomas Hadley, John Morris.
                                      25. 148

COMPTON, MATTHEW, SR., Charles Co.   19 Mar, 1744/5
                                      15 Sep, 1747
To son SAMUEL COMPTON, all that pt of my estate he possessed
with in Virginia and 2 s. sterl.
To dau SUSANNA WHITELY, 2 s. sterl.
To dau dau ELENDER SLYE, 2 s. sterl.
To grandson MATTHEW COMPTON Parker, 2 s. sterl.

122

To son Matthew Compton, rest of estate.
Wit: George Briscoe, William Howard.
25. 150

GRANGER, CHRISTOPHER, Kent Co., planter.   21 Jul, 1747
                                              4 Sep, 1747
    To bro. JOHN GRANGER, 1 slave, and at his decease to my cousin
JOHN GRANGER, son of Thomas Granger.
    To cousin ELIZABETH BRYAN, dau. of James Bryan, cattle.
    To cousin WILLIAM GRANGER, cattle.
    To SARAH GRANGER, dau. to my wife ANN GRANGER,
    To wife ANN GRANGER, extx.,
Wit: John Sudler, Emory Sudler, Joseph Sudler.
                                              25. 151-152

SHIRBURN, CLARE (CLEAR), St. Mary's Co.   21 Feb, 1745
                                              6 Aug, 1747
    To sons RICHARD BROOKS and BAKER BROOKS SHIRBURN, cooper
kettle and furniture.
    To son NICHOLAS SHIRBURN, rest of estate, ex.
Wit: John Miles.   25. 152-153

BINKS, JOHN, St. Mary's Co., planter.   22 Aug, 1747
                                              31 Aug, 1747
    To worthy friend, Richard Molyneax, slaves, furniture.
    To Hannnah Dorsey, black horse and 1/2 her mother's wearing
apparell; also my green chest besides what is belonging to her
from her father's estate.
    To godson JOHN BURNE, son of James Burne, horse at Mr.
Locker's stock.
    To goddau SARAH FITZJEFFERY, livestock.
    To godson MISERY GRIGGS, son of GEORGE GRIGGS, SR., livestock.
    To friend JANE BENDING, bed and blankets.
    To JOHN DORSEY and PATRICK BOYD, personalty.
    To WM. HARRISON, son of WM. HARRISON, horse.
    To JOHN DORSEY, my late wife's son, and BRIDGET ROADS and
HANNAH DORSEY, his two sisters - rest of my estate.
Vitus Herbert and John Dorsey, exs.   25. 153-155

ONEALE, PETER, St. Mary's Co.   17 Apr, 1745
                                              16 Sep, 1747
    To wife ANN ONEALE, land and plantation, being pt of a tract,
"Crachbone." If she remarries land goes to
    son JOHN ONEALE. If he has no heirs then to
    son PETER LAMAR ONEALE. If he has no heirs then to
    son JAMES ONEALE. If he has no heirs then to my daus
(unnamed).
    To dau ELIZABETH ONEALE, personalty. If no heirs then to my
dau MARY ONEALE.
Wit: Mevl. Loch, Ja. Wood, John Suete.   25. 155-157

GULLY, THOMAS, Talbot Co.   23 Aug, 1747
                                              27 Oct, 1747
    To wife RACHEL GULLY, my dwelling plantation, pt. of "Ashby";
at her decease to son CHARLES.

To son THOMAS, stock.
To son BARTHOLOMEW, stock.
To my 2 daus., ANN and RACHEL, cattle.
Wit: Robert Goldsborough, John Sutton, Sarah Moore.
25. 157-158

HUNT, THOMAS, Calvert Co.   14 Aug, 1747
                                             14 Nov, 1747
    To wife, the plantation, but at her decease to son THOMAS, but
my moveable estate divided amongst my wife and children.
    Wife, extx.
Wit: Wm. Hardesty, Job Hunt, Thos. Rhodes.   25. 158

TAYLOR, EVERARD, Calvert Co.   25 Sep, 1747
                                             16 Nov, 1747
    To son BRYAN TAYLOR, my library.
    Wife SARAH, extx.
Wit: Charles Clagett, John Rigby, Amy Batson.   25. 159

HATTON, JOSEPH, Prince George's Co.   1 Dec, 1737
                                             14 Nov, 1747
    To wife LUCY HATTON, 1/3 of my estate, 100 A. given me by my
mother, MARY HATTON, by my father, WILLIAM HATTON, last will to
such persons in that my mother in her last will bequeathed.
    To dau. MARY HATTON, a child's pt.
    To son JOSEPH HATTON, 400 A., on Cowpen Branch, near the
plantation of Thomas Middleton, where he now lives. Same side of
creek that was appointed by my father, WILLIAM HATTON, his last
will to divide a parcel of land that he bequeathed to my sister,
PENELOPE MIDDLETON, from the land he bequeathed to me.
    To son NATHANIEL, 200 A. in the plantation I now live on.
    To son RICHARD, 200 A.
    My 4 sons: JOSEPH, NATHANIEL, RICHARD and JOSHUA; dau.
ELIZABETH.
    Wife Lucy Hatton, extx.
Wit: John Frazer, Mary Whitmore, Margaret Whitmore.
25. 159-161

FRANKLIN, JOHN, Anne Arundel Co., planter   9 Oct, 1747
                                             11 Nov, 1747
    To son-in-law JOSEPH CHEW, a gun.
    To son JOHN FRANKLIN, 1 horse.
    To son ROBERT, stock.
    To dau ELIZABETH, when she marries or is age 17.
    Wife ISABELL FRANKLIN, extx.
Wit: William Fisher, Wm. Matthews.   25. 161-162

HOLLIDAY, ROBERT, surgeon, Baltimore Co.   2 Dec, 1745
                                              2 Oct, 1747
    To wife ACHSAH HOLLIDAY, all bonds, monies, 2 lotts in
Baltimore-Town, # 2 and 3 and plantation called "Goshen
Resurveyed."
    To unborn child, lot in Baltimore-Town, No. 4 and stocks and
servants.
    To bro JAMES HOLLIDAY, entire estate if wife deceased without

heirs.
    Capt. Charles Ridgely, ex.
Wit: Lyde Goodwin, John Ensor, John Haddin (or Hedding).
                                                25. 163

HITCHCOCK, GEORGE, Baltimore Co.   23 Aug, 1747
                                           4 Nov, 1747
    To grand-son GEORGE TYE, my dwelling plantation house, mills
and improvements, and for want of hrs., to his sisters, ELINORS
TYE.
    To grand-dau. ELINOR TYE, 50 A, conveyed to me by Wm. Knight,
granted to Knight and called "Knight's Addition."
    To grand-son GEOREGE TYE, slaves.
    To grand-dau. SUSANNAH TYE,
    To son and dau. JOHN and PRESOSCIA TYE.
    Wife MARY HITCHCOCK, and son-in-law JOHN TYE, exs.
Wit: Henry Saylor, John Cook, Aquila Carr.   25. 164-165

STRINGER, SAMUEL, Queen Anne's Parish, Anne Arundel Co.,
    practioner of physick.   20 Jul, 1744
                                           5 Dec, 1747
    To wife LYDIA, pt of "Warfields Contrivance," dwelling houses,
and at her decease to son RICHARD; wife's land called "Hobb's
Park," in sd. county.
    To son SAMUEL, my brick house in Annapolis, lots and
improvements, when he arrives at age 21 years.
    To dau. ANN, and son RICHARD, to descend to son RICHARD when
of age.
    To son SAMUEL, and my daus. LUCY and ANN, then and their hrs.
forever, tract called "Ivy Church" in Little Pipe Creek, Prince
George's Co., divided equally.
Wit: Joseph Hall, Benj. Warfield, Joshua Warfield, son of
Alexander.   25. 165 - 167

LEE, ANNA MARIA, Prince George's Co.   8 Sep, 1746
                                            1 Sep, 1747
    To CAPT. THOMAS ADDISON, in General Bragg's Regiment, 2
slaves, and appoint him ex.
Wit: A. Murdock, Mrs. Elinor Addison, Rev. Henry Addison.
                                                25. 167

PIBORN, JOHN, SR., Prince George's Co.   23 Sep, 1747
                                            25 Nov, 1747
    To son JOHN, stock.
    To son BENJ., stock.
    Dau. RUTH PIBORN, shall have her choice.
    Daus.: MARY PIBORN, RACHEL CALVIN, SARAH PRATHER, 1 s.
    Son BENJAMIN PIBORN, shall have the orphan boy, Charles Hyatt
until he is age 21.
    Sons JACOB and BENJAMIN PIBORN, exs.
Wit: Benj. Chitty, Charles O'Neal, George Nichols.
                                                25. 168

SMOOT, JOHN, Prince George's Co., planter. 20 Oct. 1747
                                            25 Nov, 1747

To son JOHN, 100 A. called "Sealls Desire."
To son EDWARD, 100 A. called "Crumford."
To wife MARY, her thirds.
To dau. MARY, stock.
Wit: Solomon Stinton, James Harrison, Thomas Birdwistle.
25. 168

CROCKETT, JOHN, Baltimore Co.   3 Aug, 1747
                                  2 Dec, 1747
    To sister HANNAH CROCKETT, 500 A., land called "Isles of
Capehea."
    Mentiions SAMUEL STANDEFORD.
    To wife MARY CROCKETT, 50 A. bequeath to MARY DORSEY, dau. of
my bro.-in-law ELY DORSEY.
    Remaining pt. of tract called "Marino," providing that DAVID
COPELAND be suffered to live on that pt. he lately leased from
me.
    To NATHAN RICHARDSON, son of my bro.-in-law, Nathan
Richardson, of Baltimore Co.
    To wife MARY, remaining pt. of my estate and appoint her extx.

Wit: Daniel Richardson (Quaker), Thomas Sprigg, Thomas Lingen,
Edward Sprigg.   25. 171-172

WRIGHT, THOMAS HYNSON, Queen Anne's Co.   11 Sep, 1747
                                            12 Oct, 1747
    To wife MARY WRIGHT, 1 slave.
    To sons: NATHAN SAMUEL TURBUTT and THOMAS WRIGHT, and
grand-dau. SARAH WRIGHT, equally, my personal estate.
    Appoint the last 2 named, exs.
Wit: Chas. Downes, Jno. Jackson, John Wilkinson.
                                            25. 173

NEEDLES, THOMAS, Queen Anne's Co.   13 Aug, 1736
                                      13 Oct, 1747
    To son JOHN NEEDLES, 1 s.
    To dau. MARY JOHNSON, same.
    To dau. PRISCILLA NEEDLES, same.
    To wife, my debts and legacies being first paid, the remainder
to her and appoint her extx.
Wit: John Johnson, John Hollingsworth, Charles Hynes.
                                      25. 174 - 175

HALL, LAURANCE, Queen Anne's Co., planter.   20 Sep, 1747
                                               15 Oct, 1747
    To son JOHN HALLS, 75 A. whereon he now lives, called "Hog
Harbour."
    To son WM. HALL, 75 A., pt. of sd. tract.
    To son LAWRENCE HALL, 75 A.
    JOHN and WM. HALL, exs.
Wit: John Brown, John Folkner, Burton Francis Faulkner.
                                               25. 176

EMORY, ARTHUR, Queen Anne's Co., gentleman.   18 Jul, 1747
                                                25 Nov, 1747

To son THOMAS EMORY, 10 pounds.
To son JAMES EMORY, pt. of 2 tracts called "Trustram Addition," and "Corsey" upon Wye containing 200 A.
To son GIDION EMORY, pt. of 3 tracts called "Fortune," "Saint Paul," and "Carramans Creek."
To son JOHN EMORY, 5 s.
To son ARTHUR EMORY, 5 s.
To my daus.: ANN SUDLER, SARAH CARTER, JULIANA KEMP and LETTETLIER KIRBY, 5 s.
To son GIDION EMORY, 5 slaves.
To wife JAQUELIENNE (?) EMORY, several slaves.
To son JAMES EMORY, 5 slaves.
Wife and son JAMES EMORY, exs.
Wit: Wm. Emory, Thomas Emory, John Emory.   25. 177

JACKSON, GEORGE, Queen Anne's Co.   22 Sep, 1747
                                                 27 Nov, 1747
To son THOMAS JACKSON,
To dau. ELIZABETH SEAGER, slaves.
To MOSES FLOYD, stock.
Mentions "my wife's thirds."
Son BENJAMIN JACKSON, ex.
Wit: Daniel Chapman, James Sloss, Francis Jackson.
                                                         25. 179

DICKENSON, HANNAH, Talbot Co.   23 Sep, 1747
                                                 11 Nov, 1747
To son WM. DICKENSON, use of slaves, and at his decease, to grand-son JAMES DICKENSON.
To grand-son, afsd., at his father's decease, and if my son WILLIAM DICKENSON shd. decease before my grand-son comes to age 21, then the slaves to be put in the hands of Pollard Edmondson.
To dau. ELIZABETH WALKER, 3 slaves; at her decease, to my 2 grand-sons ANTHONY and THOMAS RICHARDSON, and if they die without issue, then to my sd. dau. ELIZABETH WALKER.
To sd. grand-son ANTHONY RICHARDSON, silver bowl.
To unborn child of dau. ELIZABETH, some slaves.
To dau. MARY EDMONDSON, use of 2 slaves., and at decease, to grand-child.: LUCRETIA, ANN and MARY, equally.
To grand-son JAMES EDMONDSON, 1 slave.
To dau. ANN DICKENSON, 3 slaves, and in case she die, then to my son WILLIAM DICKENSON.
Mentions grand-son JAMES DICKENSON.
Mentions my dau. ANN DICKENSON, in discharge of her pt. of her dec'd. father JAMES DICKENSON'S estate; desire my dau. ANN be put to school at Philadelphia for 2 years.
To son-in-law POLLARD EDMONDSON, use of slaves, while she is in school, and the money (sterl. money I have at Philadelphia and 2000 pounds tobacco, providing that he take care that my dau. ANNE DICKENSON, be well kept at Philadelphia); my plate and household stuff, which I gave sd. dau. ANN, remain in care of my dau. ELIZABETH WALKER, until she is of age.
Son-in-law PHILIP WALKER,
To son WM. DICKENSON, 6 pounds sterl. that I have in England.
Wit: David Jones, Priscilla Abbott, Samuel Abbott. 25. 180-1

LOVEDAY, SARAH, Talbot Co., housekeeper 1 Jan, 1743
               24 Nov, 1747
 To grand-dau. SARAH PROUSE, 1 s. sterl.
 To son THOMAS LOVEDAY, my personal estate.
 Thomas Loveday, ex.
Wit: Hannah Dobson (Quaker), John Needles, Isabel Dobson, Isaac
Dobson.   25. 184

WALES, JOHN, Talbot Co.   1 Oct, 1747
              27 Nov, 1747
 To son JOHN, land lying on St. Michael's River.
 To son ROBERT WALES, furniture.
 Dau. ELIZABETH BLADES,
 Wife and son JOHN, exs.
Wit: Jo. Hopkins, John Hews, Mary Blades, Sr. 25. 185

TREW, WILLIAM Sr., Kent Co.   25 Feb, 1747
              25 Jun, 1747
 To cousin WILLIAM TREW, son of my bro. JOHN TREW, late of Kent
Co. dec'd., my now dwelling plantation and all lands belonging to
the same. Land belonging to the same being the uppermost pt. of
a tract of land called "Cornelius Comgys's Choice," and the whole
tract resurveyed by myself and Morgan Brown, and in the resurvey
provided and the sd. tract being equally divided bet. Morgan
Brown and myself, of 420 A.
 To Morgan Brown and hrs., upper pt.
 To cousin WILLIAM TREW and hrs.,
 Mentions cousin JOHN TREW,
 To cousin WM. TREW, JR., 3 slaves.
 To friend REBECCA THOMAS, widow, 1 slave.
 To cousin WILLIAM CLARK, my clothing.
 To grand-dau. ANNA WILMER, my slaves.
 To HANNAH BODEAN, 6 head of sheep and cattle.
 Cousins WM. TREW, JR. and JOHN TREW, exs.
Wit: Robert George, Joseph George, Isaac Milton. 25. 186

CORSE, JAMES, Kent Co. 22d day, 1st mo., 1747
             8 Jul, 1747
 To wife ANN, 1/2 dwelling house, during life.
 To son JAMES and hrs., my dwelling plantation, and if he die
without hrs., to son MICHAEL COURSE and hrs., and if he die
without hrs., to son DAVID.
 To dau. RACHEL REDGRAVE, cattle.
 To dau.: ANN ENGLAND, ELIZABETH HOWARD, and HANNAH BRISCOE,
sheep.
 To dau. OFFLEY, 1 pound money.
 Dau. MARY CURRY,
 My child. to have balance equally; names as follows: JAMES,
MICHAEL, CALEB and DAVID CORSE.
 Son JAMES, ex.
Wit: Michael Corse, John Dunn, Peter Ball, John Corse.
              25. 188

BARNEY, FRANCIS, Kent Co., carpenter.   22 May, 1747
                                          8 Aug, 1747
    To 2 grandsons, ISAAC PERKINS and BARNEY CORSEY, tract called
"Barney's Forest," and a tract purchased of Wm. Debrular, called
"Essex."
    To grand-dau. ARAMINTA PERKINS, 100 A., pt. of tract called
"Richard's Adventure."
    To grand-dau. MARY PERKINS, tract called "White Marsh."
    To son-in-law EBENEZER PERKINS, 100 A. and slave named Mingo;
my dau. SARAH PERKINS, his wife.
    To kinsman MOSES ALFORD, my sword and belt.
    To 4 grand-child.: ISAAC, ARAMINTA, MARY PERKINS and BARNEY
CORSE, balance.
    Sons-in-law, EBENEZER PERKINS and JAMES CORSE, exs.
Wit: Benj. Burgin, James Cann, Thos. Bowers, Jane Roberts, Wm.
Atwox.   25. 189

HOWARD, AMBROSE, Kent Co., planter.   6 Nov, 1746
                                          8 Aug, 1747
    To wife BARBARA HOWARD, my dwelling plantation, but if she
shd. die, then to sons JOHN GOULD HOWARD and GEORGE HOWARD. If
son GEORGE HOWARD shd. marry MARY STANLEY or any of that family,
that my will is that he shall have none of afsd. plantation, but
it shall be all for son JOHN GOULD HOWARD.
    To son JOHN GOULD HOWARD, stock.
    My 3 sons: AMBROSE, DAVISON and CHRISTOPHER HOWARD; dau. MARY
STEVENS.
    Wife, extx.
Wit: Thos. Gould, Thos. Hausworth, Mary Hawsworth.
                                          25. 191

BOWERS, WILLIAM, Kent Co.   7 Oct, 1747
                                - - - - - -
Noncupative will of WILLIAM BOWERS, dec'd. Oct. 7, 1747.
Depositions of James Roberts, who states he was at the house of
WILLIAM BOWERS, who sd. it was his will that his 2 sons shd. be
at their own disposing as soon as they arrive at age 18.
Deposition of William Cannady states he was at sd. house of WM.
BOWERS, who then was exceedingly ill, who stated the same.
Wit: Wm. Cannady, Kent Co.   25. 193

FOWLER, THOMAS, Prince George's Co.   20 Nov, 1742
                                          9 Jan, 1747
    To wife ELIZABETH, land and slaves.
Wit: Leonard Wayman, Robert Constable, Thos. Edney.
                                          25. 194

FOTTRELL, EDWARD, Baltimore Co.   17 Feb, 1741/2
                                      27 Feb, 1741
    To son EDWARD FOTTRELL, land on Jones Fall, near Baltimore
Town.
    To son ED., land I bought of Wm. Peel.
    To son THOMAS, 3 lots in Baltimore Town.
    To cousin ACHSAH FOTTRELL and hrs,
    Basil Dorsey and Alexander Lawson, exs.

Wit: T. Sheredine, Francis North, Elinor Smith, William Payne.
Late of the City of Cork, have the use and management of the mill
house and all the appurtenances belonging to that tract of land
(except the mill), and to get firewood from land I bought of Mr.
Peel, for and in consideration that he, the sd. Wm. Payne, shall
take care of my 3 child., within mentioned and bring them up at
his own proper charge until they are of age.
    To son THOMAS, 1 slave, who was intended to be bound to Wm.
Payne.
    To son EDWARD, 1 slave.
    To dau. ACHSAHA, 1 slave.
    Desire that Wm. Payne not tend over 30,000 hills in corn in
any one year.   25. 194

Wit: Bourdillon, Benedict; Bourdillon, Jannette Jansen; Maynard,
Lawrence.   18 Apr. 1742
                                             23 Jan, 1744
Came Alexander Lawson before the subscriber, Commissary General
of the Province, and renounced the Executorship of the afsd.
testament, and therefore letters testamentary are to be granted
in due form to the other executor, Basil Dorsey, 5-6-1742.
                                                     25. 196

WHITE, FRANCIS, Somerset Co.   9 Jul, 1747
                                             26 Sep, 1747
    To wife, MARY WHITE, 1/3 pt. of moveable estate.
    To son FRANCIS, WHITE, JR., my dwelling plantation, and tract
called "Outlett," he to let his sisters, MARY, MARGARET and SARAH
WHITE, to live on sd. plantation as long as they are single.
    To child.: JOHN, THOMAS, FRANCIS, HENRY, PRISCILLA HOPKINS,
MARY, MARGARET and SARAH WHITE, remainder of my moveable estate,
equally divided bet. them.
    Wife Mary, and son THOMAS WHITE, exs.
Wit: George and Samuel Jones, John Roberts.   25. 197

MAC GRAH, ROBERT, Somerset Co., planter.   27 May, 1747
                                             19 Nov, 1747
    To mother JANE MAC GRAH, my dwelling house and plantation,
whereon I live, and land adjoining left me by my father OWEN MAC
GRAH'S, last will.
    To mother JANE MAC GRAH, personal estate.
Wit: Henry Ballard, Wm. Miles, John Parker.   25. 198

FRAIN, JAMES, Somerset Co.   22 Dec, 1747
                                             11 Jan, 1747
    Son-in-law JAMES HARDY,
    To 2 grand-child., TEMPERANCE and MARY FRAIN, dau. of JAMES
FRAIN, each of them, 100 pounds money, at age 20.
    To sister MAGDALIN SMITH, 1 slave.
    Use of slaves for support of 2 grand-child., TEMPERANCE and
MARY FRAIN, until they are of age.
    To dau. TEMPERANCE ACWORTH, cattle.
    To dau. ANN FRAIN, slaves.
    To grand-son ROGER FRAIN, now living with me, remainder of my
estate.

Cousin WILLIAM SMITH, and Day Scott exs.
Wit: Robert Given, Robert Farington, Levin Farington.
25. 199
DIXON, THOMAS, Somerset Co., gentleman.   8 Sep, 1747
24 Feb, 1747/8
To wife, SARAH DIXON, my plantation, with houses and orchards,
whereon I now live, during life, and at decease, give sd.
plantation to son THOMAS DIXON.
To son ISAAC DIXON, land bet. my bro. WILLIAM DIXON and
myself, and bounded corner tree belonging to Capt. Thomas
Williams and myself, and land taken out of land called "Dixon's
Addition," of 167 A., 136 A. of which I give son ISAAC, as before
mentioned.
To son ISAAC DIXON, 1050 A. of marsh taken out of patented
land called "Dixon's Lot."
To dau. ELIZABETH TURPIN, 20 s.
To dau. MARY PURNELL, 20 s.
To dau. SARAH DIXON, 1 slave.
My friend, Capt. Thomas Williams, and my son-in-law William
Turpin, guardians of my 3 child.: THOMAS, ISAAC and SARAH DIXON.
Wife and son ISAAC, exs.
Wit: Wm. Smith, Outerbridge Horsey, Wm. Fordred.
25. 201

RULF, SARAH, Baltimore Co., widow.   7 Jul, 1747
19 Nov, 1747
To son RICHARD RULF, my servant man.
To dau. HANNAH BULL, slaves.
To dau. MARY RULF, furniture.
To dau. SUSAN RULF, cattle.
To son HENRY RULF, furniture.
To son DANIEL RULF, tobacco.
My 6 child.: RICHARD, DANIEL, HANNAH BULL, MARY, SUSAN, AND
HENRY RULF.
Son RICHARD RULF, and son-in-law JOHN BULL, exs.
Wit: Wm. Bradford, George Bradford.   25. 202 - 203

DORSEY, COMFORT, Baltimore Co.   8 Jan, 1747
23 Jan, 1747
To child.: SARAH, VENICE and JOSHUA DORSEY, 1 s. sterl.
To son GREENBERRY DORSEY, 1 s. sterl.
My estate to be divided bet. VINCENT DORSEY, JOHN HAMMOND
DORSEY and JOHN DORSEY, son of GREENBERRY DORSEY.
To COMFORT DORSEY, dau. to GREENBERRY DORSEY, pair of gold
earrings.
A mortgage due me by my son JOSHUA DORSEY, of value 41 pounds,
I desire it left to ELIZABETH DORSEY, dau. of JOSHUA DORSEY.
To JOHN DORSEY, son of GREENBERRY DORSEY, furniture.
JOHN HAMMOND DORSEY, ex.
Wit: Daniel Kenley, John Day, Stephen Orion.   25. 204

WHEELER, LEONARD, Baltimore Co.   1 Sep, 1747
30 Jan, 1747
To wife ANN, 1/3 of real estate.
To dau. ELIZABETH, the half of all lands.

To unborn child,
Bro. THOMAS WHEELER, and wife ANN, exs.
Wit: Robert Clark, Jr., Robert Clark, Sr., Mary Clark.
                                        25. 205

DENTON, WILLIAM, SR., Baltimore Co.   17 Dec, 1744
                                            2 Mar, 1747
     The 3 tracts in my possession called "Batchelor's Hope,"
"Batchelor's Meadow" and "Salt Peter Neck," on the south side of
Gunpowder River, equally into 2 pts., 1/2 to my eld. son WILLIAM,
now living on sd. tract.
     To grand-son JAMES DENTON, and in default of hrs., to his bro.
WILLIAM DENTON, that if my son WM. DENTON, shd. have any sons by
his present wife, that the half pt. of my land aforesaid shd.
descend unto the eld., and if he dies without hrs., to descend to
my son WM. DENTON'S dau. and unto her hrs.
     Son JOHN DENTON shd. enjoy 1/2 of my 3 tracts when equally
divided into 2 pts., being the place my sd. son JOHN DENTON now
lives, upon on Gunpowder River, the easternmost pt.
     If my son JOHN, shd. die, give the same to his eld. son JOHN
DENTON.
     I give the same unto the next son.
     My sd. son JOHN DENTON, shd. have, and if my sd. son JOHN
DENTON,
     Mentions my son JOHN'S, eld. dau. PRISCILLA DENTON.
     To my grand-dau. RACHEL BEVANS, 20 pounds money; mentions her
dec'd. mother, my dau. RACHEL, which 2 sums amounts to 50 pounds
to sd. RACHEL BEVANS.
     My grand-son ABRAHAM ANDREWS,
     Balance of estate bet. sons WM. and JOHN and my daus. JANE
DALLAHYDE and PROVIDENCE DENTON.
     Sons Wm. Denton and John Denton, exs.
Wit: John Taylor, Walter Dallas, Joan Bevan, Jr. 25. 207 - 208

SWIFT, JOHN, Queen Anne's Co.   8 Nov, 1747
                                          23 Dec, 1747
     To wife ANN SWIFT, and son GIDEON SWIFT, slaves.
     To grand-dau. ELIZABETH SWIFT, dau. of my son GIDEON SWIFT,
stock.
     To grand-daus.: ELIZABETH SWIFT and MARTHA SWIFT, hrs. of son
JOHN SWIFT, and my dau. ELIZABETH, land equally.
     Gideon Swift, ex.
Wit: Robert Crump, Thos. Hill, Jno. Holt. 25. 208 - 210

BOURROUGHS, WILLIAM, Queen Anne's Co.   29 Jun, 1747
                                          23 Jan, 1747
     To wife HANNAH, my dwelling plantation.
     50 A. I bought of my son EDWARD, my son WILLIAM, to be
equally,
     To son VALENTINE, 50 A. of "Borough's Park."
     Eld. sons: THOMAS, GEORGE and JOHN.
     To wife, my crops.
     To dau. HANNAH, furniture.
     To grand-son ABRAHAM BUROUGHS, my son RICHARD, my clothing.
     To grand-son WILLIAM BURROUGHS, now dwelling with me, stock.

Son THOMAS, ex.
Wit: Andrew Carrer, John Carrer, John Norris.   25. 210

HOPPER, MARY ANN, Queen Anne's Co.   20 Dec, 1747
                                           28 Jan, 1747
    To dau. ANN HOPPER, land called "Larkin" of 200 A., and tract
called "Guilford," 200 A., in sd. county.
    To son WILLIAM HOPPER, my dau. MAY ANN HOPPER, 200 A. called
"Coursey Point," alias "Smith Mistake" (being pt. of tract
heretofore given to MOSEY, my father, THOMAS HYNSON WRIGHT), in
sd. county.
    My son THOMAS HOPPER.
    If my husband WILLIAM HOPPER, will purchase 200 A. of equal
value to the 2 hundred called "Coursey Point," alias "Smith
Mistake" and give same to my sd. dau. MARY ANN HOPPER and hrs.,
then my will is that my son THOMAS HOPPER, have the 200 A. called
"Coursey's Point" and sd. son THOMAS HOPPER, his hrs., to my sd.
dau. MARY ANN, in case of death without lawful issue.
Wit: Wm. Carman (spelled William Carrman in the body of the
probate), John Alexander, Joseph Lane.   25. 212

JARRMAN, WILLIAM, Queen Anne's Co., planter.   8 Jan, 1747
                                              18 Feb, 1747
    To son STEPHEN JARMAN, land called "Hogg Harbor" formerly laid
out for Solomon Clastard, or east side marsh, called "Long
Marsh."
    To dau. SUSANNA, 1 slave.
    Wife, extx.
Wit: John Burk, Jr., John Fisher, John Darnton.   25. 213

SEENEY BRYAN, Talbot Co., planter.   19 Dec, 1743
                                           12 Dec, 1747
    To mother SARAH SEENEY, my lands called "Sultans Addition" and
"Hardship," and appt. her extx.
Wit: Trustram Thomas, Solomon Sharp (Quaker), John Prewett.
                                                   25. 214

BOUNTIN (or BOUNTON), THOMAS, Talbot Co.   5 Oct, 1747
                                            1 Jan, 1747
    To wife, land; at her decease, to my 2 sons, THOMAS and JOSEPH
BOUNTIN.
    To son THOMAS BOUNTIN, my silver buttons and etc.
    To son JOSEPH BOUNTIN, my silver shoebuckles.
    Wife REBECCA BOUNTIN, extx.
Wit: Wm. Richardson, Joseph Waite, Wm. Bush.   25. 215

ANGLEY, JOHN, Talbot Co.   4 Nov, 1747
                                           15 Jan, 1747
    To grand-dau. MARY ANN ANGLEY, my personal estate.   Thomas
Helsby, ex.
Wit: Adam Brown, Mary Anderson.
Testament at request of sd. testator, before me Thos. Bullen.
                                                   25. 216

ORUM, ANDREW, Talbot Co.   16 Dec, 1747
                                                  22 Jan, 1747
     To son ANDREW ORUM, pt. of tract called "Adventure."
     To sons JOHN and LEVI, tract called "Orume Delight."
     To LEVI, my dwelling plantation.
     Personal estate, left to me by my mother, to be equally
divided.
     To 2 daus. MARY and ELINOR ORUM, all moveable estate.
     Wife ELIZABETH, extx.
Wit: George Eubanks, Anthony Gregory, George Parratt.
                                                  25. 217

TAYLOR, ISABELL, Talbot Co., gentlewoman.   15 Aug, 1747
                                              1 Feb, 1747
     To grand-child.: HENRY, JAMES, REBECCA and CATHARINE TAYLOR,
slaves.
     Give WILLIAM STEVENS,
     Two daus. in Dorchester Co.
     Dau. REBECCA TAYLOR, and John Walker, exs.
Wit: Mary Marchent, Mary Jones, Margaret West.   25. 218

MACKEY, WILLIAM, Talbot Co.   22 Jan, 1747/8
                                              29 Feb, 1747
     To wife RACHEL MACKEY, extx., and my 2 sons HEZEKIAH and
PHILIP MACKEY, my 2 slaves.
     To son ROBERT MACKEY, slaves.
     To son PHILIP MACKEY, my gold ring.
     Balance to be divided bet. 3 sons: HEZEKIAH, PHILIP and
ROBERT.
Wit: James Barnett, Samuel Richard, Richard Barnett.
                                                  25. 219

HALL, RICHARD, Talbot Co.   10 Oct, 1742
                                              5 Mar, 1747/8
     To bro. THOMAS BAYNARD, my lands.
     To my mother SARAH SPINNAL (or SPRINNAL), furniture.
     Mother and my bros., exs.
Wit: John Nichinson, Michael Meloney, J. Gore.   25. 220

HUTCHINS, THOMAS, Talbot Co.   31 Dec, 1747
                                              3 Mar, 1747
     Wife PRISCILLA HUTCHINS, extx.
Wit: Jacob Gore, David Harrington.   25. 221

BACON, HENRY, St. Mary's Co.   4 Oct, 1747
                                              20 Feb, 1747
     To grandau ANN BACON SMITH, furniture and tobacco.
     To grandson HENRY BACON SMITH, tobacco.
     To dau FRANCES BACON, slaves, furniture.
     To dau ANN BACON, slave, Rose and her sons, Machlin and
Andrew, furniture and a boatswains chest.
     To dau CHRISTIAN SMITH, 1 s.
     That remaining estate to two daus ANN and FRANCES and that Ann
the eldest of the two have first choice.
     Dau ANN BACON, extx.

134

Wit: George Innes, Joseph Wright, Thomas Keartley.   25. 222

PATTYSON, JANE, Calvert Co.   16 Nov, 1747
                                                2 Feb, 1747/8
    To grand-dau. ELIZABETH JOHNSON, my slaves.
    To grand-son SAMUEL JOHNSON, grand-dau. JANE GRAY, grand-son
SAMUEL GRAY, certain slaves.
    My grand-child., whose names are: JOHN JOHNSON, JEAN JOHNSON,
FRANCES JOHNSON, MARGARET GRAY, HANNAH GRAY and REBECCA GRAY, my
stock of cattle.
    To daus. ELIZABETH JOHNSON, and JANE GRAY, clothing.
    Grand-son JOHN JACKSON, grand-daus. JANE JOHNSON and MARGARET
GRAY.
    Son-in-law JOHN GRAY, ex.
Wit: Wm. Sharples, John Bond (John Bond was a Quaker, and
affirmed instead of swearing oath.).   25. 224

KING, JOHN, Calvert Co.   25 Nov, 1746
                                                26 Feb, 1747
    To son IGNATIUS KING, after decease of my wife, SARAH KING,
1/2 of my lands.
    To sons THOMAS and SAMUEL KING, remainder of my lands, after
decease of my wife SARAH KING.
    Wife, extx.
Wit: Richard Stallings, James Jarvise, Thomas Hinton, Henry
Murry.   25. 225

ERWIN, JOSEPH   27 Feb, 1747/8
                                                24 Mar, 1747/8
    To son WILLIAM ERWIN, pt. of land I live on, already divided.
    To son ROBERT ERWIN, remainder of tract I live on called
"Linton," as by deed of gift, may appear.
    To sons WM. and ROBERT, my moveable estate.
    To dau. HESTER FORD, 5 s. sterl.
    To dau. ELIZABETH DURANCE, 5 s. sterl.
    To grand-son JOSEPH FORD, 8 lbs. money.
    To grand-son ROBERT FORD, 8 pounds money.
    To grand-dau. ISABELLA FORD, cattle.
    To grand-son JAMES FORD, cattle.
    To son WM., 1/2 of meadow ground, share equally with his bro.
ROBERT.
    Son Wm., and James Thorp. exs.
Wit: Richard Chapman, Wm. Nilley.   25. 226

MANKIN, STEPHEN.   18 Dec, 1747
    Matthew Breeding, ex., to receive remainder of estates after
debts are paid.
Wit: James Gray, Andrew McKenny, Probated in Charles Co.
                                                   25. 227

COURTS, JOHN, Charles Co..   16 Jan, 1747
                                                28 Jan, 1747
    To wife ELIZABETH COURTS, slaves Amelia, Thomas Dyut, Sarah
Baell (Baelt?), the latter two to served from their arrival into

this country five years and then to be set free.
That son WILLIAM COURTS and John Martine to allow carpenters
named James and Jack to perform work for wife.
Son JOHN to receive slave Jemmy and Penn after wife's death or
marriage; also negro woman called young Hannah dau to old negreo
James and Hannah; also negro Jenny, mulato Nun's dau; negro
carpenter called Sam.
To son WILLIAM COURTS negro carpenter called Jack and Negro
James Father to carpenter Jemmy; also negro woman called Hannah
wife of said negro James last mentioned, also mulatto Nun as also
old negro Sarah, also Chapley, negro Harry and Negro Pegg at
Nanjemoy Quarters.
To son ROBERT HENLY COURTS, negro blacksmith called Luke,
negro Bobb, negro Bess and negro boy called Nero and negro man
called Lilliputt.
To dau ANN COURTS, negro Sarah, nbegro Ned and negro Hannah,
the said Ned's wife.
To dau CHARITY ADAMS, tobacco.
To dau MARY ANN MARTINE, negro carepenter called Jemmy,negro
boy at Matawoman Quarter called Ben.
To dau ELIZABETH JONES negro Pompy; also Moll and Martine.
To son WILLIAM COURTS, intail all my lands in William and Mary
Parish, Charles Co.
To son JOHN COURTS, land in Prince George's Co. near Rock
Creek called "Clean Drinking."
To son ROBERT HENLY COURTS, land on Matawoman Run in Prince
George's Co., 500 A.; also tract in Charles Co. upon Potowmack
River known as "Martins Freehold."
To son WILLIAM COURTS 1/2 the lotts at Nottingham purchased by
me of Isaac Cecil for Daniel Dulany Esq. and myself in partner-
ship, the moyety of which lots I give to son WILLIAM.
To friend Nathan Harris, suit of mourning of about 10 s. price
per yard.
To my bro. CHARLES COURTS use of negro called Charles.
To Friend John Pen, Sr., suit of mourning.
To Joseph Woodman suit of mourning.
To friend James Pland, 100 A., near my land and towards Edward
Ford's.
Residue to be equally divided between William Courts, John
Courts, Robert Henly Courts, Ann Courts, Mary Ann Martine and
Elizabeth Jones, my children.
William Courts, John Martine and Charles Jones, exs.
Wit: Jos. Douglass, Edward Ford, Robert Hall.   25. 228

DORMOND (or DORMAN), SAMUEL, Somerset Co.   22 Nov, 1747
                                             17 Mar, 1747/8
To son JOHN DORMOND, plantation where I now live, at decease
of my wife.
To dau. SARAH DORMOND, furniture.
To dau. ELENOR DORMOND, furniture.
To dau. TABITHA DORMOND, furniture.
To son SAMUEL DORMOND, furniture.
Wife CATHARINE DORMOND, ex.
Wit: John Peden, John Broughton, Nehemniah Tillmar.
                                             25. 231

COX, WM., Somerset Co.   19 Jan, 1745
                                               17 Mar, 1747/8
    Wife, MARY COX.
    To son JOHN COX, after decease of my wife, MARY COX, slaves.
Son SAMUEL COX,
Dau. ELIZABETH COX,
To dau. MARY COX,
    To 3 daus.: SARAH, ELIZABETH and MARY, the balance of the
slaves.
    My 5 child.: JOHN, SAMUEL, SARAH FLEMMON, ELIZABETH and MARY
COX.
    Wife MARY, extx.
Wit: Wm. Taylor, Charles Dickenson, Robert Boywer, Samuel Adams.
                                                    25. 233

SMOCK, HENRY, Somerset Co.   20 Jul, 1740
                                                 6 Nov, 1747
    To son JOHN SMOCK and son WILLIAM SMOCK, land that is on the
other side of Quapancoe Road, being pt. of "Batchlor's Lot."
    To son SAMUEL SMOCK, my old plantation whereon I formerly
lived and being pt. of "Batchlor's Lott."
    To son HENRY SMOCK, the plantation where on I live being pt.
of "Yorkshire," and pt. of "Convenience" with all appertenances
belonging.
    To son THOMAS SMOCK, remainder of lands called "Conveniency,"
adjoining on the head of the Prase Swamp.
    To wife ELIZABETH SMOCK, the whole right of the plantation
whereon I live.
    If son JOHN SMOCK, shd. die in his present illness, then sd.
land bequeathed him to be the right of son THOMAS SMOCK, and
land bequeathed son THOMAS be right of son HENRY SMOCK.
    Balance equally bet. my child.
    Wife ELIZABETH SMOCK, extx.
Wit: Thomas Poynter, Richard Blizard, Edward Round.
                                                    25. 235

FASSITT, WM., Sussex Co., on Delaware, in the Province of
Pennsylvania, gentleman.   14 Dec, 1744
                                                31 Oct, 1747
    To wife NAOMI FASSIT, 1/3 pt. of my estate.
    To my unborn child, tract formerly held by Richard Hinman in
right of his wife, in Sussex Co., afsd., and by me purchased of
Jacob Kollock, Comfort Kollock, relict of Simon Kollock, late
dec'd. and Jeremiah Claypole to sd. child unborn.
    Child. hereafter mentioned: WILLIAM, DAVID, SOPHIA, LEVIN, and
the 3rd, which is unborn. 3rd?
    To son DAVIS FASSIT, a certain tract or land lying in
Worcester Co., MD., in Synapuxin Neck, 500 A. called "Carmell" on
the uppermost side of sd. neck, devised me by my father to him
the sd. DAVID FASSIT.
    To son LEVIN FASSIT, pt. of land "Buckingham" in Worcester
Co., 700 A.

To dau. SOPHIA FASSITT, land in Worcester Co., "Buckingham,"
525 A., which appears on record in Somerset Co., to her.
HINMOND and JOHN READES shall have cattle.
ROUS FASSITT, my bro. shall be guardian of my children.
Wife to have sole management of my estate in Sussex Co., PA.
Bro. ROUS FASSITT, management of my estate in Worcester Co., MD.
Wife NAOMI FASSITT, and bro. ROUS FASSITT of Worcester Co.,
exs.
Wit: John Lowes, Joseph Hemblin, Wm. Shankland, Sussex Co.
Dec. 31, 1747, then came Wm. Shankland, John Lowes and Joseph
Hamblen, witnesses, and state they saw WM. FASSITT, sign his
will.
Note: Memorandum, the testator, dying in Sussex, on Delaware, his
will was then proved and recorded and letters testamentary to his
widow was granted, but inasmuch as the testator had land in
Worcester Co., MD, it was thought necessary sd. will shd. be
proved in the county afsd.   25. 236 -
238

MUMFORD (or MUMPHORD), JAMES, SR., Worcester Co.   10 Mar, 1746
                                                   2 Feb, 1747/8
     To wife, the plantation whereon I live.
     To son JAMES MUMFORD, land whereon I live, pt. of tract called
"Rochester," it being all that I bought of Catharine Purnell.
     To dau. CATHARINE, furniture.
     My child.: ANN MERIDITH, GODFREY, SARAH, ESTHER, ELLEN,
CATHARINE, TABITHA and JAMES.
     At the decease of wife, SARAH MUMFORD,
     To NICHOLSON MUMFORD, gun and 30 s.
Wit: E. Round, Henry Turner, Wm. Brazier.
On the back of the foregoing will was thus written, 2-2-1747/8.
                                                   25. 239

WALE, WILLIAM, Jr., Worcester Co.   22 Apr, 1744
                                           2 Mar, 1747/8
     Wife MARY WALE.
     To dau. VASHTI, plantation where I now dwell in sd. county,
but if she die without issue, my young. dau. LEAH WALE, have
same.
     To dau. MOLEY, furniture.
     To son ZEDEKIAH WALE, my gun.
Wife, extx. Wit: Charles Rackliffe, Daniel Conner, Charles Whale.
At the foot of foregoing will thus written: Came Daniel Conner
and Charles Wale, 2 of the witnesses, and state on oath they saw
sd. WM. WALE, sign his will.   25. 240 - 241

MARTIN, JAMES, Worcester Co.   12 Dec, 1747
                                           3 May, 1747/8
     To wife MARY MARTIN, the use of my dwelling plantation, and at
her decease, to son THOMAS MARTIN.
     To dau. ELIZABETH, slave.
     To son WILLIAM, 2 lots in Snow Hill Town, Nos. 17 and 18, for
the making over of which I have Wm. Duke's and Thomas Gray's
bonds.
     To son JAMES, the 1/2 lott of land in Snow Hill Town,

purchased by Alex Bunele and myself of one John Martin, hr. to
Edward Martin, conveyance whereof is amongst the records of
Somerset Co.   Son-in-law JOHN MARTIN CONVEY.
Make over to my son GEORGE, a lot of land in Snow Hill Town,
which he promised to convey to me, but never has done it.
To son GEORGE, my slaves.
To son WM., my Mulatto boy.
To son JAMES, a Molatto girl.
To sons THOMAS and WILLIAM, clothing.
Mentions my dau., name not given.
To wife, remainder of my moveable estate.
Wife MARY, extx. Wit: John Neill, Patrick Allison, John Done.
Date on back of foregoing will 1747/8 May 3; came John Neil,
Patrick Allison and John Done, who state they saw JAMES MARTIN,
sign his will.   25. 242

KNIGHT, WILLIAM, Cecil Co., gentleman.   14 Apr 1746
                                               7 Jun, 1746
     To wife RACHEL, my estate, during life; at decease, to my
dau, REBECCA; my plantation, at head of Bohemia River in Cecil
Co., there together with land I purchased of James Paul Heath,
land called "Clifton," at head of Bohemia River in Cecil Co.; to
my dau. SARAH, at her decease without hrs., then to my dau.
REBECCA, and if my daus. shd. die without hrs., then to my nephew
JOHN LEACH KNIGHT, and in default of hrs., to my nephew ROBERT
STOAKES.   Wife RACHEL, and my friend James Paul Heath, exs.
1746 on the back of the will was thus written 6-7-1746. James
Flanagan, Charles Coatts and James Harper, who make oath they saw
the testator sign his will.   25. 243 - 245

RHILY, REBECCA, Prince George's Co.   24 Sep 1747
                                              21 Jan 1747/8
     To son Hugh Rhiley, plantation, 250 A., to be laid out by
William Beall, and if he dies without heirs then to be equally
divided between his elder bro Pharo and his two sisters Elizabeth
and Hannah.
     To son Pharoa, 151 A., pt of "Dan."
     To dau Elizabeth, 100 A.
Wit: Francis Abston, William Frasee.   25. 245

BRIGHTWELL, PETER, Prince George's Co.   27 Nov, 1747
                                              23 Dec, 1747
     To wife ANN, and dau. ELIZABETH, tract called "Nest Egg." Wit:
Thomas Morton, John Brightwell, George Naylor. Codicil to will of
PETER BRIGHTWELL, I give my dau. CATHARINE, stock, leave my
son-in-law JOSEPH CAGE, plantation which is now sitting for 3
years. Wit: Thomas Morton, William Watson, James Watson. At the
foot of the above Codicil was thus written: Prince George's Co.,
1-29-1747/8, who state they saw PETER BRIGHTWELL, sign the
Codicil to his will. At the bottom of sd. will: Prince George's
Co., 1-28-1747/8, then came Thomas Morton, John Brightwell and
Geo. Nailer, the 3 evidences to the foregoing will, and made oath
they saw PETER BRIGHTWELL sign same.   25. 246 - 247

DOWNES, NATHANIEL, Queen Anne's Co., planter. 24 Feb, 1747
                                                 1 Mar, 1747
    To dau. MARY DOWNS, tract called "Smith's Neglect," 150 A.
    To nephew JAMES DOWNES BENNETT, son of my sister ELIZABETH
BENNETT,
    To father-in-law, WILLIAM GREENWOOD, my violin.
    To dau. MARY DOWNES, personal estate.
    My bro.-in-law GEORGE BENNETT, have the bringing up of my dau.
until 16 years of age.
    Bro.-in-law George Bennett, ex.
Wit: Abraham Williams, Nathaniel Wright, Peter Rich.
At the foot of the foregoing will, thus written: Queen Anne's Co.
3-1-1747.   25. 248

KEYS, RICHARD, Queen Anne's Co., carpenter.   20 Jan, 1747
                                               10 Mar, 1747
    To son GEORGE KEYS, tract called "Jamaica Addition" of 50 A.,
but if it happens that my sd. grand-dau. shd. die without hrs.,
then I give same to my nephew RICHARD KEYS, son of my bro. JOHN
KEYS.
    To son GEORGE KEYS, stock.
Wife MARY KEYS, extx. Wit: George Bennett, George Lewis, Thos.
Wilkinson.   25. 249 - 250

JARMAN, ROBERT, JR., Queen Anne's Co.   13 Jan, 1747
                                           22 Mar, 1747
    To son ROBERT JARMAN, my plantation where I now live, called
"Newport," 284 A.
    To son JOHN JARMAN, tract called "Swanford."
    To son WILLIAM JARMAN, and hrs., remainder of "Bradford,"
whereof James Baker now dwells, 100 A.
    To dau. SOPHIA JARMAN, stock.
    My several child: ROBERT, JOHN, WILLILAM, SOPHIA, and MARY
ANN, ANN, MARY and ESTHER JARMAN.   Wife MARY ANN JARMAN, extx.
Wit: John Burk, Jr., Stephen York, John Emory. At the foot of the
will was written thus: Queen Anne's Co. 3-22-1747.
                                                  25. 251

ROBERTS, JAMES, Queen Anne's Co.   15 Jan, 1747/8
                                           24 March, 1747
    To eld. son BENJAMIN, pt. of 2 tracts called "Lows Desire" and
"Shepherd's Redoubt," 100 A. each.
    To son JAMES, 100 A.
    To son ABRAHAM, 100 A.
    To son DAVID, tract called "Robert's Neck."
    To son JOHN, set of smith's tools.
    To son BENJAMIN, son JAMES, dau. SARAH, dau. MARY, dau. ANN,
and dau. HANNAH, slaves.
    To wife ANN, slaves.
    To 4 daus.: SARAH, MARY, ANN and HANNAH, 5 pounds each when
age 16.
    Child.: BENJAMIN, ELIZABETH, SARAH, JAMES, JOHN, ABRAHAM,
MARY, ANN, DAVID, HANNAH.
Wife ANN, and sons BENJAMIN and JAMES, exs.

140

Wife ANN, and sons BENJAMIN and JAMES, exs.
Wit: Anthony Bowe (or Rowe), Benj. Blower, Colomon Heney.
Written on the back of the foregoing will was thus: Queen Anne's
Co., 3-24-1747.   25. 252

CHANCE, RICHARD, Queen Anne's Co.   17 Apr, 1746
                                               30 Mar, 1747
   To son RICHARD CHANCE, "Harper Lot" in Dorchester Co.
   To JOHN CHANCE, his bro. ROGER, my 2 sons ELIJAH CHANCE and
BATCHELDER CHANCE, tract called "Bare Point"; ELIJAH to have 1/2
where he now lives, and BATCHELOR the end he now lives on.
   To son BOON CHANCE, land called "Littlefoots" and "Addition"
bought of me by Benjamin Moor.
   To wife ELENOR, plantation where I now live.
   To dau. RACHEL SWIFT, grand-son THOMAS WITTINGTON, grand-dau.
ELINOR JORDAN, my personal estate equally.
   To son WILLIAM, 1 s.
   To son WARNER CHANCE, 1 s.
   To dau. ELIZABETH BARTTLET, 1 s.
   To dau. RUTH JORDAN, 1 s.
   To dau. JULANA PEARSON, 1 s.
   To sons.: RICHARD, JOHN, ELIJAH, BALCHELDER and BOON, 300
pounds tobacco, every year, each.   Wife, extx. Wit: Peter Rich,
Susanna Rich, Sidney Rich. Date on back of will, 3-24-1747.
                                                            25. 256

COOK, JAMES, Queen Anne's Co.   1 Mar, 1747
                                               14 Apr, 1748
   To eld. son JOHN COOK, 1 slave.
   To sons WILLIAM and SAMUEL COOK, my dwelling plantation called
"Cempersons Choes [Camperson's Choice] " and "Addition of
"Cemperson Chos," equally.
   To son JOSHUA COOK, 1 slave.
   To son THOMAS COOK, 1 slave.
Wife ELIZABETH COOK; dau. RACHEL COOK, extxs.
Wit: Thomas Cooper, Abrahm Hurelock, Wm. Harrington. Date on back
of wills: 3-24-1747.
The widow made her election to take her third, 4-14-1745.
                                                            25. 257

HOLLIDAY, JAMES, Queen Anne's Co.   11 May, 1738
                                               30 Mar, 1747
My tract of land at Patuxent in Prince George's Co., commonly
called "Billingsley's Point," 1000 A; my other tract of land in
Talbot Co. called "Faulkner's Folley," 100 A., we sold for my
wife, SARAH HOLLYDAY.
Tract on Chester River in Queen Anne's Co. called "Readburn,"
14040 A., and also 200 A., pt. of "MacLenborough," which I bought
of John Hawkins, Jr., my son HENRY HOLLYDAY, and being after
decease of his mother, pt. of tract "Readbourn Rectified," the
plantation where Jacob Bailey was settled, when I bought sd.
land.
   To son JAMES HOLLYDAY, tract called "Readburn," lying north or
south eastward of the Branch; the deed is dated 2-4-1734, of land

To son HENRY HOLLYDAY, 114 A., pt. of sd. tract.
To wife SARAH HOLLYDAY, remaining pt. of my estate.
Wife, extx.
At the foot of the will was thus written: Queen Anne's Co.,
3-30-1747.
Wit: John Hawkins, Edward Brown, Deborah Hawkins and Mirimi
Hawkins. (Her name was later called "Minnie Gould"; at the time
of the execution of the foregoing will, named "Minnie or Minni
Hawkins."   25. 258

BERRY, MARGARET, Queen Anne's Co.   9 Feb, 1747
                                        31 Mar 1748
     To nephew THOMAS MATTHEWS, my dwelling plantation.
     To JOHN IRONS (?), 5 pounds for his bringing executor, pay for
same.
     Desire my executor pay to THOMAS WILKINSON, 12_0 pounds
tobacco, being his utmost to dock the entail of my father's will.
     Balance of estate to nephews: WILLIAM and THOMAS MATTHEWS.
     Friend John Irons, ex.
Wit: John Green, Jr., Nathaniel Tucker, Peter Rich.
The foot of the will was thus written: Queen Anne's Co.
3-31-1748.   25. 260 - 261

WRENCH, WILLIAM, Queen Anne's Co.   31 Mar, 1740
                                        31 Mar, 1748
     To wife REBECCA WRENCH, all of my plantation where I now live,
called "Hawkin's Farm," during her life; son WILLIAM WRENCH, at
decease of my wife, my dwelling plantation.
     To son HENRY WRENCH, remaining pt. of tract called "Wrenches'
Lot."
     To son JAMES WRENCH, pt. of tract called "Wrenches' Farm," 200
A., where Richard Emerson formerly lived.
     To son PETER WRENCH, 200 A. land adjoining John Vanderford's
plantatiion; to sd. son, furniture and slaves.
     To dau. MARGARET CHAIRS, 20 s.
     To son-in-law JOHN VANDERFORD, and dau. MARY VANDERFORD, 200
A., being pt. of "Wrenches' Farm," where they now live.
     To dau. REBECCA PRATT, 1 horse.
     To son WM. WRENCH, slaves.
     Wife and son WM., exs. At the foot of foregoing will, was thus
written: Queen Anne's Co., 3-31-1740.
Wit: Thomas Hynson Kelly, John Gordon and Thomas Wilkinson, saw
the testator WM. WRENCH, sign his name.   25. 262

LOVEJOY, JOSEPH, Parish of St. Pauls, Prince George's Co.,
planter.   20 Feb, 1743
                                         6 May, 1748
     To wife ANN LOVEJOY, my estate, real and personal.
     To son SAMUEL LOVEJOY, after my sd. wife's decease, to have
estate.
     To SAMUEL LOVEJOY and hrs., right to my estate.
     To son JOSEPH LOVEJOY, also lands wherewith I am now
possessed, and slaves.

To dau. ANN BERRY, wife of Humphrey Berry, slaves.
My child.: SAMUEL and JOSEPH LOVEJOY, and ANN BERRY, wife of
Humphrey Berry.
Wife and son Joseph, exs.
On the back of the foregoing will was thus written: Prince
George's Co., 5-6-1748. Wit: Thomas and John Tucker, Edward and
Francis Moserly, on oath say they saw JOSEPH LOVEJOY sign his
will.   25. 264

NAYLOR, JOHN, Talbot Co., planter.   19 May, 1743
                                             8 Apr, 1745
     To son JOSEPH NAYLOR, tract called "Morefield's Addition," and
10 A. of "Morefield," which I had of Thomas Vickers, and if
JOSEPH die without hrs., then son DAVID NAYLOR, shall have sd.
land.
     To loving ANN NAYLER, my personal estate, and appoint sd.
wife, extx. Wit: Grace Williams, James Gad, Thomas Vickers.
                                                        25. 265

SHARP, SAMUEL, Talbot Co.   - - - - - -
                                            12 Apr, 1748
     To wife ANN SHARP, my estate. On the back of the foregoing
will was thus written: Talbot Co., Ann, the wife of Wm. Troth,
being one of the people called Quakers, made her solemn
affirmation and declared she saw SAMUEL SHARP, dec'd., write his
name to the within will; John Dickenson being one of the people
called Quakers, made his affirmation, and declared he was
acquainted with sd. SAMUEL SHARP, dec'd.; Thomas Barnett, Jr.
made oath who states he was acquainted with the sd. SAMUEL SHARP;
the widow made her election.   25. 267

COBEN, JAMES,   11 Mar, 1747
                                           15 Apr, 1748
     To eld. son JAMES COBEN, 1 s. sterl.
     To 2nd son THOMAS COBEN; my eld. dau. ELIZABETH COBEN; my 3rd
son WM. COBEN, and all equal executors of my estate.   All my
child. have an equal pt., except my eld. son.   Mentions his
wife, but not by name. Wit: Joshua Hopkins, John Watt, Mary Hold.
At the foot of the foregoing will was thus written: Talbot Co.,
John Watt and Mary Floid, 2 witnesses say they saw JAMES COBEN
sign his will.
25. 268

PINKSTONE, PETER, Talbot Co., planter.   5 Jan, 1747
                                           15 Apr, 1748
     To my friend, ISAAC DIXON, my personal estate, and the debt
due me from William Kelly for my crop, made upon Robert Hall's
plantation in the year of "Christian Account" 1747, and that debt
of 200 pounds of tobacco due from Richard Start. Wit: John Dixon,
James Rudinson, Wm. Williams. On the back of sd. will: Talbot Co.
before sd. witnesses, 4-15-1748.   25. 269

HANN (or HENN), JOHN, Prince George's Co.   12 Mar, 1747
                                            15 Apr, 1748
     Money to be divided bet. my children.

To wife SARAH HENN, the plantation I now live on until my son
JOHN HENN, is age 21.
To dau. HANNAH HENN, 30 pounds out of my estate as her birth
right.
To son JOHN HENN, when he is age 21, the plantation, and if
shd. happen that my dau. HANNAH, shd. die before of age, to my
dau. ELIZABETH HENN.
The names of my child.: ANNAH, ELIZABETH, CATHARINE, SARAH and
JOHN.
Friends, Capt. John Middaugh and Wm. Burrock, exs.
Wit: John Diel Henn, Robert Elexoad, James Wilson. 25. 270

RATCLIF, FRANCIS, St. Mary's Co.   6 Oct, 1747
                                                 4 Mar, 1747
To wife MARY, half the land I live on.
To son JOHN RATCLIFF, other part of my land known as
"Ratcliffs Hope," where he now lives; also pt land of my wife at
her decease. For want of heirs to fall to my granddau MARY ANN
RATCLIFF.
To dau ANN WILSON, 1 s. sterl.
Wife MARY extx.
Wit: Thomas Greaves, Sr., John Baptis Greaves, John Booker.
                                                      25. 272

KANNADY, William, Forrest of St. Mary's Co. 26 Feb, 1745/6
                                             26 Mar, 1748
To bro. RICHARD FORREST and my sister CATHARINE HEBB, all my
estate.
Brother in Law WILLIAM HEBB and bro RICHARD, exs.
Wit: James Waughop, Mazeren Fargoe, Martha Jenkins. 25. 273

MACKEY, SARAH, St. Mary's Co.   13 Feb, 1747
                                                28 Mar, 1748
To son THOMAS JANE, tobacco.
To son WILLIAM CHALLENER JANE, tobacco.
To daus, MARY and ANN JANE, remainder of estate.
Capt. James Bissco, ex.
Wit: John Stevens, Isaac Parett, Isabel Cook.   25. 274

BAXTER, Edward, St. Mary's Co.   2 Jan, 1747
                                                 30 Mar, 1748
To wife KATHARINE BAXTER, extx, all my estate.
Wit: Thomas Verrin, James Kndrick, Robt. Acquaintence. 25. 275

DONALDSON, JOHN, St. Mary's Co.   20 Dec, 1747
                                                  6 Apr, 1748
To wife ELIZABETH DONALDSON, extx, all my land, having
provided for all my children.
To dau. MARY MAGDALENE COOK, tract, 247 A., she now lives on.
To dau. SABINA STODDART, remainder of land and her heirs, now
in being, vizt. ELIZABETH STODDART, MARY MAGDALENE STODDART and
ANNE STODDART.   25. 276

PAYN, THOMAS, St. Mary's Co.   18 Jan, 1747
                                                 19 Apr, 1748

To dau MARY, personalty.
To son ISAAC PAYN, personalty.
To rest of my children: JOSEPH PAYN, THOMAS PAYN, JOHN PAYN,
DIANA PAYN, ELIZABETH PAYN, equal shares of my estate.
Wife ELIZABETH, extx.
Wit: William Griggs, Joseph Fitzjeffery.   25. 277

DAINBRY, RICHARD, St. Mary's Co.   30 Mar, 1748
                                            28 Apr, 1748
   To Friend Edward Passons, ex., all my estate.
Wit: Timothy Barnhouse, Rodolph Barnhouse.   25. 278

COOPER, BASIL, St. Mary's Co.   24 Apr, 1748
                                             2 May, 1748
   To bro. MARK COOPER, 1 s. and to his son 1 s.
   To Levin Dorsey, son of John Dorsey, 1 s.
   To Mary Ann Egerton, dau of James Egerton, 1 s.
   To James Egerton, 1 s.
   To John Dorsey, 1 s.
   To Henrietta White, dau of Mark Cooper, 1 s.
   To Matthew Cooper, dau of Mark Cooper, 1 s.
   To Ann Cooper, dau of Mark Cooper, 1 s.
   To Nathan Cooper, son of Nathaniel Cooper, 1 s.
   To Friend William Locer, ex. to have use of my effects during
his lifetime, allowing Mrs. Ashby 20 s. per year.
Wit: Joseph Leigh, Thos. Standworth, John Hudman.   25. 278

HUTCHINS, FRANCIS, Calvert Co.   21 Dec, 1747
                                            29 Dec, 1747
   To friend ANNA HARRIS, 1/3 pt. of my personal estate.
   To sister ELIZABETH HUTCHINS, balance of estate, but if sd.
sister ELIZABETH, shd. die without issue, then I give my estate
to my uncle LITTLETON WATERS, and my Aunt SARAH WATERS.
Uncle Littleton Waters, ex.
Wit: Hutcheson Parker, Alethea Parker, Sarah Parker.
                                                        25. 280

PARRISH, ELIZABETH, Baltimore Co.   16 Nov, 1745
                                            20 May, 1748
   Husband JOHN PARRISH.
   To dau. MARY, silverware.
   My 7 child.
Appoint Joseph Taylor ex., to the care of friends.
Wit: Samuel Hopkins (Quaker), Dorothy Lawson.   25. 281

STUMP, JOHN, Cecil Co.   7 Sep, 1747
                                            16 Nov. 1747
   To son JOHN STUMP, tract called "Harts Delight," that I now
live on; son JOHN STUMP, 67 A. which I have a lease for.
   To son HENRY STUMP, land "Harts Delight," 50 A., which I
bought of George Black; son HENRY STUMP, 50 pounds money of this
province; son HENRY STUMP, a mare colt.
   Wife MARY, and 2 sons exs.
Wit: Benjamin Chew, Thomas Ellet, Elizabeth Ellet.
                                                        25. 282

HUSBANDS, JOHN, Cecil Co.   - - - - - -
                                         20 Jan, 1747/8
   James and Mary Poor declare that a few hours before JOHN
HUSBANDS died, he declared they shd. take notice that his will
was that all his personal estate shd. be equally divided bet.
sister-in-law ELIZABETH PARR, and EPHRAIM MEEKING, truly begotten
in wedlock by his sister SARAH MEEKINGS, wife to Joshua Meekings.
   Likewise, that his personal and real estate be divided bet.
sd. ELIZABETH PARR and EPHRAIM MEEKING, and that he appoint his
sister-in-law Elizabeth Parr, and Joshua Meekings, exs.
   That he died about two of the clock Thursday, 19th instant,
Jun.   25. 283

DOUGLASS, WM., Cecil Co.   21 Dec, 1747
                                          26 Jan, 1747/8
   To sister LARABA ALMAN, my whole executor and heir.
Wit: Edward Armstrong, Valentine Douglass, Alexander Stewart.
                                                  25. 283

WARD JOHN, Cecil Co.   25 May, 1745
                                          13 Mar, 1747/8
   To wife MARY WARD, 1/3 pt. of my estate.
   To son PERIGRINE WARD, my dwelling plantation.
   To grand-son JAMES CHATHAM WARD, son of my son JOHN WARD,
dec'd. for 300 A., pt. of tract "Greenfield," where my son now
lives, on the main road from Cecil Town to Fredrick Town, with
the plantation where Jeremiah Grigley formerly lived. To my sd.
grand-son JAMES CHATHAM WARD, the above 300 A., pt. of
"Greenfield"; then to my grand-son JOHN WARD, the son of HENRY
WARD and HANNAH, his wife.
   To grand-son JOHN WARD VEAZEY, and REBECCA his wife, my house
and lot in Frederick Town, under care of his father.
   To 2 sons, PEREGRINE WARD and HENRY WARD, and my grand-son
JAMES CHATHAM WARD, tract called "Partnership," 1500 A.
   To 4 grand-sons JOHN WARD, son of PEREGRINE WARD; JOHN WARD
VEAZEY, son of JOHN VEAZEY and REBECCA his wife; JAMES CHATHAM
WARD, son of JOHN WARD dec'd.; and JOHN WARD, son of HENRY WARD,
my personal estate.
Wife MARY WARD, and sons PEREGRINE and HENRY WARD, exs.
Wit: William Ellis, John Bellarmin, Thomas Hynson, Jr., Hartley
Sappenton.   25. 284

COSDEN, ALPHONSO, Cecil Co.   6 Feb, 1747
                                          2 Apr, 1748
   To eld. son ALFONSO COSDEN, 100 A.
   To son THOMAS COSDEN, 100 A.
   To EASALIN COSDEN, my bro, 200 A.
   Mentions an unborn child and his dau. ALETHIER.
Benjamin Terry, ex.
Wit: Cornelius Brady, John Smith, Augustine Terry.   25. 287

RITCHEY, JOHN, Cecil Co.   7 Mar, 1747/8
                                           7 Apr, 1748
   To son JAMES RITCHEY, my plantation.

To son ALEXANDER RITCHEY, 7 pounds.
To dau. MARY, my furniture; chest of drawers formerly
belonging to her mother and a side saddle that was her sister's.
To young. son ROBERT RITCHEY, 15 pounds money of Pennsylvania,
to be paid when my ex. JAMES RITCHEY, out of my real estate,
against the time of his maturity.
All of my wearing apparel be equally divided among my 4 sons.
My son JAMES RITCHEY, the benefit of JACOB DEAHOUR.
Furniture divided bet. 3 young. child.: Dau. MARY, and sons
JOHN and ROB.
Plantation divided bet. sons JOHN and ROBERT.
Appoint bro. ROBERT RITCHEY, and friend THOS. KILLGORE,
overseers.
Son JAMES RICHEY, ex.
Wit: Robert Ritchey, Thomas Kilgore and Thomas McCrery.
25. 288 - 290

CANNADEY, MARY, Cecil Co., widow.   22 Apr, 1748
                                           10 May, 1748
To son EDWARD CANADEY, 1/2 of my estate.
The other 1/2 bet. young. daus. JANE and ELENOR.
Thomas Cook, ex.
Wit: David, John and Rachel Williams.   25. 290

BOWLDING, RICHARD,   25 Mar, 1748
                                          10 May, 1748
To sister ELIZABETH, the plantation lying on Back Creek.
To my bro. WILLIAM, my other plantation on Elk River.
To my mother's young. dau. MARTHA, my personal estate.
Uncle WILLIAM PRICE, and bro.-in-law, JAMES FOSTER, exs.
Wit: James Boulding, Henry Renin, Martin Alexander. (This will
seems to have been written in Cecil Co.)   25. 291

RICHARDSON, ANN, Kent Co.   12 Nov, 1747
                                          10 Feb, 1747
To grand-son WARNER MIFFLIN, stock.
To dau. MARY MIFFLIN, clothing.
To dau. JOANNA THOMAS, stock in pt. of what shall arise or
become due from her father, DAVID THOMAS, his estate, and that
she be brought up under care of DANIEL MIFFLIN and MARY, his
wife.
To son THOMAS RICHARDSON, slaves.
To son JOSEPH RICHARDSON, slaves of my late husband's estate,
but if his bro., my son THOMAS RICHARDSON, shall equally divide
the land that was his father's lying in Cecil Co., bet. him and
his bro. JOSEPH RICHARDSON, as his father died intestate, then I
desire that all of the remaining pt. of my dower and debts
mentioned divided bet. sons THOMAS and JOSEPH RICHARDSON. I
desire sons THOMAS and JOSEPH, be brought up under the care of
their uncle DANIEL RICHARDSON, and if they die without issue,
then my dau. JOANNA THOMAS,and my grand-son WARNER MIFFLIN, to be
equally divided bet. them.
To cousin MARY MASSEY, a slave and stock.
To my friend Hannah Hull, side saddle that Joanna Thomas used
to ride on, and an old side saddle that I left down in Talbot Co.

to Mary Hull.
   That the slave Betty at George Dunhan's, may remain with him
during sd. Dunhan's life.
   To my friend THOS. BOWERS, 100 pounds tobacco.
   Dau. JOANNA THOMAS, is left to the care of son DANIEL MIFLIN
and MARY, his wife.
   Cousin WM. RASIN, ex.
Wit: George Rasin, Joseph Hull.   25. 292 - 293

HYNSON, CHARLES, Kent Co.   19 Aug, 1747
                                               11 Apr, 1748
   To wife TERUNCINA, my estate, plantation called "Harrises
Forest," and lands adjoining to my dear child. MARGARET, dau. of
MRS. MARGARET _____, of Philadelphia, and my houses
and lots in town.
   Wife, extx.
Wit: Wilthanna Hynson, Margaret Corwardine, John Baddison.
                                               25. 294

POWELL, WILLIAM, Kent Co.   12 Jan, 1747/8
                                               18 Apr, 1748
   To dau. MARY, 4 sheep.
   To dau. ANN, furniture.
   To dau. HANNAH, furniture.
   To dau. MARTHA, furniture.
   Friend, WILLIAM GRAVES.
Wit: David Bell, Wm. Graves, Benjamin Green.   25. 295

HOSIER, HANNAH, Kent Co.   20 Feb, 1748
                                                9 May, 1748
   To son HENRY HOSIER,
   To dau. MARY DICKENSON, wife of DANIEL DICKENSON of Talbot
Co., 12 pounds money, current gold and silver, and if she die
without issue, sd. money to go to my son RICHARD HOSIER.
   Son HENRY, ex.
Wit: Edward Comegys, Morgan Brown, Rebecca Brown. 25. 297

MUIR, ADAM, Dorchester Co., merchant.   10 Nov, 1747
                                               16 Apr, 1748
   To eld. son JAMES MUIR, my lands, mills and personal estate in
Worcester Co., and debts due to me from any person whatsoever in
Maryland, Great Brittain, Island of Maderia or any other place.
   That my sd. son JAMES, do pay to my dau. ANN, when at age, the
sum of 500 pounds money sterl., and if she die without issue, to
son JAMES.
   To son CHARLES MUIR, my lands in Dorchester Co.
   Bro. THOMAS MUIR, ex.
Wit: Jos. Ennalls, Samuel Griffith, Thomas Weems. Sd. witnesses
saw ADAM MUIR sign his will and further declare that it is his
will that his vessels of what kinds belong to his son JAMES.
(This codicil probated 11-10-1747.)
Wit: Jos. Ennalls, Samuel Griffith.   25. 298

LOWE, JOHN, Talbot Co.   5 Mar, 1747
                                               17 May, 1748

called "Grafton's Manor," and 1 tract called "Piney Neck."
     To dau. ELIZABETH LOWE, 110 A. being pt. of "Grafton's Manor,"
lying bet. the head of Grace Creek and William Web Haddaway's;
and I further give to sd. dau., 50 A. called "Haddaway's Lott"
bet. the creek and Wm. Web Haddaway's, which sd. parcel of land
remain to her and hrs., and if she die without issue, my dau.
ESTHER LOWE, shall have and enjoy sd. lands.
     If my dau. ELIZABETH lives to age 18, to take the land I have
bequeathed her, but prior to that time, same to remain with her
mother, my son JAMES LOWE.
     To dau. FRANCES LOWE, 10 pounds money.
     To dau. MARY LOWE, 10 pounds money.
     To dau. SARAH LOWE,
     To dau. ESTHER LOWE, 10 pounds money.
     Neighbor Wm. Web Haddaway, wife Mary Lowe, son James Lowe,
exs. Wit: Thomas Smith, W. Webb Haddaway, John Harrison. The date
on the back of the will, 5-17-1745 (or 1748), Talbot Co. sct.
The widow of the dec'd. made her election and abides by the will,
5-17-1748.   25. 300

GOW, JAMES, Charles Co., planter.   5 Jan, 1747/8
                                        16 May, 1748
     To son JAMES GOW, tracts called "Tower Hill" and "Godfreys
Chase." If he should die without heirs then to dau ANNE, "Tower
Hill" and 10 a. out of "Godfreys Chase," and to dau MARY,
remainder of "Godfreys Chase."
     To son JAMES, Negro boy Daniel and other.
     To dau ANNE, negro Juno and other.
     To second dau MARY, Negro named Warrey amd Negro Ben, and
other.
     Edward Millstead and dau of Mary, exs.
Wit: Daniel Bourne, Simon French.   25. 302

JAMES, JOHN, Prince George's Co., planter.   17 Apr, 1747
                                              13 Apr, 1748
     To wife MARGARET-PETER BECRAFT, to have management of estate
until my son comes to age 21.
     To son DANIEL JAMES, 100 A. called "Allaway" lying on
Lingdnore. Wit: Henry Young, Richard Wright, John Ward.,
4-13-1748.
     25. 304

CHARLTON, JOHN, Prince George's Co., gentleman.   29 Mar, 1748
                                                  21 Apr, 1748
     To wife and child., my estate.
     To son JOHN, personalty.
     To son THOMAS, my sword, and if the above 2 child. die before
of age, sd. personalty to be divided amongst surviving bros. and
sisters.
     To bro. ARTHUR, my great riding coat.
     To JOHN DARLING, my silk Camblet coat.
     To my servant DANIEL MC CRORY, a suit.
     To bro.-in-law THOMAS CHARLTON, stock.
     THOMAS, and HENRY CHARLTON, my bro.-in-law, exs.
Wit: Eleanor Charlton, Joseph Perry, James Downey. Date on back

Wit: Eleanor Charlton, Joseph Perry, James Downey. Date on back
of will, 4-21-1748.   25. 305

CHARLTON, EDWARD, Chester Co., Province of Pennsylvania.
                                                     3 Jun, 1747
                                                    28 Apr, 1748
    To bro. JOHN CHARLTON, 20 pounds, Pennsylvania currency.
    To bro. THOMAS CHARLTON, 31st pounds Pennsylvania currency.
    To bro. HENRY CHARLTON, lands.
    To sister MARGARET CHARLTON, 2 pounds Pennsylvania currency.
    To sister LETTICE CHARLTON, 30 pounds Pennsylvania currency,
provided she marries with the consent of my exs.
    To HENRY CHARLTON, son of my bro.-in-law, JOHN CHARLTON, 10
pounds Pennsylvnia currency.
    To THOMAS CHARLTON, son of my bro. JOHN CHARLTON, 10 pounds
Pennsylvania currency.
    Bros. THOMAS and HENRY CHARLTON, exs.
Wit: Robert Fleming, William Stewart.   25. 305

HEDGES, ANDREW, Prince George's Co.   13 Mar, 1747
                                              2 May, 1748
    Wife MARY, shall have all that what she brought with me as
also all the pewter, that belongeth to the house and the 1/3 pt.,
as also a bay mare; wife to have money to school the child.
    To 2 sons THOMAS and ANDREW.
    3rdly, my great Bible shall be given to son THOMAS.
    To bro. PETER HEDGES, my riding saddle.
    To bro. JOSEPH HEDGES, my plough.
Wit: Stephen Julian, Peter Stitly, Peter Stull.   25. 307

GALLOWAY, JAMES, Anne Arundel Co., (late of Philadelphia).
                                              4 Dec, 1747
                                              - - - - -
    To dau. SARAH FISHBOURN, 400 pounds money of Pennsylvania.
    To dau. JENEY GALLOWAY, 500 pounds of money of Pennsylvania.
    My son SAMUEL.
    Mother-in-law MARTHA ROBERTS, and SUSANNA DILLWYN of
Philadelphia.
    Dau. to be under care of son-in-law SAMUEL GALLOWAY, until she
is age 18, and then to be removed to Philadelphia.
John Dillwyn, James Pemberton, exs.
Wit: Joseph Galloway, Ann Harris, Susanna Galloway, Dr. John
Hamilton, June 16, 1745.   25. 308

BORDLEY, THOMAS, Annapolis, but intending this day to depart for
Great Brittain.   4 Jun, 1747
                                                   16 Jun, 1748
    Desire all debts paid, particularly that to Mr. Wahelin Welsh,
with interest.
    The rest and residue of personal estate to MRS. MARGARET
SMITH, haberdasher, of Mark Lane, London, for the tenderness,
care and friendship I have always met with from her and her
family.
    To bro. JOHN, my undivided moyety of our 4 lotts in Annapolis.
I am desirous that my 4th pt. of "Augustin Mannor" shd. descend

in course to bro. MATTHIAS BORDLEY, which I take to be agreeable
to my father's inclination as well as mine.
    The balance of estate in the Province of Maryland, to sister
ELIZABETH BORDLEY, and bro. BEAL BORDLEY.
    Martin Smith of Mark Lane, ex., desiring Mr. Jennings and bro.
STEPHEN, assist him in execution hereof.
Wit: John Carpenter, Samuel Wood, Beal Nicholas.   25. 310

YOUNGER, MARY, Talbot Co., widow, dec'd.   30 Apr, 1748
    The depositions of Eve MacDaniel widow, and Elizabeth Holt
spinster, all of Talbot Co., being sworn upon the Evangels of
Almighty God, deposes that about sometime in March last, deponent
being at the house of MARY YOUNGER, the sd. dec'd., she being
then very sick, James Barnett, of the county afsd., came to see
the sd. dec'd., and in her sickness, did then desire sd. James
Barnett that he might have all what little was remaining after
payment of what she owed and the expense of funeral, except a
lennen wheel, which she gave ELIZABETH NORTH.   25. 311

GALLOWAY, JOHN   19 Feb, 1747/8
John Galloway adds a Codicil to his will; desires that the
executors not charge any commissions on the several legacies
above bequeathed, either to my wife JANE GALLOWAY, or my dau.
JENNY GALLOWAY, and order that if my dau. MARY CHEW, shd. die
within the space of 12 months after the receipt of the 1/4 pt. of
the residue of my estate, bequeathed above to her without issue,
or if she shd. die leaving issue, within the time afsd., the
money return to my son-in-law BENJAMIN CHEW, to be divided among
my 3 other child. Wit: Jola Milton, Ann Harris (the latter being
a Quaker), Oct. 12.   25. 312

WOODING, JOHN, Anne Arundel Co., planter.   22 Jul, 1741
                                              12 Dec, 1747
    To son JOHN WOODING, tract "Parishes Range," 270 A., in
Baltimore Co.
    To son SOLOMON, my dwelling plantation, 50 A., pt. of "Mary's
Mount"; to sd. son SOLOMON; my dau. ELIZABETH BATTEE, 1 slave.
Sons John and Solomon Wooding, exs. Wit: John Jacobs, Robert
Davis, Willilam Davis. At the foot of the will was written:
12-12-1747, came John Jacobs, Robert Davis and William Davis,
the 3 witnesses.   25. 313

WATTS, JOHN, Anne Arundel Co., planter   3 May, 1747
                                              13 Jan, 1747
    To sons RICHARD and JOHN WATTS, and MARGARET PERKINS, my
personal estate.
    My just debts and funeral charges are to be divided bet. sons
RICHARD and JOHN.
    Appoint JOS. COWMEN, guardian to my 2 sons RICHARD and JOHN;
desire Joseph Cowman to put my sons to some good trade.
    Son-in-law JOHN PERKINS, ex.
Wit: John Ramsay, Joseph Cowman, Jr.   25. 314

DORSEY, JOSHUA, Anne Arundel Co.   14 Nov, 1747
                                      6 Feb, 1747
    To wife Anne,250 A., my dwelling plantation called "Major's
Choice."
    To son HENRY DORSEY, my 2 tracts, one called "Dorsey's
Anglis," 200 A., the other called "Dorsey's Hills," 200 A., both
tracts lying in the county.
    To son PHILEMON DORSEY, 1/2 tract called "Brothers'
Partnership," taken up jointly bet. my bro. JOHN DORSEY, and
myself, 632 A.
    To son JOSHUA DORSEY, 250 A.
    To son NICHOLAS DORSEY, tract "Huntingstowne Quarters," 266
A., original tract was some years ago resurveyed by my
bro.-in-law HENRY RIDGEBY.
    To dau. RACHEL WARFIELD, 20 s. sterl.
    To dau. ELIZABETH DORSEY, 20 pounds.
    To dau. ANNE DORSEY, slaves.
    To dau. SARAH DORSEY, 1 slave.
    To son CHARLES DORSEY, my dwelling plantation and 250 A.
Mentions his young. child., and to support NICHOLAS and
CHARLES with provision at their own stock.
    Wife and 2 eld. sons, exs.
Wit: Henry Ridgely, Basill Dorsey, Richard Simpson, Elizabeth
Ridgely, Ephraim Howard, Henry Howard.   25. 315 - 318

BURLE, MARY, Anne Arundel Co.   19 Nov, 1747
(The named is signed BURLY)   15 Feb. 1747
    To bro.-in-law NATHANIEL STINCHCOMBE, and if he die without
hrs., to my sister HAMMUTALE STINCHCOMBE, and my bro. THOMAS
STINCHCOMBE.
Wit: John Marriken, Sr., Philip Pettybone, Samuel Fowler.
Memorandum: The Testatrix, MARY BURLY, by the information of
Philip Pettibone, who intermarried with her mother, would have
been 16 years of age, if she had lived until March, next, and no
more. Certified 2-15-1747.   25. 319

MAPP, FRANCIS, Anne Arundel Co.   18 Mar, 1744/5
                                    7 Mar, 1747
    All my relations living in England. I think it not worth this
trouble to seek after it; therefore, my will and pleasure is as
follows:
    To my worthy friend MR. ASHBURY SUTTON, my slave girl.
    To ELIZABEYTH GILLISS, dau. of EZEKIEL and MARY GILLISS,
Ezekiel Gilliss, ex.
Wit: Richard Young, Thomas King, Samuel Budd.
Wit. to Codicil Thomas King and Samuel Mitchelson, 12-12-1747.
                                        25. 320

THACHEREL, THOMAS, Anne Arundel Co., planter. 5 Feb, 1747
                                    11 Mar, 1747
    To wife MARY THATCHEREL, my estate and appoint her extx.
Wit: Jane Clark, Jane Perry, Thomas Baldwin.
On the back of sd. will: 3-11-1747.   25. 321

152

CHESHIRE, JOHN, Anne Arundel Co.   31 Dec, 1747
                                                11 Mar, 1747
   To wife, 1/2 of my estate.
   The other 1/2, to my 2 cousins in Great Brittain: WILLIAM
CHESHIRE and RICHARD POOH, to be sold here, and the produce to be
sent home and equally divided bet. them and my wife and friend
MR. STEPHEN WEST,, SR., Admr. on my estate.
Wit: Wm. Ford, Thomas Watson, Nicholas Norman.   25. 322

LINSTEAD, HANNAH, Anne Arundel Co.   14 Apr, 1747
                                                 10 May, 1748
   To son JOHN ACHORS, my goods and chattels.
O'Neal Roboson, Sr., planter, Anne Arundel Co., ex.
Wit: O'Neal Roboson, Jr., Edward Mattox.
At the foot of sd. will, was written: May 10, 1748.
                                                   25. 323

SMITH, SAMUEL, Anne Arundel Co.   16 Oct, 1747
                                                 23 May, 1748
   To 2 sons, JOHN and ANTHONY SMITH, my tracts lying on the
north side of Susquehanna in Cecil Co., one called "Heath's
Adventure," 200 A., and the other called "Holland," 650 A.,
equally divided bet. them and the hrs. of their body; but in case
son ANTHONY shd. die before he arrives age 21, then my will is
that his pt. of sd. land be equally divided bet. my sons SAMUEL
and JOHN SMITH.
   To son SAMUEL SMITH and hrs., 1 slave named Jack.
   To son JOHN SMITH, 1 slave.
   To son ANTHONY SMITH, 1 slave.
   To daus.: ANN and DINAH SMITH and hrs., 1 slave; also a new
side saddle and furniture to be sent for from England by my
executors.
   To dau. JANE SMITH and hrs., 1 slave.
   To dau. ELIZABETH SMITH, 1 slave.
   To cousin DINAH HANCHETT, 5 pounds money.
   To grand-daus.: MARY and ELIZABETH SMITH, cattle.
   To grand-son SAMUEL SMITH, 2 head of cattle.
   To wife ELIZABETH SMITH, 1 slave.
   Wife and son Samuel, exs.
Wit: Joseph Ward, Margaret Watkins, Thomas Ijams, Elizabeth
Ijams.   25. 324

TEPEDO, MARY, Anne Arundel Co., widow.   17 Apr, 1744
                                                 18 Jun, 1748
   To son JOSEPH TEPEDO, all my 50 A. where I now live, lying
near Herring Creek in sd. county, called "Knighton's Choice."
   Order that grand-son JOSEPH MUMFORD, enjoy sd. tract.
   Son JOSEPH TEPEDO, ex.
Wit: James Trott, Thomas Borer, John Gardner.   25. 326

DOLBE, PETER, Worcester Co., planter.   26 Dec, 1747
                                                  8 Apr, 1748
   To wife MARY, 1/2 of my estate.
   To son JOHN DOLBE, the plantation I live on called "Double

To son JOHNATHAN DOLBE, land called "Venter," 100 A.
To son PETER DOLBE, land called "Second Choice."
To dau. LEER, cattle.
To grand--son HUMPHREY MARSHALL, 1 heifer, 3 years old.
Son JOHN DOLBE, ex.
Wit: John Hamm, Thomas Walter, Daniel Boyce.   25. 327

MERCY, JOHN, SR., Worcester Co.   14 Mar, 1747/8
                                            12 Apr, 1748
     To eld. son JOHN MERCY, land whereon I live, 100 A., called
"Good Sweep," which sd. land I bought of Thomas Aydelott, with
the houses and orchards.
     To son EZEKIEL MERCY, 2 lots, next the ship yard, and to be
held by him and hrs.
     To son JOSEPH MERCY and hrs., 100 A., it being on the south
side and adjoining to his bro. WILLIAM, and on the back side, and
to be holden by my sd. son JOSEPH, and his hrs.
     To ATTHINS MERCY, 1 s. sterl.
     To son JEDIAH MERCY, 1 s. sterl.
     To son DANIEL MERCY, son WM. MERCY, the plantation where I
formerly dwelled.
     To son WM., dau. SARAH MERCY, and wife ANN MERCY, to them 100
A. that lyeth at the seaside.
Wit: Joseph Miller, Thomas Hamey, Joseph Carter.   25. 328

GRAY, ZACHARIAH, Baltimore Co., planter.   9 Oct, 1742
                                            18 Mar, 1747
     To son EPHRAIM GRAY, the dwelling plantation.
     To son ABSOLOM GRAY, the other pt. of that tract called
"Nashes Rest."
     To son ZACHR. GRAY, a tract of land lying upon a branch called
Bull Neck Branch, called "Part Willis," and that called "Madrins
Outlet."
     To dau. ELIZABETH GRAY, 100 A. on the north side of Back
River, called "Goosberry Neck."
     To my dau. ANN BAZE, 15 pounds of my estate.
     The thirds of my wife REBECCA GRAY, after death, shall equally
be divided among her child.
     It is my desire that if my sons ABSOLOM GRAY or EPHRAIM GRAY,
shd. die without issue, that their parts shd. belong to the
longest liver of them.
Wit: John Finex, Robert Willkinson, John Willson. 25. 330

ALLINDER, JOSHUA, Cecil Co.   6 Mar, 1748
                                            15 Apr, 1748
     To wife MARY ALLINDER, 50 pounds of money.
     To eld. son WILLIAM ALLINDER, 50 pounds money.
     To dau. MARY ALLINDER, 50 pounds Pennsylvania money.
     To son JOSHUA ALLINDER, 50 pounds money.
     To young. son NICHOLAS ALLINDER, 50 pounds money of
Pennsylvania.
     To bro's. son JOSHUA ALLINDER, 5 pounds money.
     To friend THOMAS ELLETT,
Wit: Wm. Allen, Henry Good, Thos. Kenedy.   25. 331

AUGHARD, JOHN, Baltimore Co.   27 Nov, 1746
                                                 26 May, 1748
    To bro. WILLIAM HODSWORTH, and sisters: ANN, REBECCA, HANNAH
GODWIN, ELIZABETH HODSWORTH and SARAH HODSWORTH, an equal share
of my estate as follows: tract of 50 A. over Deer Creek, stock,
clothing.
    Benjamin Goodwin and Wm. Reice, bros.-in-law, exs.
Wit: Samuel Wells, William Foxley, Abraham Jerrett.   25. 332

ELLETT, GEORGE, Baltimore Co.   26 Apr, 1748
                                                  8 Jun, 1748
    To DARBY HENLEY, my ex., and SARAH HENLY, my dwelling
plantation.
    To MARAH JAMES, cattle.
Wit: Joseph Norris, Wm. Wright.   25. 334

RUTTER, RICHARD, Cecil Co.   8 Mar, 1747
                                                 28 Apr, 1748
    Wife MARY RUTTER, and son MOSES RUTTER.
    If wife or son MOSES, shd. die, then my estate to descend to
RALPH RUTTER, the son of Ralph Rutter, late of Cecil Co., dec'd.
and in default of hrs., the same to descend unto THOMAS RUTTER,
son of Thomas Rutter of sd. county, dec'd.
    Balance of estate to JOHN JONES' daus.: ELIZABETH, CATHARINE
and MARY, son MOSES.
    Friend Zebulon Holinsworth, ex. [who resigned executorship,
assigning it to Mary Rutter, widow, on 28 Mar 1748].
Wit: Elinor Jones, Job Everstoon, John Herbert.   25. 334-6

RYLAND, JOHN, SR., Cecil Co., planter.   4 Jun, 1747
                                                 11 Apr, 1748
    To son JOHN RYLAND, all my claim to certain tract of land
lying in Kent Co., Maryland called "Strawberry Bank," and also
other lands in sd. county.
    To young. son SYLVESTER RYLAND, the tract I live on called
"Mulberry Mold" and "Mulberry Dock," also my right and title to
lands in Cecil Co.; in default of issue, same to my 2 daus.
REBECCA and ELIZABETH RYLAND.
    Balance divided among my 4 child.
    Wife, extx.
Wit: Edward John White, Charles Bowen, Ann Bowen.
Date on the back of the will above: 4-11-1748.   25. 336 - 338

ARMSTRONG, JAMES, Cecil Co.   27 Feb, 1747
                                                 10 May, 1748
    To wife MARTHA, 1/3 of my real and personal estate.
    To 4 child.: JOHN, WILLIAM, JAMES and my dau. that is at her
mother's breast, the remainder of my estate.
In witness whereof, I have hereto set my hand and seal this 28th
day of Feb., 1747/8.
    Bro.-in-law Fergus Smith and my cousin JOHN RITCHEY, exs.
Wit: Robert Gordon, Wm. Smith, John Ritchey.
Date on back of the book; on the back of the will: 5-12-1748.
                                                 25. 338 - 339

FOSTER, JAMES.   12 Apr, 1748
                                        10 May, 1748
   Wife ELIZABETH.
   To son JAMES, when he arrives age 21, my dau. MARY, 5 s.
   To daus. SUSANNA and REBECCA, their equal portions.
   My wife's uncle JAMES BOULDING, to have the binding of son
JAMES, according to his discretion to a trade, to be bound past
till he is age 20 years or else bound to William Price.
   Wife, extx.
Wit: Thomas Cowan, James Price, Martin Alexander.
                                        25. 339

IRONS, JOHN, Queen Anne's Co., planter.   - - - - - -
                                        10 May, 1748
The deposition of James Everett of Kent County, upon Delaware,
planter, and of John Cheshire of Queen Anne's County, Maryland,
planter, on oath say that on the 1st of March, 1747, being at a
the house of Margaret Berry, where a certain JOHN IRONS of Queen
Anne's County, planter, had for some months before that time been
resident, and who was then lying on his death bed, where he died
the day following: the sd. JOHN IRONS called to these deponants
and did them bear witness that he was going to say his last will,
and then spoke the following words: I leave to my sister HESTER
MOONEY, all that I have.
Signed: Wm. Tilghman, Deputy Comry. of Queen Anne's Co.
                                        25. 340

BRANTHWHATE, JOSEPH, Queen Anne's Co., joyner. 19 Apr, 1744
                                        12 May, 1748
   To DANIEL BRANTHWHATE, bro., my sett of joyner's tools.
   To SARAH BRANTHWHATE, wife, remainder of my personal estate.
   Wife, extx.
Wit: Elizabeth Fisher, Henry Templeman, William Fisher.
                                        25. 340

SATTERFIELD, WILLIAM, Queen Anne's Co.   27 Apr, 1748
                                        2 Jun, 1748
   To wife DINAH SATTERFIELD, my estate, my land "Winfield," shd.
be divided bet. my 2 sons NATHANIEL and WILLIAM SATTERFIELD;
NATHANIEL to have no pt. of land where my son WM, is now settled.
   To son JAMES, furniture, at decease of my wife.
   To son THOMAS, furniture.
   To dau. ALICE, furniture, at decease of my wife.
   Balance to be divided bet. my 3 child.: JAMES, ALICE and
THOMAS SATTERFIELD.
   WILLIAM SATTERFIELD, son, ex.
Wit: Wm. Emory, Wm. Hurd, Stephen Yoe.   25. 341

EATON, THOMAS, Talbot Co.   9 May, 1748
                                        8 Jun, 1748
   To son RICHARD EATON, and dau. SARAH EATON, 1 s. sterl., each
of them and no more to be paid by my exs.
   To son ANDERTON EATON, PETER EATON, ESTHER BLEADS and MARY

156

EATON, my estate equally, when my son RICHARD and my dau. is paid
off.
    Son ADDERTON EATON and son PETER EATON, exs.
Wit: Arthur Rigby, David Fitzpatrick, Eleanor Fitzpatrick.
                                      25. 343

ELLIOTT, EDWARD, Talbot Co., planter.   2 May, 1748
                                    9 Jun, 1748
    To dau. SARAH SPENCER, wife of Thomas Spencer, my dwelling
plantation, consisting of the following tracts: "Chance," "Sarahs
Garden," my pt. of "Benson's Enlargement," until such time as her
son JOHN SHANNANAN shall have arrived to age 21, and at her
decease, to my grand-dau. MARIAH SPENCER.
    To grand-son JOHN SHANNAHAN, slaves, at the death of his
mother SARAH SPENCER, and for want of issue to his mother, and
his mother SARAH SPENCER, and for want of hrs. to my son EDWARD
ELLIOTT.
    To grand-son WILLIAM ELLIOT, slaves.
    Son Edward Elliot, ex.
Wit: Joseph Hopkins, Richard Keighley, William Corsey.
                                      25. 344

SINKLER (or SINKLAIR), WILLIAM, Talbot Co. 26 Oct. 1747
                                    11 Jun, 1748
    To sister-in-law RUTH WILSON, the loom that she works on.
Balance estate to wife and 2 child., equally.
    Sister VIOLETTE, have her 2 child., that I have, without any
charge from me or my estate.
    Wife SARAH and friend PERRY BENSON, exs.
Wit: Ruth Wilson, Wm. Wile, Peter Benson.   25. 345

MEDLEY, JOHN, Sr., St. Mary's Co.   2 Dec, 1743
                                    5 Apr, 1748
    To son in law THOMAS GREENWELL, the land where he lives; after
his decease to my grandson, GEORGE GREENWELL and for want of
heirs to JAMES MEDLEY son of JAMES MEDLEY.
    To son JOHN MEDLEY, 1 s.
    To son GEORGE MEDLEY's hrs., and the rest of his children, 1
s.
    To son WILLIAM MEDLEY, 1 s.
    To son THOMAS MEDLEY, 1 s.
    To son JAMES MEDLEY, 1 s.
    To heirs of dau MARY, 1 s.
    To dau. ANN COLE, feather bed.
    To wife, SARAH, 1/3 of estate.
And the rest of my estate to my three children, CLEMENT, JEAN
and HENRIETTA MEDLEY.
    Wife SARAH and son CLEMENT, exs.
Wit: James Waughop, Enoch Combs, Cornelius Maning.
                                      25. 346

TEPPET, JOHN, St. Mary's Co.   25 May, 1748
                                    5 July, 1748
    To dau. MARY DUNBAR, 1 s.
    To grandson JOHN DUNBAR, Negro girl called Jane.

To wife ELIZABETH TEPPETT, slaves called Pegg and Samuell
To son EDWARD MADDOX TEPPET, Negres Joseph and Terey, and
other when he reaches age 18.
Wit: John Maddox, Edman Bolen, Hue Mackmilon.   25. 348

GREAVES, John, SR., St. Mary's Co.   27 Jan, 1746
                                             5 July, 1848
     To George Thompson, St. Mary's Co., right to plantation he now
lives on, called "Rockey Point."
     To son THOMAS GREAVES, plantation he lives on, called
"Hopewell," and pt of "Hardships Addition" and at his decease to
my grandson THOMAS GREAVES, JR; and for want of heirs to my
grandson JOSHUA GREAVES, and for want of his heirs to his brother
JOHN GREAVES, and for want of his heirs to my granddau HENRIETTA
ANDERSON, and for want of her heirs, so on to the youngest of my
son THOMAS's children. For want of such heirs then to fall to
grandau. TABITHA GREAVES, dau to JOHN GREAVES, JR., deceased, and
for want of such heir to her brother JOHN GREAVES, and for want
of his heirs to his brother JESSE GREAVES and for want of such
heirs to fall to my son GEORGE GREAVES.
     To grandson JESSE GREAVES the plantation his father lived on
when he died being pt of "Greaves Chance."
     To grandson JOHN GREAVES son of JOHN GREAVES, JR., deceased,
tract called "Greaves Lott."
     To son GEORGE GREAVES, "Greaves Swamp."
     To grandson JESSE GREAVES and JOHN GREAVES to be under care
and tuition of son GEORGE GREAVES until age 18.
     To dau ELENOR GREAVES, "Hardships Addition," and for want of
heirs to dau ANN GREAVES, and for want of her heirs to granddau
MARU ANN NELLSON, and for want of her heirs to granddau CHLOE
NELSON, and for want of her heirs to grandson SENECA NELSON, and
for want of his heirs to dau ELIZAB. NELSON, and for want of
heirs to dau MARGARET STANDIDGE.
     To dau ELIZABETH NELLSON, tract, "Doepark," and 50 A.,
"Doepark's Addition."
     To dau MARGARET STANDIDGE, pt. of tract "North addition of
Doepark."
     To dau in law, MARGARET GREAVES.
     If any of the children or grandchildren forsake the Protestant
religion then they are to be disinherited.
Wit: Richard Weakling, Robert Drury, John Booker.   25. 349

DAVIS, THOMAS, Back River, Baltimore Co.   1747/8
                                            28 Jul, 1748
     Desire that the mortgage on a tract of land lying on Back
River Neck and county, afsd., be paid and Daniel Dulany, Esq. or
his assigns, being 10 pounds sterl., sd. land containing 200 A,
and the original tract called "Norwick" and after sd. mortgage is
paid and discharges, give sd. 200 A. equally bet. my sons,
ROBERT, WILLIAM and DANIEL DAVIES.
     Give my dwelling plantation, called "Dukes' Discovery,"
containing 80 A. to wife MARY DAVIS, during her life, and at her
decease, to son THOMAS DAVIS.
     After my wife's 3rds are taken out, the balance to my 5 sons
and daus.

158

Wit: Christopher Duke, Sarah Duke, John Garner, Walter Dallas.
25. 354

RELLET, EDWARD, Charles Co.
Charles Co. 30 Jun 1748 came Doctor James Ferguson and made oath
that he was with Edward Rellet(?) when he lay sick of the
sickness whereof he died; that Edward Rellet desired that the
deponant to make his will; that his estate after debts were paid
was to be given to Sarah Becknell dau of Mary Becknell. Also
confirmed by David Lanter.   25. 356

MADDOX, JOHN, Charles Co.   11 May, 1748
                                                 28 Jun, 1748
    To wife SARAH MADDOX, all lands and tenements, all Negroes.
Slaves named:
Sam born Dec 1736 and Peter born Jan 1747 to JOHN MADDOX son of
NOTELY.
Judith born 1734 to NOTELY son of NOTELY MADDOX.
Jane born Apr 1737 to WILLIAM son of NOTELY MADDOX.
Robert born May 1739 to CHARLES son of NOTELY MADDOX.
Elizabeth born Jan 1745 to TOWNLY son of NOTELY MADDOX.
Susanna born Apr 1734 to SAMUEL son of JOHN MADDOX.
Yalla born Jun 1739 to JOHN son of JOHN MADDOX.
Lydda born Oct 1741 to NOTELY son of JOHN MADDOX.
Mary born 1743 to THOMAS son of JOHN MADDOX.
Ned born Feb 1723 to JOHN son of NOTELY MADDOX.
James born 1725 to NOTELY son of NOTELY MADDOX.
To WILLIAM son of SAMUEL MADDOX, wearing apparel.
Wife SARAH, extx, to have slaves during her lifetime.
                                                             25. 356

DOWNING, JAMES, Prince George's Co.   14 Jun, 1747
                                                 12 May, 1748
    To son JAMES DOWNING, 70 A., pt. of a tract "Doublin" in
Sapling Branch, and give him the balance of my estate at decease
of wife ANN DOWNING, provided he shall pay my other 3 sons: HENRY
DOWNING, 200 pounds of tobacco; and he pay to JOHN DOWNING and
NATHANIEL DOWNING, 2000 pounds of tobacco, when JOHN and
NATHANIEL DOWNING shall come to age 21.
    Wife, extx.
Wit: Richard Marlow, Josiah Wynn, Richard Blue.
                                                             25. 358

HITCH, SOLOMON, Somerset Co.   14 Mar, 1747/8
                                                  5 Apr, 1748
    The plantation I now live on, and the land I took up adjoining
to it, and the land belonging to the plantation.
    To son SOLOMON HITCH, my land I bought of James Storey's hrs.,
and half of land at Rockawakin, equally divided bet. him and son
WM. HITCH; and if LEVIN die without issue, then my son WM., have
all land and plantation at Rockawakin.
    To son SOLOMON, 2 slaves.
    To dau. ANN HITCH, the land that made over to me by Wm.
Weatherwell, called "Powell's Folly."

To dau. EVE HITCH, 1 slave.
To dau. REBECCA HITCH, 1 slave.
To friend JOSHUA INGLISH, son of William English, cattle.
To HILGET HITCH and ROBERT GIVEN, slaves; and they to be
overseers of my estate.
Son SOLOMON HITCH, ex.
Wit: Joseph Wetherly, Thomas Alswoth, Robert Farrington.
4-5-1748, came witnesses to above will, and made oath they saw
the Testator, SOLOMON HITCH, sign his will.   25. 360

SAMUELS, ANN, Stepeney Parish in Maryland, Somerset Co.
                                    18 Apr, 1748
                                    10 May, 1748
     To grand-dau. SARAH SAMMONS, the dau. of PETER SAMONS, my son,
furniture.
     To dau. ELIZABETH HOPKINS, 20 s.
     To dau. SARAH WATTER (or WALTER), 20 s.
     To dau. MARTHA WALLIS, and her son SAMUEL WALLIS, and her dau.
GRACE WALLIS, equally, to be divided bet. the 3.
The above is the copy of ANN SAMOUS' will which was signed,
sealed and acknowledged on 4-18-1748; signed "ANN SAMOUS."
Wit: Magdalen Pollet, John Spence, Teaque Dickeson.   25. 361

HORSEY, NATHANIEL, Somerset Co.   6 May, 1748
                                          25 Jun, 1748
     To grand-son NATHANIEL, son of OUTERBRIDGE HORSEY, all my
lands and slaves.
     To son OUTERBRIDGE HORSEY, 1 s.
     To dau. ELIZABETH, the wife of JOHN HORSEY, 4 slaves.
     To dau. SARAH BEAUCHAMP, wife of ISAAC BEAUCHAMP, 1/3 of my
household goods, cattle and etc.
     To dau. MARTHA, wife of AMBROSE DIXON, 1/3 of my household
goods.
     To grand-son NATHANIEL HORSEY, and 3 daus., equally, divide
the slaves.
Friend Wm. Coulbourn, son of Wm., son Outerbridge, exs.
Wit: Thomas Jones, Michael Holland, Thos. Montgomery, George
Caton.   25. 362

GRANGER, EDWARD, Dorchester Co.   13 Nov, 1747
                                          16 Nov, 1747
     To dau. REBECCA WILLISS, 1 s.
     To THOMAS HEATHER, 1 s.
     To son WM. GRANGER and PRICE WARD, my estate.
Wit: Edward Trippe, Wm. Green, Oven Sillivan.   25. 364

PATTISON, JAMES, Dorchester Co.   7 Jul, 1747
                                          5 Mar, 1747
     To JOHN PATTISON, 100 A. on James's Island, being pt. of the
land called "Armstrong Hogpen."
     To wife MARY, land with my now dwelling plantation.
     To dau. ANN, land on Taylor's Island, called "Dover," that

lyeth on the last side of the Lend Cove.
    To ELIZABETH PATTISON, "Dover" tract on west side of Long Cove.
    To JACOB PATTISON, 100 A. on James's Island, being east pt. of land caalled "Armstrong's Folly," lying on Little Choptank River.
    To THOMAS PATTISON, 100 A. on James's Island, being pt. of afsd. land called "Armstrong's Folly," where his father lived, to him and his hrs. forever.
    To wife MARY, 1/3 pt. of my estate.
    To ANN and ELIZABETH, 2/3, but will that at my wife's decease, her pt. to go to ANN and ELIZABETH.
    To RICHARD, my mill, desk and surveyor's books.
    To JACOB PATTISON, 28 A. on Taylor's Island, being tract, "Marshey Hope," except pt. that I have sold to John Aaron.
    To PRISCILLA DRIVER, 5 s.
Wife MARY, extx.
Wit: Wm. Geoghegan, John Barns, Thomas Spicer, Daniel McCay.
                                                    25. 365

REALY (REILY), CORNELIUS, Dorchester Co.   9 Nov, 1747
                                                  2 Apr, 1748
    To wife ELENOR, my dwelling plantation, and after decease, all land called "Raley's Discovery," 96 A. to my dau. ANN, and my best furniture.
    To daus.: CORNEALY, REBECCA and RACHEL, my moveable estate.
    To dau. REBECCA, 50 A., which I bought of Joseph Fisher, being pt. of land called "Long Range."
    To dau. RACHEL, 50 A., which I bought of Joseph Fisher, land being pt. of tract of land called "Goodhead Mannor."
    John Oldfield and son-in-law JOHN BURTON, exs.
Wit: Hugh Sherwood, Elizabeth Sherwood, Mary Woolcott.
                                                    25. 366

DOHORTY, JOHN, Dorchester Co.,   1 Apr, 1748
                                                  15 Jun, 1748
    To son GEORGE DE HORTY, land called "Dolfin's Hill," in Dorchester Co., near my now dwelling plantation; slaves; stock.
    To son JOHN, land called "Horse Ridge"; stock.
    To dau. MARY, 100 A. remainder of tract, "Turkey Point"; stock.
Wife CATHARINE DEHORTY, extx.
Wit: John White, Mathew Driver.   25. 367

CANNON, THOMAS, SR., Dorchester Co.   24 Jan, 1746/47
                                                  15 Jun, 1748
    To eld. son THOMAS, 100 A. called "Poplar Hills."
    To JAMES and CLEAR, the son and dau. of my son JAMES, 60 or 70 A.
    To son JOSEPH, 50 A. of land out of that tract called "Cannon's Thicket"; 50 A. called "Cannon's Long Square," in Worcester Co.
    To son ABSOLOM, the remainder pt. of that tract of land called "Cannon's Thicket."
    To son STEPHEN, 72 A. of "Cannon's Sovana."
    To son LOWDER, a tract called "Cannon's Venture," and 20 A.

out of the resurvey of tract called "Efard."
    To son LEVI, remaining pt. of "Efard."
    To dau. SARAH, 1 slave, at decease of wife.
    Wife CATHARINE, extx.
    Wit: Wm. Clarkson, Sr., Wm. Clarkson, Jr., James Clarkson, Thomas
Clarkson.   25. 369

MILLER, JOHN,   27 Jul, 1746
                                             27 Jun, 1748
    To wife DOROTHY MILLER, 1/2 of my estate.
    To MARY WHITELY, the dau. of Arthur Whitely, 1 heifer.
    To JOHN HATFIELD, my clothing.
    To the child. of John Hatfield, living in Kent Co., Delaware,
all the remainder of my estate to be equally divided amongst
them.
    Wife and John Hatfield, exs.
    Wit: Thomas Vicars, John Vicars.   25. 370 - 371

ROSON, CHARLES, Dorchester Co.   2 Mar, 1748
                                            14 Aug, 1748
    To son JOHN ROBSON, tract called "Surveyor's Point"; tract
called "Robson's Pasture."
    To my unborn child, tract called "Robson's Chance."
    To wife and son JOHN, moveable estate.
    Wife ELIZABETH ROBSON, extx.
    Wit: Thomas Chapman, Edward Keene, Edward Keene (probably Sr. and
Jr.).   25. 371

FISH, MARY, Dorchester Co., widow.   4 Dec, 1747
                                                     1748
    To son HENRY WILLIGOT, 3 slaves.
    To son JOHN BOWDLE, 2 slaves, but if he shd. die without hrs.,
to return to HENRY WILLIGOT.
    To dau. SARAH DELLEHAW, 1 slave, until her son THOMAS
DELLEHAY, comes of age 21.
    To dau. ELIZABETH LITTLETON, 1 slave, and for default of hrs.,
to return to JOHN BOWDEN.
    To grand-child.: WILLIAM JONES, MARY WILLIGET (or WITHGET),
MARY FEASTON, 1 ewe.
    To grand-dau., MARY JONES, 1 heifer.
    To ex., my slave woman to be sold.
    Son HENRY WITHGETT, ex.
    Wit: John Anderton, William Jones, Mark Littleton, Jane Dellehay,
Wm. Littleton.   25. 372

BILLINGS, JAMES, Dorchester Co., gentleman. 18 Nov, 1746
                                              7 Dec, 1748
    To wife ANN,
    To eld. son THOMAS, all lands that are his sd. mother's
inheritance, with the land I have made in Nanticoke River, being
pt. of tract "Weston" given to me by the last will of Capt.
Charles Rider; tract I bought from Wm. Hemsly, called "Scotch
Folley," lying on damn bet. my now dwelling house and Dr.
Smith's; land upon the northwest fork of Nanticoke River, called
"Addition To Fullam," adjoining to tract called "Fullam," by his

grandfather Col. John Rider. In his lifetime, to him conveyed
unto his bro. JAMES, and his hrs. and assigns forever, which is
very modest (or moderate) matter for my sd. son THOMAS, to comply
with if he duly considers the expense I have been at in England
for his education, also.
Tract called "Scotch Follyard," the buildings on Nanticoke,
have been to me to the prejudice of my 2 young. child; therefore,
if son THOMAS does not comply with the term above mentioned, then
I devise to sd. JAMES, son, the afsd. pt. of sd. tract called
"Weston," as afsd. to me devised by the will of Capt. Charles
Rider; the sd. tracts to sd. son JAMES; also the tract on
northwest fork of Nanticoke River, whereon John Brown now lives,
called "Orms Kirk."
To dau. ANN, and hrs., in case son JAMES shall not comply with
the sd. proviso, and the tract I purchased of widow Anderton and
hrs.
There are deeds of gift to each of my child., from their
worthy grandfather, for slaves that he gave them.
Wife ANN, and 3 child.: THOMAS, JAMES and ANN.
Wife ANN, guardian. The last request of a dying friend, that
Col. John Henry and Mr. James Edge will advise and assist my
extx. in her troublesome office.
Wit: John Henry, Thomas Smith, Elizabeth Tolley.   25. 373

BENNETT, JOHN, Queen Anne's Co.   21 Feb, 1747/8
                                         16 Jul, 1748
    That the accounts due me and JOHN BENNETT, make this my deed
of gift to wife MARGARET.
Wit: Daniel Smith, John Cadenhead.   25. 376

WEBB, TIMOTHY, Long Neck, Queen Anne's Co. 18 May, 1748
                                         21 Jul, 1748
    To wife MARY, if she remain single, dwell with son GEORGE,
during her life.
    To son GEORGE, the plantation, but if he die without hrs.,
same to dau. JANE.
    To dau. NENAH, furniture.
    Son GEORGE, ex.
Wit: Thomas Mooth, Wm. Wiott, Samuel Phillips.   25. 377

WILLSON, WILLIAM, Queen Anne's Co.   1 Dec, 1747
                                         23 Jul, 1748
    To bro. ABRAHAM WILLSON, my clothing.
    To nephew NEHEMIAH WILLSON, 5 s. sterl.
    To wife ANN WILLSON, 1 slave.
    To dau. MARY WILLSON, tract I purchased of John Machonikin
(?), and in default of hrs., to nephew WM. WILLSON., son of
Abraham Willson, shd. enjoy same.
    To dau. MARY WILLSON, 1 slave.
    To nephew WILLIAM WILLSON, my dau's. estate here given her.
Friend John Emory, Jr., as guardian to my dau.
    To wife ANN WILLSON, the 3rd pt. of my estate.
    Wife, extx.
Wit: Littleton Ward, James Clayland, John Clayland, Jr.
                                         25. 379

FISHER, THOMAS, Queen Anne's Co., planter. 16 Jun, 1748
                                            29 Jul, 1748
     To son JAMES FISHER, pt. of a tract situated in the forks of
Choptank River on the east side of the main branch of Tuckahoe
Creek, called "Fisher Meadows."
     To wife ESTHER FISHER, the use of all remaining pt. of
"Fisher's Meadows," which I have not before given to son JAMES
FISHER.
     To son RICHARD FISHER, remaining pt. of "Fisher's Meadows,"
which I have not before given son JAMES FISHER, at decease of his
mother, ESTHER FISHER.
Wit: Christopher Wise, Abigail Wise, Elizabeth Fisher, John
Mayne.   25. 380

COMEGY, CORNELIUS, Queen Anne's Co., planter.
                                             8 Apr, 1748
                                            16 Aug, 1748
     To wife MARY COMEGYS, the furnishings.
     To eld. son JOHN COMEGYS, my dwelling plantation called
"James's choice," of 150 A., and if he die without issue, to
descend to my 2nd son GIAS BARTAS.
     To my eld. dau. MARY COMEGYS, tract near Beaver Dam Branch
called "Salem," 350 A.
     To dau. JANE COMEGYS, land called "Crump's Chance," Nigh The
Cat Tails Branch, 50 A.
     Unborn child mentioned.
     The remaining pt. of my personal estate to wife's pt., being
sub-divided, I will shall be equally divided amongst my 4
above-named child.: JOHN, GIAS, BARTAS, MARY and JANE. (The name
"Gias" has a comma after it, even though he mentions "4" child.,
and in the first pt. of the will, the 2 names are shown to be one
person.)
     Cousins CORNELIUS COMEGY and EDWARD COMEGY, of Kent Co., exs.
Wit: John Harris, Davenport Wells, John Holt.   25. 382 - 383

CHAIRS, THOMAS, Queen Anne's Co., planter.   28 Mar, 1748
                                              25 Aug, 1748
     To son THOMAS CHAIRS, land called "Batchelor's Adventure," the
land I now live upon, and 100 A. lying on Tuckahoe Branch in
Queen Anne's Co., called "Storey's Park"; and if son THOMAS,
fails to have issue, then to my dau. RACHEL CHAIRS; and in
default of her hrs., same to dau. CATHARINE CHAIRS; and in
default of hrs., to dau. SARAH CHAIRS.
     To dau. ANN, my slaves.
     To dau. MARY, certain slaves.
     To dau. SUSANNA, certain slaves.
     Mentions his younger children.
     Leaves son THOMAS, under care of son-in-law, John Olston.
     Leaves dau. RACHEL, under care of dau. MARY.
     Son-in-law John Olston (?), and daus. CATHARINE and SARAH,
exs.
Wit: Wm. Ellbert, Thomas Carradine, John Given.   25. 383

RIDDLE, CORNELIUS, Queen Anne's Co.   5 Jan, 1747
                                    1 Aug, 1748
    To son CORNELIUS RIDLE.
Wit: John Roberts and Earle Burton.   25. 385

WARD, LITTLETON, Queen Anne's Co., cooper.   2 Jun, 1748
                                 29 Aug, 1748
    To sons PHILIP and JAMES WARD, land called "Colre" (or
"Colne"?), 286 A. lying in sd. county.
    To dau. RACHEL WARD, stock.
    To bro.-in-law HENRY BANNER, my cooper tools, if he will live
with and serve my wife until the time is expired. He was bound
by Talbot Co. Court to serve me as an apprentice.
    Wife MARY WARD, extx.
Wit: Wm. Bannan, Richard Tucker, Charles Webb, Thomas Harris.
                                         25. 386

BROWN, JOHN, Queen Anne's Co.   29 Mar, 1748
                                  29 May, 1748
    To wife SARAH BROWN, 2 slaves.
    To son ELISHA BROWN, 2 slaves.
    To son JOHN BROWN, my now dwelling plantation, pt. of
"Batchelor's Hope" and pt. of "Neglect"; and in default of issue,
to son NATHAN BROWN.
    To dau. MARY BROWN, 5 s.
    To son CHARLES BROWN, tract called "Marsha Croock" in sd.
county.
    Balance of estate divided bet. wife and child., (my dau. MARY
BROWN, excepted).
    Wife SARAH, extx.
Wit: Thomas Davis, Dorcas Wright.   25. 387

OFFUTT, MARY, Prince George's Co.   9 Mar, 1747/8
                                  11 Sep, 1748
    To son EDWARD OFFUTT, 1 slave.
    To son JAMES OFFUTT, 5 pounds sterl. money.
    To son SAMUEL OFFUTT, 5 pounds sterl.
    To each of my dec'd. son, WM. OFFUTT'S child., 5 pounds money.
    To each of my dec'd. son JOHN OFFUTT's child., 5 s.
    To each of my dec'd. dau. JANE WARRINGS' child., 5 s. money.
    To each of my dec'd. dau. MARY BOWEY's child., 5 s.
    To dau. SARAH HARRIS, my clothing.
    To son NATHANIEL OFFUTT, 1 slave.
    My 2 sons: EDWARD and NATHANIEL OFFUTT.
    Nathaniel Offutt, ex.
Wit: Richard Burgess, John Brown, Braizer, Thomas Shreve.
                                   25. 388 - 389

PHELPS, WILLIAM, Anne Arundel Co.   12 Jul, 1748
                                  20 Aug, 1748
    To son RICHARD PHELPS, 1 slave; one tract called "Phelps'
Adventure," 25 A. on branch called Flat Creek Branch; one tract
called "The Upper Part," Clark Cromwell laid out for 50 A.
    To 3 sons: JOHN, BENJAMIN and ZACHARIAH PHELPS, to be fairly
divided on creek called Flat Creek.

My personal estate to be divided bet. my 5 sons: WILLIAM,
JOHN, RICHARD, BENJAMIN and ZACHARIAH.
Wife, extx.
Wit: Samuel Day, Elizabeth Cheney; Wm. Rogers, Deputy Commry.
25. 389

PEIRPOINT, CHARLES, Anne Arundel Co.   1 Jan, 1747
                                          1 Aug, 1748
    To son CHARLES PIERPOINT, my land in Baltimore Co., granted by
name of "Cannon's Lott," 200 A.
    To son JOSEPH PIERPOINT, my tract in Anne Arundel Co., granted
me by name of "Stoney Hillside," 15 A., with grist mill, and
"Pierpoint's Pleasure," at decease of my wife SIDNEY PIERPOINT.
    To son JOSEPH, 1 slave.
    To son MISAEL PEIRPOINT, 100 A., whereon he now is situated
being pt. of tract called "Benson's Park" in Anne Arundel Co.
    To son ABRAHAM PEIRPOINT, and dau. MARY PIERPOINT, remaining
pt. of sd. tract called "Benson's Path," by a division of same;
my afsd. son ABRAHAM bounding on and with his bro. MISACH (?);
    To dau. MARY, with the premises and appurtenances thereunto
belonging.
    To ABRAHAM, 1 slave.
    To son HENRY PEIRPOINT, 1 slave.
    To dau. CHEW PEIRPOINT, 1 slave.
    To dau. MARGARET PIERPOINT, 1 slave.
    To dau. SIDNEY PEIRPOINT, 1 slave.
    To dau. BATHSHABA PIERPOINT,
    To wife SIDNEY PEIRPOINT, my dwelling plantation.
    To 2 of my sons and 6 of my daus.: JOSEPH, ABRAHAM, CHEW,
MARGARET, CALIS, SIDNEY, BATHSHABA and MARY, equally, remainder
of estate.
    Wife and son JOSEPH, exs.
Wit: Joseph Taylor, John Taylor, Basil Deavor.   25. 390 - 391

KIDD, ALEXANDER, Anne Arundel Co.   8 Aug, 1748
                                      11 Aug, 1748
    To wife ELENOR KIDD, 1/2 pt. of my estate.
    To dau. HANNAH KIDD, cattle.
    To dau. ELINOR SASFORD, 1 s.
    To dau. SARAH CREASE, 1 s.
    To son SAMUEL KIDD,
    Wife and son SAMUEL, exs.
Wit: Edward Parrish, James Urry.   25. 392

HYATT, ALVAN,   - - - - - -
                                       - - - - - -
    New Castle County, on Delaware. By the tenor of these
presents, I, John Curtis, Esq., register of the Probate of Wills
of Granting Letters of Admr., for the county of New Castle, upon
Delaware, by virtue of a commission from the Hon. George Thomas,
Esq., Lieutenant Governor of and Commander in Chief of the
counties of New Castle, Kent and Sussex, upon Delaware and
Province of Pennsylvania. Make known to all men, that on the
24th Nov, 1748, at New Castle in the county of Newcastle, afsd.,
was proved the last will of ALVAN HYATT, late of sd. county,

dec'd., having divers, places within sd. county. Know all men by these presents, that I, the will of ABRAHAM HYATT, of St. George's Hundred, in the county of New Castle on Delaware, Esquire, to the last will of my bro. ALVAN HYATT, late dec'd. of same place, appoint in my place my friends Samuel Allyne of Maryland in Cecil Co., and Matthias Bordley of Annapolis, Maryland, to collect whatever is in the hands of Mr. John Evitts of Annapolis, afsd. from the estate and executor of the sd. dec'd. by any manner of means.
Signed: ABRAHAM HYATT, executor to the last will of his bro. ALVIN HYATT; signed 1748/9.
25. 393

THOMAS, JOSEPH, Baltimore Co., planter.   4 Jul, 1748
                                            7 Sep, 1748

That freehold estate lying in Baltimore Co. on a creek called Saltpeter Creek, called "Thomas," is resurveyed purchase, to my dau. RUTH SING (or LING), to her hrs., and another tract "Joseph's Priviledge," whereon there is a resurvey warrant. Desire that all of the vacant land adjoining shd. be included, and the property to be the above sd. RUTH SING'S, and hrs.
   To dau. RUTH SING, 1 slave.
   Wife DARKS THOMAS, and dau. RUTH SING, joint extxs.
Wit: Richard and Wm. Jones, W. Bond.
25. 395

BOWEN, BENJAMIN, Baltimore Co., planter.   17 Dec, 1745
                                             1 Jul, 1746

To GREENBURY BOWEN BAXTER, son of ELIZABETH BAXTER, land called "Goose Harbour," then to fall to BENJAMIN BAXTER, son of ELIZABETH BAXTER.
   That JOSHUA SMITH, son of ANN SMITH, shd. have a year of schooling out of my personal estate.
   Balance to be divided bet. ELIZABETH BAXTER, and her 2 sons GREENBURY BOWEN BAXTER, and BENJAMIN BAXTER.
   Bro. EDWARD BOWEN and ELIZABETH BAXTER, exs.
Wit: A. Eaglestone, Samuel Harryman, Robert Green, Edward Perijoy.
25. 396

HOPKINS, THOMAS, Talbot Co.   3 Jan, 1745
                                          2 Aug, 1748

Desire to be buried at Dundel Chapple.
   To 4 daus. of John Ray; (ELIZABETH, MARY, RACHEL and SARAH), which he had by my dau. ELIZABETH, 28 pounds current money.
   The balance of my estate to my 2 daus. KATHRINE WILLSON and REBECCA ROBERTS (or ROBARTS), equally.
   Son-in-law Thomas Robarts, ex.
Wit: Samuel Cochayne (or Cockayne), John Willson, Patience Ward, (Patience Butler, wife of John Butler, lately called Patience Ward).
25. 397

REW (RUE), ISAAC, Talbot Co.   8 Apr, 1747/8
                                          8 Apr, 1748

2 sons CHARLES, for himself at the age of 18, and son MORGAN, at the age of 18, both to be for themselves, and likewise my son MARK, to be for himself, at age 18.
   To son CHARLES, stock.

To son CHARLES, stock.
To son MORGAN, cattle and shoemaker's tools.
To son MARK,
The names of various persons debts due: Dr. Wm. Brown Vickers
to ISAAC REW; GEORGE VICKERS, JOHN THORNTON, ROBERT STONESTREET,
RACHEL TRANTON, MARY EVENS, ABNET TURNER, JAMES BELL, GEORGE
BAXTON.
Wit: Adam Williams.
Widow of dec'd. MARY REW (RUE), made her election and took her
1/3 pt.   25. 398

JOHNSON, PETER, Worcester Co.   3 Mar, 1747
                                                     8 Aug, 1748
     To son PETER JOHNSON, that pt. of my land on which my son
JOHN, formerly lived.
     To son ARTHUR JOHNSON, that pt. of my land where my son
LEONARD formerly lived, bounded as follows: beginning at a marked
white oak, the first boundary of my son PETER'S land, and running
that first mentioned course, bet. Capt. Parramore's line.
     To son ARTHUR JOHNSON, land called "Purgetory."
     My personal estate to be divided among my 8 child.: JOHN,
PETER, ARTHUR, TABITHA, ANN, JOYCE, CHARITY AND SARAH, which I
give to them and their hrs.
     Sons John, Peter and Arthur Johnson, exs.
Wit: Stephen Hall, Samuel Hopkins, Ezekiel Wise.
                                                   25. 399 - 400

TOWNSEND, CHARLES, Worcester Co., planter.   6 Apr, 1748
                                                     2 Aug, 1748
     To dau. EALIE BEAVENS, 1 s.
     To son CHARLES TOWNSEND, 1 s.
     To dau. ANSLY TOWNSEND, 1 s.
     To son ELIAS TOWNSEND, 1 s.; 200 A. at decease of my wife,
then to SOLOMON TOWNSEND.
     To son WILLIAM TOWNSEND, 1 s.
     To dau. MARY TOWNSEND, 1 s.
     To dau. SARAH TOWNSEND, 1 s.
     To dau. ELIZABETH TOWNSEND, 1 s.
     To wife MARY TOWNSEND, my estate.
     Son JOSEPH TOWNSEND, and wife, exs.
Wit: Peter Taylor, Saul (Saml.?) Townsend, Wm. Donoho, Wm.
Donoho. (Two of them, probably a Jr. and a Sr.)   25. 401

ONEAL, JAMES, Worcester Co.   24 Jun, 1748
                                                     21 Aug, 1748
     To eld. son RICHARD O'NEAL, my dwelling plantation, I now
dwell in called "Rume Ridg," and 50 A. others called "Sedar
Swamp," and 50 A. called "Ketches Savaner."
     To son THOMAS O'NEAL, 200 A. lying in Persons Neck.
     To son JAMES O'NEAL, 50 A. called "Dry Savaner," and 60 A.
called "Cruched Ridge."
     To dau. ELIZABETH, 50 A.
     To dau. ISABEL O'NEAL, land called "Water Ford," lying on Cool
Branch.
     To dau. ESTER O'NEAL, 1 slave.

To my loving RACHEL O'NEAL, as long as she remains a widow,
and afterwards to be divided among my child.
Wit: Frances Lank, John O'Neal, Mary O'Neal.   25. 402

KANKEY, JOHN, Elk River, Cecil Co.   12 Mar, 1748
                                            13 May, 1748
    To son JOHN KANKEY, tract of land bought of Theolaus Jucaye,
formerly; now called by name of "Jones' Land." My desire is that
he shall begin at James Veazey's northernmost bounded corner, and
running thence west and etc. to the extent of Sin Johns Maner,
and all the land of the southwest side of that line, belonging to
me, being pt. of St. John's Maner, I will do and bequeath unto
son JOHN KANKEY; and bequeath to son JOHN KANKEY, 1 bond I have
of Edward Johnson and Zidlen Hollingsworth and Thos. Johnson for
200 pounds money, dated 1746., with interest.
    To son HARMON KANKEY, the home plantation.
    I desire that William Husband, Samuel Gilpen and Michael Lum,
or any 2 of them, shall be the appraisers of my moveables.
Wit: Edward Johnson, Joseph Wallace, Michael Lum, Racel Alrichs.
                                                    25. 404

COX, JOHN, SR., Cecil Co., planter.   1 May, 1748
                                             1 Jun, 1748
    To son WILLIAM COX, my plantation which is a tract called "The
Level," 100 A. in Cecil Co.
    To son BENJAMIN COX, 100 A., pt. of tract called "Cevility,"
lying in Cecil Co.; authorize BENJAMIN COX to make over unto
Philip Stoop, Sr., tract called "Becks Medows" lying in Cecil Co.
    To dau. REBECCA COX, 1 slave.
    To dau. MARY COX, the rent of the afsd. plantation called
"Cevility," for the term of 4 years, beginning on the 28th Dec.,
and sd. MARY shall pay annually, quit rents.
    To son THOMAS COX, 1 s. sterl.
    To son JOHN COX, 1 - furniture.
Wit: Mary Gilmore, David Ricketts, Benedict Pennington.
                                                    25. 404

PHILLIPS, NATHAN, Elk River, Cecil Co.   24 May, 1748
                                                 2 Jul, 1748
    To wife JANE PHILLIPS, stock, and at her decease to JAMES
BOULDEN and JOHANES ARREANS, equally.
    To son SAMUEL PHILLIPS, my slave.
    To JOHN ROSTER, cattle and lease.
    To grand-child. JOHN PHILLIPS, 5 pounds money.
    The name of JOHANAS ARREANCES, instead of ARREANS, is
mentioned.
    SAMUEL PHILLIPS, eld. son, dec'd., is mentioned.
Wit: Michael Lum, Thos. Ross, Manadon Phillips.
                                                    25. 407

TERRY, HUGH, Cecil Co.   9 Jun, 1748
                                1 Aug, 1748
    My land in Kent Co. called "Molton," and my land in Cecil Co.
called "Swanharber," equally bet. my child.: WILLIAM, ALISHA,
THOMAS, AUGUSTIN, VACHEL, RUTH, BEATRICE, TERISHER TERRY.

I order that the whole estate shall be kept on the
plantations.
Son WM. TERRY, and dau. RUTH TERRY, exs.   25. 408

ROBARTS, KING, Cecil Co.   27 May, 1748
                                             5 Aug, 1748
    To bro. JOHN ROBARTS, 10 pounds money.
    To SAMUEL GILPIN, remaining pt. of my effects.
Wit: Joseph Gilpin, Joseph Richardson, Eliner Phillips.
                                                  25. 409

PETERS, CHRISTIAN, Cecil Co., gentleman.   13 Jun, 1748
                                             9 Aug, 1748
Born in Harborugh in the Duckdom of Lunebudin, Germany; in
consideration of my mortality, I declare my will.
    To the son of my dec'd. sister, MARY ELIZABETH HARTMANN, 1 s.
sterl.
    The same sum to my sister ANNA LOUISE REMER, or her child.
    To wife UNITE, all the moveable estate in America.
    The land not in use, to be given to build a schoolhouse for
the child. of poor people without any pay and shall be instructed
in the principles of our Christian religion.
    As for what estate actions and demands which I have in
Germany, I leave all to my half-sister, the widow MATFIELDS, in
Lavenbury, or her child., if she dies before I do; May, 1746.
    Wife, extx.
Wit: Wm. Scott, Jonas Brown, David Pean (or PAIN).
                                                  25. 410

MEAKINS, JOSHUA, Cecil Co.   1 Apr, 1748
                                              6 Sep, 1748
    To JOHN WAGONER, stock.
    My child.: RICHARD, JOSHUA, SARAH and ELIZABETH MEAKINS.
    My will is that my dau. SARAH, live with Rev. Mr. Hugh Jones,
and his spouse, until she arrives of age.
    Dau. ELIZABETH, live with Mrs. Rebecca Heath.
    My executor let my son RICHARD have any reasonable pt. of his
share of my estate, if he binds himself to John Stogden or any
good tradesman.
    I appoint Benjamin Pearce, ex., and also to settle the admin.
of John Husband's estate, jointly with Elizabeth Parr, and leave
son JOSHUA, to my executor.
Wit: Nicholas Price, Rebecca Price, Alser Walley. (Alie Wally,
one of the witnesses, on oath, states they saw the Testator
JOSHUA MEAKINS sign his will.)   25. 411

HANSON, ROBERT, Charles Co.   5 Apr 1746
                                             27 Sep 1748
    To son WILLIAM HANSON, 100 A. called "Abergame" which I
included in a tract called "Roburtus" granted to me by escheat,
pt of his now dwlling plantation; also tract called "addition to
Robertus," 28 A.; also my instruments and mathematick books.

To son ROBERT HANSON, my youngest son, all land and plantation I now dwell on, 100 A., pt. of "Bettys Delight" left me by the will of my father JOHN HANSON, decd. and 69 A. of land which I bought of William Chandler being pt. of tract called "Chandlers Hill"; also 4 lots formerly laid out in Charles Town, two of which I bought of Richard Rogers, 1 of John Brown and 1 of Thomas Sanders; also 1 lot laid out in the said town in my own name; also 1 lot laid out for me in Charles Town whereon I have now a tobacco house; also 100 A. called "Corkers Hog hole."

To my dau DOROTHY HERRISON, wife of RICHARD HARRISON, 250 A., pt. of tract called "Hansonton," to be laid off the eastern most part of it.

That remaining part of said tract called "Hansonton" and also 124 A., pt. of tract callled "Robertus" adj said "Hansonton" to be sold.

To dau MARY HANSON, tract called "Habberdeventure" laid out for 150 A. which I bought of John Lambeth; also other tract called "Hansons Plain," 75 A.

To son SAMUEL HANSON, sword, pistol and silver seal.

To grandson ROBERT HANSON son of SAMUEL and MARY HANSON, watch made by Tomlinson.

To son BENJAMIN HANSON, watch made by Royle and horse.

Remainder of estate to be divided amongst son BENJAMIN HANSON, son ROBERT HANSON, dau MARY HANSON, dau SARAH HANSON and dau VIOLETTA HANSON.

Nephew WALTER HANSON to have the guardianship and tuition of my son ROBERT HANSON.

Sons SAMUEL, WILLIAM and nephew WALTER, exs.

Wit: Edm. Porteus, Sam: Hanson Jr., Daniel of St. Thomas Jenifer.

                                                    25. 412

COX, WILLIAM, SR., Calvert Co.   5 Dec, 1743
                                                 9 Dec, 1748

To wife CATHERINE COX, son JOHN COX.
All moveable estate to be divided amongst all my child.
Wit: John Grover, Sr., John Grover, Jr., John Bradley, Sr.
                                                    25. 415

DOYNE, EDWARD ALOYSIUS, St. Mary's Co.   6 Jul 1748
                                                 3 Aug 1748

To bro. IGNATIUS DOYNE, 6 Negroes: Ned, Joshua, Bob, Nan, Sarah and Nanny and remainder of estate.
To Ignatius Spalding all his debts due me.
To Benjamin Jameson all debts due me.
To Robert Brent all debts due me.
To sister MARY JAMESON, large dyaper table clauth and 6 napkins.
To Sophia Doyne riding horse silver.
Bro. IGNATIUS DOYNE, ex.
Wit: Baptist Barber, Luke Gardiner, A. Thompson.   25. 416

PRICE, Henry, St. Mary's Co.   14 Jul 1746
                                                 15 Aug 1748

To nephew THOMAS COOK, heifer and furniture.

To nephew WILLIAM PRICE, heifer, gunn.
To mother JOHANNAH PRICE, remainder of estate and after her
death to sister FRANCES PRICE and if she died without heirs, then
to bro. WILLIAM PRICE.
Mother JOHANNAH PRICE, extx.
Wit: George Clark, Richard King, Ignatius Bryan.   25. 417

PHILBERT, JOHN, Charles Co.   22 Apr 1748
                                            9 Jul 1748
    To son LUKE, land I am now possessed of called "Philberts
Chance," and if he dies without heirs then to male heirs of son
ARCHIBALD.
    To son WHORTON, tract called "Philberts addition" whereon my
dwelling is and if he dies without heirs then to male heirs of
son JOHN.
    To wife ELIZABETH, stock, furniture; and at her death to sons
ARCHIBALD, JOHN and MARK and dau. ELIZABETH.
Wife ELIZABETH, extx.
Wit: Jo: H: Harrison, Thomas Hudson, Josaph Ratliff.   25. 418

BARKER, JOHN, Charles Co.   21 Aug 1746
                                           15 Jul 1748
    To wife ELINOR BARKER, 4 Negroes: James, John, Austin and
Jenny, 1/2 of household furniture, cattle and horses.
    To son JOHN BARKER, 2 Negroes, Jeoffry and Jockey, parcel of
land in Charles Co. near the Great Dams called ___blank___, 100 A.
    To son WILLIAM BARKER, land on which I live, 4 Negroes:
Fortune, Carpenture, Robin and Joe, but to allow my sister
CATHERINE WILLSTEAD have Negro Robin during her lifetime. That
he bind Joe at age 15 to learn trade of a joyner or bricklayer,
at his discretion for term of 7 years.
    To neice CATHERINE BARKER, dau. of PETER BARKER, late of
Charles Co., 1 Negro called Benn and if she dies without issue
then Negro Benn to her sister ELIZABETH BARKER and if she dies
without issue then to nephew GEORGE BARKER son of aforesaid PETER
BARKER.
Wife ELIJOR BARKER and son JOHN BARKER, exs.
Wit: William Dent, Jno. Elgin, Richard Bent, Mary Bent.   25. 419

ADAMS, SAMUEL, Charles Co.   1748
                                           10 Sep 1748
    To wife CHARITY ADAMS, Negroes, Harry and Jack, cattle.
    To dau. TABITHA, tract called "Adames Retirement," 100 A.,
tract called "Adamses Outlett," 50 A., tract called "Adamses
Pasture," 34 1/2/ A., Negro Charles, furniture.
    To daus CELIA and ATHEAHLEAH, being twins, tract called
Batchelors Hope, 277 A., Negro woman named Seened(?), mullato
Rachell, furniture.
    To dau. CLOE, tract called "Leverpool Point," 32 1/2 A., tract
called "Crosmons Entrance" which I claim by escheat and 3 pounds
sterl. to clear the said land, Negro girl Violetto, cow and calf.
    To JOHN COURTS WADE, cow and calf, small gunn.
    Bro. BENJAMIN ADAMS to make my coffin.
    To servant man named Andrew Robertson 1 year of his indented
time.

172

Wit: James Crawley, Anne Crawley, John Elgin.   25. 421

WHARTON, HENRIETTA, Charles Co.   10 Feb 1747/8
                                             19 Sep 1748
   To bro. FRAS. WHARTON, 4 Negroes: Joss, Terry, Nedd and Henry;
if he should return from beyond seas without entering into holy
order but if otherwise then to my 4 sisters: MARY BRENT, JANE
PARNHAM, ELIZ: PILE and ANN SMITH.
   To sister ELEAR. WHARTON, Negro woman Sarah.
   To sister PARNHAM Negro girl Lettice.
   To bro. JESSE WHARTON, Negro woman Sue and her girl Monica to
bro. JESSE WHARTON's child his wife is now big with but if he
should die without heirs then to my nephew HENRY PILE.
   To neice POLLY BRENT, furniture.
   To Dr. PARNHAM, horse.
   To bro. PILE, horse.
   Dr. Fras. Parnham and Jos: Pile, exs.   25. 423

WEST, ROBERT, SR., Baltimore Co., planter.   9 Apr, 1747
                                              7 Sep, 1748
   To wife SARAH, during life, and estate to be divided among our
child..
   Wife SARAH, extx.
Wit: Enoch West, Wm. Cox.   25. 424

JEWKES, FRANCIS, Baltimore Co.   14 Sep, 1745
                                              7 Oct, 1748
   To dear bro. LANCELOT JEWKES.
   Dr. James Mather, ex.
Wit: Thos. Chase, Edward Degan, Eliz. Jones.   25. 425

RENSHAW, THOMAS, Baltimore Co.   13 Aug, 1748
                                             13 Oct, 1748
   To 1st born son JOHN RENSHAW, 250 A., being pt., of tract
called "Brothers' Discovery."
   To 2nd son ABRAHAM RENSHAW, 250 A. called "Brothers'
Discovery."
   To 3rd son THOMAS RENSHAW, 250 A.
   To 4th son JOSEPH RENSHAW,
   To dau. JANE RENSHAW,
   Wife JANE RENSHAW, extx.
Wit: Samuel Brice, James Brice, Sarah Ellwood.   25. 426

WALTHAM, CHARLTON, Kent Co.   15 Mar, 1746/7
                                              4 Jun, 1748
   To bro. JOHN WALTHAM, slaves.
   To bro. THOMAS WALTHAM, estate lands I live on and which I
have leased of WILLIAM HARRIS.
   To nephew JOHN WALTHAM, son of bro. JOHN,
   To my kinswoman RHODE HALL, furniture.
   To sister HANNAH, furnishings.
   To CHANDLER HALL, bro. to RHODE, cattle.
   Bro. JOHN, ex.
Wit: Jno. Gresham, Gustavus Hanson, John Battershell.
                                                  25. 428

GWENAPP, RICHARD, Kent Co.   29 Nov, 1743
       4 Jul, 1748
    To ELIZABETH BANTAM, estate, to be paid by Lewis Williams.
Lewis Williams, ex.
Wit: Elizabeth Nowland, James Nowland.
Signed JA Calder, deputy Comry. of Kent Co.   25. 429

SMITH, CHARLES, Kent Co.   13 Aug, 1748
       1 Sep, 1748
    To son JOHN SMITH, 50 A. on upper end of tract, taking in the
house where Thos. Cookk lives.
    To son JOSEPH SMITH, my dwelling plantation, and rest of my
land; and right of a pew in the new addition in St. Paul's
Church, Kent Co.
    But to prevent mistakes, my dau. MARY, is to have 50 A. of
land laid out of JOSEPH'S land, at the end of JOHN'S 50 A.
    To cousin JOHN SMITH, 3 sheep.
    Balance of estate to be divided equally bet. 2 sons and 2
daus.
    Only 6 pounds to be taken out of my dau. MARY'S, pt. and
divided bet. my 2 sons and my dau. RACHEL, to make a reduction
out of her pt. to the value of what she or her husband has had
already.
    Son JOSEPH, ex.
Wit: Jno. Smith, William Hagnes, Richard Meaders. 25. 430

HARRIS, WILLIAM, Kent Co.   17 Jun, 1748
       2 Sep, 1748
    My lands lying on both sides the head of Farloe Creek be sold
and money to pay my debts.
    To wife ANANA MARGARETTA HARRIS, several slaves.
    To son JAMES HARRIS, slaves.
    To dau. ARIANA HARRIS, slaves.
    To son JAMES, my land in Kent Co., when he lives to arrive at
age 21.
    To dau. ARIANA, land in Cecil Co., except my pt. of what lyes
near Little Elk, in partnership with Messrs. Brice and Cheston,
and my pt. of land called "Harris' Venture," adjoining to Mr.
Brice's pt.
Wit: Daniel Cheston, Matt Arris, J. Bordley.   25. 432

PERKINS, DAVID,   10 Aug, 1749
       18 Oct, 1748
    To wife REBEKAH, 1/3 pt. of my moveable estate, and the half
of my dwelling plantation, while she lives a widdow.
    To dau. SARAH and the hrs. of her body, my lands and
improvements, now lying in New Castle Co., Pennsylvania.
    To son DAVID PERKINS and hrs., remaining pt. of estate.
    Wife REBEKAH (Quaker), and son DAVID PERKINS (Quaker), exs.
       25. 434

GLANDON, RICHARD, Chester, Queen Anne's Co., planter.
       17 Jul, 1748
       22 Sep, 1748

To wife ANN GLANDON, my stock of horses, and etc.
Wit: Jno. Coursey, Barbara Duncan, Chris Wilkinson.
25. 435

CHAPMAN, SARAH, Kent Island, Queen Anne's Co. 25 Aug, 1748
22 Sep, 1748

To SUSANNAH SLINEY, gold ring.
To SUSANNAH MATON, gold ring.
To ANN SMYTH, personalty.
To MARY DAVIS, clothing.
To MARY ANN STEVENS, ELIZABETH HENRY, 800 pounds tobacco.
To SARAH SLINEY, clothing.
To dau. of MARY DUN, clothing.
Balance to JOHN SALLAWAY.
John Sallaway, ex.
Relationship of any of the above names was not given, except dau.
of Mary Dunn.)
Wit: Robert Basnett, Josiah Sallaway.   25. 436

NEALE, HENRY, of Philadelphia, Pennsylvania.   7 Jan, 1741/2
6 Oct, 1748
To friend, JAMES QUIN, of Queen Anne's Co., Maryland, my
estate, and if he dies before I do, then to friend THOMAS PULTON
(?) of Charles Co., Maryland.
James Quin, ex., but if he is dec'd., then appoint Thomas
Pulton.
Wit: Richard Molyneux, Jno. Tay Blake, John Rawon.
Probated in Queen Anne's Co., Maryland. The oath of witnesses
was taken in presence of Edward Neal, Heir at Law, to Testator.
He did not object to probate.   25. 437

LLOYD, THOMAS, St. James Parish, Anne Arundel Co., merchant and
storekeeper.   18 Sep, 1748
10 Oct, 1748
Desire to be buried by direction of friends, The Rev. John
Lang, minister of St. James Parish, and Mrs. Margaret Lang, his
wife.
My executors have delivered into the hand of my books and
accounts, which I left in the hands of Andrew Strachan.
My dau. MARY BURNEY, wife of Capt. Warren Burney of Wapping
Parish and Hermitage Street, London, in the Kingdom of Great
Brittain.
James Dick and Andrew Strachan, exs.
Wit: Wm. Strachan, Wm. Tillard, Thomas Brown.   25. 438 - 439

ASHLEY, WILLIAM, Anne Arundel Co.   29 Jul, 1747
19 Oct, 1748
To son JOHN ASHLEY, my horse; sd. son, other stock, which I
bought of Hannah Appelby; and other stock, while his sister,
SARAH ASHLEY, lives with him.
To dau. LURANA HUMPHRIES, 45 s.
To dau. ELIZABETH ASHLEY, 1 cow and 1 calf.
To grand-son, LAURINA ASHLEY, stock which I gave his father.
To dau. SARAH ASHLEY, balance of personal estate.
Son JOHN ASHLEY, ex.

Wit: Wm. Hammons, Robert Merchell, Mary Ann Hammond.
25. 440

TUCKER, THOMAS,   2 Jul, 1748
29 Oct, 1748
    To wife, the 3rd pt. of my personal estate.
    To SARAH PANE, 1 s.
    To SUSANNAH RAWLING, 1 s.
    To MARY BEARD, 1 s.
    To ELIZABETH WHITE, 1 s.
    To son RICHARD TUCKER, 10 pounds.
    To SEALY TUCKER, 1 s.
    To EASTER HILL, 3 pounds, to be paid at age 16.
    To son THOS. TUCKER, plantation called "Friendship," lying in
Anne Arundel Co., formerly belonging to my father RICHARD TUCKER,
dec'd.
    Joseph Cowman to see that my will is performed.
Wit: Nicholas St. Lawrence, Jos. Cowman, Jr. (Quaker), Ann
Cowman.   25. 441

HELLEN, RICHARD, JR., Calvert Co.   17 Feb, 1747/8
22 Oct, 1748
    To dau. MARY HELLEN, 1 slave.
    To wife ELIZABETH HELLEN, after my debts are paid, slaves.
Wife, extx.
Wit: John Hellen, Walter Hellen, Alexander Swan, Hugh Frazer.
25. 442

WASHINGTON, JOHN, Calvert Co.   22 Sep, 1748
22 Oct, 1748
    To CAPT. JAMES HUGHE, my estate.
Wit: Richard Johns, William Askew.   25. 433

BOWIN, ELIZABETH, Calvert Co., widow.   7 Dec, 1743
8 Nov, 1748
    To son JOHN WHINFEILD, 1 slave.
    To son JONAH WHINFIELD, slaves.
    To dau. SARAH ROBINSON, slaves.
    To dau. ANN NORTHLY, slaves.
    To dau. ELIZABETH BOWIN, slaves.
    To JONAH WHINFIELD, son of Jonah Whinfield,
    To dau. ELIZABETH, furniture.
    My grand-son NATHANIEL BOWIN NORTHY.
    Son John Whinfield, ex.
Wit: Henry Austin, George Johnson   25. 444

WHINFIELD, JOHN, Calvert Co., planter.   20 Oct, 1748
8 Nov, 1748
    To my mother ELIZABETH BOWEN, my title to land and houses, and
all their premises belonging to sd. land, during her life, and
after her decease, I give sd. land to cousin JOHN WHINFIELD, but
if he die without hrs., then I give cousin JONAH WINFIELD.
    Mother ELIZABETH BOWEN, extx.
Wit: Samuel Northey, Wm. Lyles, John Robinson.   25. 445

COAN, JOHN, SR., Baltimore Co.   28 Jan, 1744
                                         2 Nov, 1745

    To son JOHN COAN, JR., 1 s.
THOMAS COAN, 1 s.
    To son WILLIAM COAN, 1 s.
    To son EDWARD COAN, my dwelling plantation, 100 A.
    To son ELIAS COAN; my dau. SUSANNAH COAN, an equal share of my
estate, and what was left of her mother's wearing apparel and 1
s. to dau. ELIZABETH.
    To dau. MARTHA COAN, 1 s.
    Desire dau. SUSANNAH, left in care of son JOHN; likewise my
dau. SARAH'S child, that is now in possesion to be given to son
THOMAS, and his care, until of age.
    Son EDWARD COAN, sold ex.
Wit: Jno. Heavin, Thoms Homer, Grace Horner. (The names of
witnesses may be HORNER or HOMER.)   25. 446

PARISH, EDWARD, Anne Arundel Co., gentleman.   5 Oct, 1748
                                     22 Nov, 1748
    To wife RACHEL PARISH, my slaves.
    To son PETER, land called "Clearest Hope," 150 A.
    To son WM., tract called "Lockwood's Great Part," containing
49 A., and tract "Lockwood's Park."
    To son ROBERT, tract whereon I live, called "Hogg Harbour,"
100 A.
    Desire that remaining pt. of my estate, after my just debts
are paid, be equally divided amongst my child., excepting dau.
ELIZABETH KNIGHT, who I cutt off with only 1 s. and no more.
    Wife RACHEL, and THOMAS NORRIS, exs.
Wit: Tho. Lingan, Sam Foard, Thos. Hobbs.   25. 447 - 448

WHEELER, ROBERT, Prince George's Co., carpenter.   7 Oct, 1740
                                     23 Nov, 1748
    To son ROBERT WHEELER, 100 A., pt. of tract called "Farmers
Marsh"; also pt. of "Addition To Farmers Marsh," to be laid out,
convenient out of both of sd. tracts to the plantation where son
ROBERT, now lives; sd. plantation to be included in the sd. 100
A, but in case son ROBERT, shd. die before his wife ANN, then I
will the sd. ANN shall have privilege to live upon sd.
plantation during her widowhood, but if she remarries again, then
the whole right and benefit of sd. land be invested in my
grand-son ROBERT WHEELER, son of ROBERT, and in case of his
death, then to become the right of my grand-dau. SARAH WHEELER,
dau. of son ROBERT.
    To son DANIEL WHEELER, 5 s. money.
    To dau. MARY, cattle.
    To son THOMAS, my tools.
    To wife GRACE, the plantation whereon I now live, pt. of
"Farmers Marsh," and pt. of "The Addition To Farmers Marsh."
    To son SAMUEL WHEELER, my personal estate, after my debts and
funeral charges are paid, he to be under the care of his mother,
until age 21; that he may have 1 hdgs. of tobacco to ship to
England annually, until he is age 21.
    To son ROBERT, a tobacco house, 50 ft. long, which now stands

upon pt. of the land which I have left, be estseemed as the right
of my wife.
Wife GRACE, and son ROBERT WHEELER, exs.
Wit: Alexander Falconar, Jacob Ingleheart, Jeams Ellett, Rignall
Odell.   25. 449

MULLIKIN, THOMAS, Prince George's Co.   15 Jul, 1745
                                             23 Nov, 1746
    To wife ELIZABETH MULLIKIN, my dwelling plantatiion; at her
decease, to son WILLIAM MULLIKIN.
    To son THOMAS MULLIKIN, slaves.
    To dau. CHARITY MULLIKIN, my slaves.
    To wife, remaining pt. of my estate.
    To child.: WILLIAM, THOMAS, ELEANOR, ELIZABETH, CHARITY
MULLIKEN, RACHEL GOODMAN and MARY HARPER.
Wit: John Bowie, Jr., Henry and Ann Hutton.   25. 451

HAZARD, DAVID, Worcester Co.   7 Jul, 1747
                                              3 Nov, 1748
    To 2 sons CORD and JOSEPH HAZARD, land that I hold in Angola
Neck, Sussex Co., and the new road that leads from the
plantation, that formerly belonged to Mr. Prickets to St.
George's Chapell, to be their division, each holding their now
dwelling plantations.
    To son CORD HAZARD, 1 slave now in his possession; also 1/3
pt. of the boat.
    To son JOSEPH HAZARD, 1 slave.
    To son DAVID HAZARD, land whereon he now lives, called
"Agreement."
    To BENJAMIN DERIXON, land I hold on the northwest side of
Herring Branch, in that patent called "Agreement."
    To sons WM. and JOHN HAZARD, 2 tracts, where I now live, one
called "North Penthinton," the other "David's Lott."
    To dau. ANN WEST, 20 s.
    To grand-child., born of dau. HANNAH COLLINGS, 1 slave, called
"Inde."
    Child.: JOSEPH, DAVID, WM., JOHN, HANNAH and ELIZABETH.
    Wife ANN, and sons JOHN and WM., exs.
Wit: Hinson Wharton, Wm. Morris, Ed Rownd.   25. 452

BOWEN, JOHN, Baltimore Co.   15 Oct, 1748
                                             25 Nov, 1748
    To son CLARKSON BOWEN, 1 s. sterl.
    To dau. ELIANOR DEAL, 5 head of sheep.
    To grand-son JOHN GREEN, 100 A. called "Bells Camp."
    Grand-son John Green, ex.
Wit: Robert Clark, Thos. Dulany, John Lyon.   25. 455

CROXALL, JAMES, Baltimore Co.   14 Oct, 1748
                                             29 Nov, 1748
    My land in Prince George's Co., called "Brothers' Generosity,"
to my bros. RICHARD and CHARLES, and to my sister: MARY RUMNEY
and hrs., equally, sd. tract 487 A.
    To mother, MILES LOVE.
    To sister, MARY RUMNEY, my servant man.

To bro. RICHARD CROXALL.
To bro. RICHARD, my riding horse.
To bro.-in-law, NATHANIEL RUMNEY, cattle.
To sister, MARY RUMNEY, household furniture.
Bros. Richard and Charles, and sister Mary Rumney, equally,
exs.
Wit: Captain Darby Lux, Doctor George Buchanan, Wm. Lux.
25. 456

PRIMROSE, BRIGGET, Queen Anne's Co.   2 Oct, 1748
                                           8 Nov, 1748
     To son JOHN NAVIL (or NEVIL), 12 penneys sterl.
     To dau. MARGARET WIATT, 12 penneys sterl.
     To dau. RACHELL NEVIL, cattle.
     To son DAVID NAVIL, and dau. CATHARINE NAVIL,
Son David, and dau. Catharine, exs.
Wit: James Ponder, John Nevil, Jr., Richard Ponder, Jr.
                                           25. 457

PONDER, RICHARD, Queen Anne's Co.   25 Aug, 1748
                                          10 Nov, 1748
     To son JAMES PONDER, 35 A. called "Ponder's Chance."
     To son THOMAS PONDER, 100 A. called "Willson's Ouldfield," pt.
of a tract called "Smith Delite," beginning at a marked poplar.
     To dau. SARAH PONDER, furniture.
     To child.: 5 sons and 4 daus.: JOHN PONDER, JAMES PONDER,
WILLIAM PONDER, DANIEL PONDER, HAMER PONDER; ANNA PONDER, RACHEL
PONDER, SARAH PONDER, ANN PONDER, all the residue of my personal
estate, equally.
     Son William Ponder, ex., giving his bros. and sisters an equal
pt. with himself.
Wit: Thos. Mounsier, Wm. Worton, James Ponder.   25. 458 - 459

BLAKE, JOHN SAYER, Queen Anne's Co., gentleman.   5 Oct, 1748
                                                   24 Nov, 1748
     To sons JOHN, CHARLES, and the child unborn, 1 tract of land
called "Russendal," and 1 tract adjoining called "Coursey's
Neck," which when intailed on me by my father CHARLES BLAKE.
     To exs., my land in Talbot Co., generally known by name of
"Grosses"; sd. land to be sold, 1/3 of my estate to wife;
remaining 2/3 to my 5 child. and unborn child.
     Wife, bro. Philemon Charles Blake, and bro.-in-law Philip
Darnal, exs.
Wit: Edward Knott, R. Porter, James Tilghman.   25. 460

LEWIS, THOMAS, Dorchester Co.   1 Oct, 1747
                                           6 Sep, 1748
     To son WILLIAM LEWIS, 50 A. called "Chance," on Taylor Island
in a neck, called "Widow's Neck."
     To son WILLIAM, my gun.
     To son THOMAS LEWIS, 58 A. called "Sharply's Pound."
     To son ELISA LEWIS,
     To wife MARY LEWIS, my personal estate, during her widowhood.
Wit: John Robson, Richard Tubman, Joseph Shinton.   25. 461

WRIGHT, ROGER, Dorchester Co.   17 Jun, 1748
                 26 Sep, 1748
 To dau. ANN PAIN, 10 s.
 To dau. BETTY, 20 s.
 Balance to be divided bet. the rest of my child.
 Wife, extx.
Wit: Elizabeth Bartleton, Thos. Hicks.   25. 462

FISHER, FLOWER, Dorchester Co.   22 Oct, 1748
                 21 Nov, 1748
 To sister MARY FISHER, 100 A. called "Cob Head Manner" in sd.
county, to be laid out adjoining the lands which I sold to
Richard Harrington, Jr.; give sd. sister MARY, 1 horse.
 To bro. WILLLIAM FISHER, my seal, estate.
 Wm. Fisher, ex.
Wit: Redmond Fallin, James Cook, William Mounticue, John Cook.
Witnesses were taken in the presence of Thomas Fisher, heir at
law.

SMITH, WALTER, St. Leonard's Creek, Calvert Co. 1 Sep, 1748
                 18 Oct, 1748
 WALTER SMITH, being in great weakness, but of sound mind,
gives to his wife ALETHEA SMITH, use of his dwelling house and
plantation.
 To son RICHARD SMITH, and grand-son WALTER SMITH, son of
WALTER SMITH, dec'd., all the several tracts of land contained in
my dwelling plantation, known by names of "Stones Land,"
"Taylor's Lands," and "Buttmores Branch," to be equally divided
bet. them; sd. RICHARD SMITH and WALTER SMITH, when WALTER arrive
to the age of 21.
 To sons JOHN and NATHANIEL SMITH, the mill, being pt. of
"Blinkhorn," pt. of "Woolfs Quarter" and "Smith's Hogpen,"
equally, (by son RICHARD SMITH), JOHN SMITH having his first
choice.
 To son CHARLES SMITH, the island lately called "Mumford's
Island," but now known by name of "Smith's Island."
 Child.: RICHARD, JOHN, NATHANIEL, CHARLES, ALETHEA PARKER, and
grand-son WALTER SMITH, son of WALTER SMITH, dec'd.
 Son RICHARD, ex.
Wit: Wm. Blackburn, Young Parran, Thomas Hellen, Oct. 18, 1748,
Calvert Co., Gabriel Parker, Deputy Comry. Memorandum that the
widow MRS. ALETHEA SMITH, renounces the will and takes the third
of the estate.   25. 455

ALLEIN, BENJAMIN, Anne Arundel Co.   9 Nov, 1748
                20 Dec, 1748
 To dau. ANN ALLINGHAM, 10 pounds money.
 To son WILLIAM ALLEIN, slave.
 To son PRINDOWELL ALLEIN, slaves.
 To sons THOMAS, JOSEPH and PRINDOWELL ALLEIN, 20 pounds money.
 To sons JOHN ZACHARIAH and BENJAMIN ALLEIN, my clothing.
 To son JAMES ALLEIN, 10 pounds current money.
 To dau. ANN ALLINGHAM,
 7 sons mentioned: JAMES, JOHN ZACHR., BENJ., THOMAS, JOSEPH,
PRINDOWELL and WILLIAM.

Wife extx., but if she dies before admin. of my estate, my son-in-law CAPT. PHILIP ALLINGHAM, be my ex., and that he put all my estate up, unless all such as I have given away, to be sold, and the money put out at interest for the benefit of my child., as they arrive of age.
Wit: James Low, Wm. Lillard.
The widow, MRS. MARY ALLEN, declared that she was content with provisions made by the will of her late husband, BENJAMIN ALLEN, 12-21-1748.   25. 466

READ, JOHN, Somerset Co.   17 Mar, 1745/6
                                                28 Nov, 1748

     To son JOHN READ, 1 s. sterl.
     To son ZACHARIAH READ, my land in Dorchester Co. called "Pokety" 50 A., and 35 A. which I took up called "Chance."
     To son OBEDIAM READ, slaves.
     To son HEZEKIAH READ, the dwelling plantation I live on and remainder pt. of that tract I bought of Charles White, and 1 s. sterl.
     To son JAMES READ, 1 slave, called "Will."
     To dau. TABITHA BOUNDS, 1 slave.
     To dau. MARY WILLIN, 1 slave.
     To dau. HANNAH HUGGINS, 1 slave.
     To wife, MARY READ, my moveable estate within doors, and without, slaves, and all at her decease to my 5 child.:
ZACHARIAH, OBEDIAH, JAMES, TABITHA and MARY.
     Son Obadiah READ, ex.
Signed: John Read, Sr.
Wit: Jacob Mezick, Covington Mezick, Joseph Dashiell. Mary Read, widow of JOHN READ, made her election, Nov. 28, 1748.
                                                25. 468

CORBY, EDWARD, Somerset Co.   10 Nov, 1748
                                                26 Nov, 1748
     To wife SARAH ANN CORBY, my dwelling plantation of 100 A., called "Corby."
     To young. bro. MATHEW, if he ever shd. arrive in this country.

Wit: Nicholas Evans Collier, Covington Mezick, Daniel Cordary.
                                                25. 469

WILLIN, EDWARD, Somerset Co.   20 Nov, 1748
                                                29 Nov, 1748
     To wife HANNAH WILLIAMS, my lands whereon I now live.
     To eld. son JOHN WILLIN, an equal pt. of my moveable estate, with the rest of my child.
     To son EVANS WILLIN, after his mother's decease or marriage, the 1/2 of my land called "Mount Hope," to be delivered to him, at the age of 21, but if no issue to fall, to son JOHN WILLIN.
     To son CHARLES WILLIN, after his mother's decease, the other 1/2 of my land called "Twin Stile," to be delivered to him, at age 21.
     To the next eld. bro. that has not inherited any pt. thereof, and so in like manner, to the young. bro., and if all my child. die without issue, to fall to my bro. JOHN WILLIN.

My child. have an equal pt. of my personal estate to be
delivered to them at age 21.
My dau. left her gold ring to bro. JAMES, when she died, and
my wife's ring she desires may be given to her son CHARLES.
Bro. John Willin, ex.
Wit: Jesse McCabe, Mary McCabe, Hannah Willen.   25. 470 - 471

GIVEN, GEORGE, Somerset Co.   15 Oct, 1748
                                                     29 Nov, 1748
      To bro. DAY GIVAN, 500 A., with my dwelling plantation; 1
slave.
      Remainder of my land to be sold, and divided bet. my bro. and
sisters.
      To sister, MARY ACWORTH, 1 slave.
      To sister, MARION BELL, 1 slave.
      To sister, CATRIEN SCOFELL, 1 molatto slave.
      To cousin THOMAS GIVEN SCOFFEL, pair of silver shoe buckles.
      Bro. DAY GIVEN, and ADAM BELL, exs.
Wit: Jno. Givan, William Alexander, Robert Twilley.
                                                         25. 472

READ, JOHN, JR., Somerset Co.   29 Nov, 1748
                                                     9 Dec, 1748
      To son JACOB READ, the plantation on which is the manor
plantation, and my desk, money; mentions his wife and children.
      To wife MARTHA READ, 1 slave.
      To dau. MARGARET READ, 1 slave.
      To dau. MARTHA READ, slaves.
Wit: Wm. Given, Patrick Quaturmus, James Read.
On the back of sd. will: 11-29-1748, then came before me the
subscriber MARTHA READ, and made her election to the within will.
                                                         25. 473

GIVEN, ROBERT, Somerset Co.   12 Oct, 1748
                                                     9 Dec, 1748
      To dau. ELIZABETH GIVEN, 1 slave.
      To son WILLIAM GIVEN, and dau. MARY GIVEN, 1 slave, called
"Tiner" and 3 children slaves.
      To son WILLIAM GIVEN, and dau. MARY GIVEN, slaves.
      To son WM. GIVEN, I give a desk.
      To wife JEAN GIVEN, 1 slave.
      To son WM., and dau. MARY, 1 slave.
      To 2 bros. GEORGE and DAY GIVEN, my clothing.
      The balance of estate to wife and 3 child.
12-9-1748. Before Nehemiah King, Deputy Comry. of Somerset Co.
was exhibited, by JEAN GIVEN, widow and relict of ROBERT GIVEN,
late of sd. county. Noncupative will of her sd. late husband,
mentioned ROBERT GIVEN, in the time of last sickness (at the
house of John Read, Jr., where he was accidently taken sick the
day after he left his own house) was heard the sd. ROBERT GIVEN,
make his noncupative will agreeable to what is contained in the
within writing. The sd. ROBERT GIVEN departed this life on
10-12-1748.
                                                     25. 474

182

LLOYD, ELIZABETH, Baltimore Co., widow   19 Nov, 1748
                                            7 Dec, 1748
    To DR. JOSIAS MIDDLEMORE, 1 slave, and at his decease, to his
son FRANCIS MIDDLEMORE.
    To THOMAS DURBIN, 60 A. on Bush River, adjoining plantation
belonging to Mathew Beck and Joseph Smith, on south side of sd.
river.
    To MARY ANDREW, wife of William Andrew,
    Desires personalty sold.
    Mentions money on interest until BILLY DURE ANDREW, dau. of
William Andrew is of age 16.
    To nephew WILLIAM ANDREW, plantation whereon I live, and
desire that now wife of WM. ANDREW, shall have any pt. of land or
personal estate.
Wit: Robert Makalwain, Samuel Smith, Rebecka Polson (or Paulson).
                                            25. 475

SMITH, RICHARD, Calvert Co.   21 Sep, 1748
                                            22 Oct, 1748
    As there is a trust left in me by the last will of my father,
lately dec'd., and my bro. WALTER not, regard to the care of my
bro. WALTER'S children.
    It is my will that whatsoever trust I have been with, shd. be
transferred and left to my bro. JOHN, so far as is left to me in
both the above-mentioned wills.
    To bro. JOHN SMITH, personal, estate and mourning ring sent me
by uncle BENNETT, after the death of his wife, who was my aunt.
    To bro. NATHANIEL SMITH, my land left me by my father on the
following terms: that he shall give up these that were left him
by our father, to my bro. CHARLES SMITH, if he complies with
these terms,
    Mentions land left him by his bro. CHARLES.
    To bro. NATHANIEL SMITH, personalty; my new wigg, which I
bought of Capt. Alding.
    Mentions uncle RICHARD SMITH, and sister ALTHEA PARKER; my
bro. WALTER'S son, WALTER SMITH.
    To my mother, my certain slaves, just left by my grandfather,
MR. NATHANIEL DARE.
    Equally divide and share my personal estate among my 3 bros.:
JOHN, NATHANIEL and CHARLES.
    Bro. ALTHEA SMITH, ex., also to succeed to my right of
administration in my father's estate.
Wit: Iola Milton, James Somervell, Elizabeth Bridgett.
                                            25. 477

HUGHS, WILLIAM, Baltimore Co., tavern keeper.   12 Mar, 1743
                                                3 Jan, 1748
    To dau.-in-law, HANNAH BANKSON, personalty, which she may have
at decease of wife.
    To wife HANNAH HUGHES,
Wit: Richard Croxall, Za. Mackubin (Zach Mackubbin), Alexr. Reid.
                                            25. 478

FORD, THOMAS, SR., Baltimore Co.   18 Nov, 1748
                                            4 Jan, 1748

To son STEAPHED FORD, some slaves, and 101 A.
To son MORDICA FORD, slaves.
To dau. MARCY BARNEY, slaves.
To her dau. MARCY BARNEY, slaves.
To son JOHN FORD, slaves.
Son THOMAS FORD, 100 A.
Son Thomas Ford, ex.
Wit: D. B. Partridge, John Tipton, Sr., Ralph Flowers.
Then came D. Bucklar Patridge, John Tipton, Sr., and Ralph
Flowers who state they saw Testator sign his will.   25. 480

COLE, JAMES, Charles Co.   27 Sep 1748
                                             2 Nov 1748
     To friend Elizabeth Love all money in Mary Love's hands.
To friend James Void(?), riding horse and mare, wearing
apparel.
     To friend Jese Love, mare and fold in possesssion of James
Talor, 300 pounds of tobacco.
To Edward Holt.
William Love, ex.
Wit: Marthy Baskket, Margit Scoffill.   25. 481

KENAM, JAMES, Charles Co.   16 Jul 1748
                                            17 Nov 1748
     To son and dau, ELAXANDER and ELIZABETH, all estate, except
legacies:
Son ELAXANDER to remain with wife until 18 yrs of age.
To Edward Ginkins, heifer.
To Mary Ginkins, heifer.
Mentions wife, unnamed.
Wit: Jno. Simpson, Agnes Smith, Ann Beck.   25. 482

ELGIN, George, Charles Co.   22 Sep 1748
                                            15 Dec 1748
     To son JOHN ELGIN, 125 A., part of tract called "Batchellors
Agreement."
     To son WILLIAM ELGIN remaining pt. above tract and another
tract called "Batchellors Rest," 100 A., after death of wife
ELIZABETH ELGIN. That if William dies without heirs then to son
JAMES and to son FRANCIS if James is without heirs.
To WILLIAM, a slave.
To dau. ELIZABETH WINTER, negro girl named Lucy.
To son JAMES, Negro named Bendo.
Wife ELIZABETH and son JOHN, exs.
Wit: William Dent, Richard Price, Jas. Ferguson. 25. 483

ASHFEALD, JOHN, Charles Co, waterman.   4 Dec 1745
                                            29 Dec 1748
     To wife ELIZABETH, extx., all my estate.
Wit: John Stromat, Anne Stromat.   25. 485

MATHEWS, ELIZABETH, Baltimore Co.   27 Nov, 1748
                                            14 Jan, 1748
     My clothing to be divided bet. 2 daus. EMILIA and ANN.
To dau. ANN, slaves.

To dau. EMILIA, slaves.
Son-in-law John Mathews, ex.
Wit: Patrick Brannan, Jeremiah Cook, Edward Hanson.
25. 485

KNIGHT, SARAH, Baltimore Co.　　　　　4 Aug, 1748
　　　　　　　　　　　　　　　　　　20 Jan, 1748
　　To son JOSEPH MARRAY, 5 s.
　　To son THOMAS MORRAY, personalty.
　　To dau. SARAH MORRAY, personalty.
　　To grand-dau. ELIZABETH MORRAY, dau. of THOMAS MORRAY,
Wit: Edward Stevenson, Joshua Cromwell, John Stevenson.
25. 486

MAC COMAS, WILLIAM, Baltimore Co.　　　1 Sep, 1747
　　　　　　　　　　　　　　　　　　30 Jan, 1748
　　To son DANIEL MAC COMAS, 50 A., where he now lives.
　　To son SOLOMON, 50 A., "Gresham Colledge," adjoining his bro.
DANIEL'S 50 A.
　　To son MOSES, 50 A. out of sd. tract.
　　To son AARON, remainder of sd. tract.
　　To sons WM. and JOHN, my dwelling plantation, pt. of tract
"Littleton."
　　To dau. ELIZABETH TREDWAY, 1 slave, named "Phillis."
　　To dau. HANNAH AMOS, 1 slave.
　　To dau. ELIZABETH MILES, 1 slave.
　　Wife HANNAH MAC COMAS.
Wit: Capt. Wm. Bradford, John Norris, son of Benjamin and Susanna
Norris.　　　　　　　　　　　　　　　　25. 488

DONAHAUE, ROGER.　　　　　　　　　25 Dec, 1740
　　　　　　　　　　　　　　　　　　31 Jan, 1748
　　To son-in-law JAMES THOMPSON, my stock.
　　To HUGH BRYARLY, 100 A., according to Daniel Preston, laid
out.
　　To ANDREW THOMPSON, 150 A.
　　To SIMON DINEY, 130 A.
　　Give son GILBERT DONEHUE, that he shall pay my son DANIEL, 10
pounds when DANIEL DONEHUE is of age.
　　Samuel Gilbert, and ELIZABETH DONAHUE, wife, exs.
Wit: Robert Bryarly, Margaret and Rebeck Bryarly. (To which was
annexed, Baltimore Co.)　　　　　　　　25. 490

SMITH, WALTER, JR., Calvert Co.　　　28 Aug, 1748
　　　　　　　　　　　　　　　　　　22 Oct, 1748
　　To wife, my personal estate.
　　Mentions unborn child.
　　Bro. RICHARD SMITH, to have management of sale of estate.
　　Son WALTER, to be brought up and educated in the Church of
England.
　　Wife, extx., only that my bro. may be employed to act in sale.
Wit: Jannett Kentt, John Tucker; 10-22-1748, came Dr. John
Hamilton and John Tucker, 2 of the witnesses, and sd. they saw
Testator, WALTER SMITH, JR., sign his will　　25. 491

185

HANCE, BENJAMIN, JR., Calvert Co.   23 Jun, 1748
                                           10 Dec, 1748
    Tract of Taney's Reserve, 312 A. and tract called "Tayney's
Addition," of 132 A., to be sold by my bro. JOSEPH HANCE, and my
bro.-in-law BENJAMIN JOHNS, or either of them, and the money
applied to my debts, giving sd. Joseph Hance and Benjamin Johns
power to sell and convey sd. 2 tracts.
    To sons BENJAMIN and KENSEY HANCE, residue of remaining pt. of
land.
    To dau. MARY HANCE, slaves.
    My 3 child. mentioned above, to share equally.
    Bro. Joseph Hance, and bro.-in-law, Benjamin Johns, exs.
Wit: Samuel Johns, Jr., Mary Johns, John Scot.   25. 492

GARDNER, JOHN, Calvert Co.   14 Nov, 1748
                                           17, Dec, 1748
    To son JAMES GARDNER, and REBECCAH SPELLMAN and SARAH AVISS,
and son WILLIAM GARDNER, for estate is fully settled.
    To son WILLLIAM GARDNER, my land where on I live called
"Johnson's Lot," and 1 other tract called "Haphazard," containing
25 A., being pt. of tract formerly held and purchased of one
James Dawkins Janer.
    Son WILLIAM GARDNER, ex.
Wit: Richard Everett, Henry Cullingbur, James Kirshan.
                                                        25. 493

DARE, MARY, Calvert Co.   7 Jun, 1748
                                           17 Dec, 1748
    To son GIDEON DARE, 1 slave.
    To dau. ALTHEA SMITH, 10 s.
    To dau. KEZIE BROME, 5 s.
    Mr. Charles Clagett's child., who were born of my dau.
DIANNAH, 5 s.
    Son CLEVERLY DARE, and hrs.
    Son Cleverly, ex.
Wit: Isaac Rawlings, John Rigby, Ellis Dixon.   25. 494

JOHNS, RICHARD, Calvert Co.   24 Nov, 1748
                                           24 Dec, 1748
    To wife MARGARET JOHNS, land and plantation where I live,
tract called "Jannott (or Jannett)." At decease of wife, sd.
land to be sold and given my kinsman, BENJAMIN JONES, and my
friend JAMES HEIGHE, or either two of them to execute deed.
    Wife MARGARET JOHNS, 1/3 of my personal estate.
    My 5 sons: ABRAHAM, THOMAS, JOSEPH, AQUILLA and JESSEY, when
        age 16, to be sent to Philadelphia, and there by my kinsman
BENJAMIN JONES, bound apprentice to some business.
    To my 9 child: (sons listed above); ELIZA, MARGARET, JANE and
PRISCILLA to be equally divided among them.
    Wife MARGARET JANE, extx.
Wit: Richard Jones of Angelica, Nathaniel Dare, Betty Hughe (or
Heighe).   25. 495

BLACKBURN, WILLIAM, SR., Calvert Co.   23 Aug, 1740
                                           26 Jan, 1748

To son WILLIAM BLACKBURN, 2/3 of my estate.
To son READ BLACKBURN, my wife 2/3 of my estate to be divided
among my 5 sons: WILLIAM, JAMES, JEREMIAH, BENJAMIN and READ.
Dau. JANE.
Sons Edward and William Blackburn, exs.
Wit: Wm. Holloway, John Maney (or Manery), Gideon Turner. Son
Edward Blackburn, released claim of all right, title or demand,
which I have as ex. to estate of my father WILLIAM BLACKBURN;
1-26-1748.   25. 496

RAWLINGS, DANIEL, Calvert Co.   7 Nov, 1748
                                                28 Jan, 1748
     To son DANIEL RAWLINGS, land where on I live on the east side
of St. Leonard's Creek, or 275 A., and 100 A. tract of land
called "Rawlings' Choice," which my father by his last will gave
me, and lies on Eltonhead Mannor.
     To son JOHN RAWLINGS, tract of land called "Rawlings' Choice,"
and tract called "Compton" on east side of Patuxant River, near
Point Patience, and tract adjoining called "Rawlings' Purchase,"
of land I lately bought of my bro. ISAAC RAWLINGS.
     Wife MARGARET RAWLINGS is mentioned, and also unborn child.
     To son DANIEL, tract my father gave me.
     To son JOHN, land I bought of my bro. ISAAC, 300 A.
     To dau. NANCY, slaves.
     To dau. REBECCA, slaves.
     Wife Margaret Rawlings and dau. Nancy, extxs.
Wit: Ellis Slater, Ann Bates, Daniel Smith, 1-28-1748.   25. 498

HOLLONSHEAD, FRANCIS, of The Clifts, Calvert Co.   30 Dec, 1748
                                                    2 Feb, 1748/9
     Grand-son WILLIAM HOLLONSHEAD, son of JOHN.
     To son THOMAS, lands called "Freshold," 200 A.
     To grand-son FRANCIS COBRITH, son of JOHN, 5 s.
     To grand-son MICHAEL ASKEW, son of BENJAMIN ASKEW, 5 s.
     Wife JESSAA, extx.
Wife, Isabella, her thirds, balance equally bet. Thomas
Hollonshead, Mary, wife of John Friwer (?), Margaret and Sarah
Hollonshead.
Wit: Job Hunt, John Stallings, James Mules (probably meant
Miles).   25. 500

BRATEN (or BRATTON), JAMES, Worcester Co.   26 Oct, 1748
                                                  10 Dec, 1748
     To son JOHN BRATEN and JAMES BRATEN, plantation I now live on,
of 200 A. on south side of my son.
     To son JOHN, 200 A. on the northeast side of sd. plantation,
surveyed by David Peak, deputy to David Wilson, equally bet.
them; James having his pt. adjoining to him; each pay their equal
pt.
     Wife MARY BRATEN, personal estate.
     Wife MARY, extx.
Wit: John Teague, John Bratten, William Bratten.   25. 501

BRATTEN WM., Worcester Co.   29 Oct, 1748
                                18 Dec, 1748
   To son WILLSON BRATTEN, land "Broughton's Chance."
   To son WILLIAM, tract called "White Oak Swamp" and
"Convenience."
   Balance of estate to 7 young. child.: WILSON, JOHN, WILLIAM,
ABERILLIA, LIDDIA, MARY and BETTY BRATTEN.
   Wm. Bratten, ex.
Wit: George Smith, Daniel Wells and Adam Spence, who state they
saw Testator (JAMES BRATTON) sign his will. (While the will is
signed by WM. BRATTON, the first paragraph of sd. will begins
with the name "Wm. Bratton," so there is an error in one of the
names.)   25. 502

BELL, ADAM, (Chirergion), Worcester Co.   -----------
                                    6 Jan, 1748
   ADAM BELL, dec'd., made his will in the presence of Adam
Spence and Mary Bratten (which sd. Mary says that WILLIAM
BRATTEN, who is since deceased, was also at first present, when
the Testator repeated the following words:
   That WALTER SMITH shd. have his gold buttons, silver stock
buckles.
   JOHN SCHOOFIELD, JAMES BRATTEN, and JOHN BRATTEN shd. have his
clothing.
   To wife, his land, and at her decease, to his bros. or their
children.
   At decease of wife, her sisters shd. have his slaves.
                           25. 503

LANG, JOHN, St. James Parish, Anne Arundel Co.   3 Jul, 1748
                                21 Feb, 1748
   I have been, for some years, bestowing upon my dau. HENRIETTA
HARRISON, a considerable share of my estate, since her
intermarriage with James Harrison, and my will is that she is
excluded from my share of her pt. of my estate; after decease,
she then to have 10 s.
   Wife MARGARET LANG, my estate.
   Wife, extx.
Wit: William Tillard, James Anderson, John Purnell. 25. 504

CUCKOE (or CUCKO), Talbot Co.   13 Oct, 1748
                                25 Nov, 1748
   To wife CATTRON COCKOE, personal estate.
Wit: Michael Melowny, George Manroe, Abner Turner. 25. 505

BARTLETT, JOHN, Talbot Co., smith.   20 Mar, 1748
                                2 Dec, 1748
   To son JOSEPH BARTLET, my dwelling plantation, tract being pt.
of "Ratliff Manner."
   My now wife, MARY, except that tract where my son JOSEPH, is
now settled.
   To dau. HANNAH BARTLETT, and to grand-son JOHN GEORGE, tract
called "Swan Brook," in Queen Anne's Co., each to have one-half.
   To dau. HANNAH BARTLET, 3 slaves.
   To grand-son JOHN GEORGE, 1 slave.

To son JOSEPH BARTLET, my copper and utensils, and all my smith tools.

To dau. HANNAH, and grand-son JOHN GEORGE, dwelling plantation.

Son JOSEPH BARTLET, and grand-son JOHN GEORGE, exs.

Wit: Abednego Bedfield, Geo. Rull, John Porter.   25. 506

DAVIS, MARY, Talbot Co.   16 Dec, 1748
                                                  8 May, 1750
    To widow of my son THOMAS, land occupied by John Robson, and if she shd. die without issue, to my dau. REBECCA, and hrs.

    To dau. REBECCA, my other 2 tenements that where John Sutten, Jr. now lives, and that where Daniel McGinny now lives, but if dau. REBECCA, shd. die, that she then to my son THOMAS and hrs.; and if both son THOMAS and dau. REBECCA, shd. die without issue, then I give my lands to son WILLIAM, and his hrs., and for want of such hrs., I give to MICHAEL EDWARDS, son of my sister ELIZABETH EDWARDS, to him forever.

    Desire my 3 child. have 1 slave each, which is due from their father's estate, and remainder of my slaves, equally divided.

    Leave dau. REBECCA, to my sister, SARAH DAWSON, to be in care of my sister SARAH, for supporting my sd. dau.

    Leave the care of my 2 sons to Perry Benson; also their estate to bring them up and support them during their none age.

    To dau. REBECCA, my clothing.

    To sister, ELIZABETH EDWARDS, 1500 pounds tobacco.

    Father-in-law Perry Benson, and my son THOMAS, exs.

Wit: Edwards Knott, Elizabeth Edwards, Edith Cook.

Talbot Co., I certify that I am under age 17, 12-16-1748; Thomas Sherwood, one of the exs.

12-15-1748, Talbot Co.: Elizabeth Edwards and Edith Mason, the now wife of Thomas Mason, who was lately Edith Cook, 2 of the witnesses of sd. will, who state they saw MARY DAVIS sign her will.

12-16-1748: Dr. Edward Knott, witness, who also states he saw her sign her will.   25. 508

SHARP, WILLIAM, Talbot Co., surgeon.   13 Apr, 1748
                                                21 Dec, 1748
    To wife ANN SHARP, my lands on the south side of Island Creek, called "Rattle Snake Point," "Saxon's Neck," "Easons Lot," "Fancy Conjure," "Sharp's Addition" and the enclosure, until son WM. is of age 21; 250 A. of sd. land for son WILLIAM.

    At decease of wife, I give son PETER SHARP, sd. lands on the north side of the creek, "Morefields Adventure" and "Dines Point."

    To son HENRY SHARP, tract; in default of hrs., give sd. land to son WILLIAM.

    To dau. ANN SHARP, 1 slave.

    Mentions: my 5 child.: PETER, BIRKHEAD, WM., HENRY and ANN SHARP.

    Wife Ann Sharp, and son Peter Sharp, exs.

Wit: Francis Chaplin, Samuel Mulliken, Sarah Webb (Quaker).
                                                25. 510

HOULT, JOHH, Talbot Co., weaver.   18 Oct. 1748
                                                27 Jan, 1748
     To wife ELIZABETH HOULT, my dwelling plantation, pt. of tract
called "Broad Oak," during life, and at her decease, my desire is
that son PETER HOULT, shd. have my land, but if son PETER, die
without issue, then my dau. ELIZABETH HOULT, shd. have sd. land.
     Reference to 2 daus. MARY and SARAH HOULT.
     Wife ELIZABETH, extx.
Wit: John McCotter, John Fleming, Tristram Thomas.   25. 512

NICHOLS, HENRY, clerk the most unworthy minister of St. Michael's
Parish of Maryland.   Thanks to God for being born in the
Christian Church and other similar good words, here given.
     Desire to be buried in my Parish Church, near my late wife
ELIZABETH NICOLS.
     To eld. son HENRY NICHOLS, declares that as I have supported
him during his residence with Mr. Fern, he would never desire any
other portion.
     To son CHARLES, land called "Partnership" in Tuckaho, divided
into 2 pts., the easternmost pt. to CHARLES.
     To son JONATHAN NICOLS, the other pt.
     To son JAMES NICOLS, my plantation and land adjoining 300 A.
     To wife DOROTHY NICOLS, her dower in my plantation called
"Galloway Michlemire" and "Bryans Lot"; and at her decease, to
son WILLIAM.
     To WILLIAM, tract "Tred Haven Creek," which I bought of John
Hopkins, to him and hrs., which sd. land he is to occupy until
after my sister ELIZABETH NICOL'S decease.
     To sister, ELIZABETH NICOLS, use of my plantation on "Tred
Haven" afsd.
     Sons: JEREMIAH, CHARLES, JONATHAN, JAMES and WILLIAM NICOLS.
Wit: W. Goldsborough, Jr., Jane Goldsborough, Ralph Elston, Mary
Miller, 2-21-1748.   Date: 9-6-1747   25. 513 - 516

DASHIELL, GEORGE, Somerset Co.   9 May, 1748
                                                 14 Nov, 1748
     To son CLEMENT DASHIELL, my 2 slaves.
     To son LOUTHER, my slaves.
     To son ISAAC DASHIELL, land where on he lives, and of his bro.
LOUTHER, including the new quarters where Polly now lives.
     To son THOMAS, tract which my father gave me by deed,
12-24-1741, called "Mitchells Improvement" on the south side of
Great Monies Creek, where my father now lives, and if son THOMAS
dies without hrs., then to son BENJAMIN.
     To son JOSEPH, land called "River Landing," which I bought of
Wm. and John Ribble, 80 A., and land of William Gray called
"Green Hill Church," where sd. Gray now lives, called "Lott
Light" in Worcester Co., and tract called "Summer Pasture."
     To son BENJAMIN DASHIELL, land called "Contention" alineated
to him by law, and his wife JANE, "The Woods Pasture," and a
tract near John Christopher and Robert Mallones, all of which I
give to son BENJAMIN.
     To young. son GEORGE DASHIELL, the plantation where on I live,
and to his eld. son, but if he dies without hrs., to son
BENJAMIN, and if he dies without hrs., to son JOSEPH.

Wife ELIZABETH, dau. ELEANOR MARTIN, grand-dau. ANN DASHIELL, grand-dau. MARY, dau. of Clement Dashiell, grand-dau. JANE, dau. of Louther Dashiell.
Balance of estate to be divided bet. CLEMENT, LOUTHER, ISAAC DASHIELL, ELEANOR MARTIN, JOSEPH DASHIELL, BENJAMIN and GEORGE DASHIELL.
Wife Elizabeth, extx.
Wit: Alexander M. Cants, Stephen Hobbs, Thomas Collins.
25. 516

KELLET, ROBERT, Somerset Co.   13 Nov, 1748
25 Nov, 1748
To wife EUNICE (Unice) KELLET, my riding horse, and 1/2 pt. of my personal estate.
To son ROBERT KELLET, dau. ELIZABETH KELLET, 1 slave.
To ELIZABETH DASHIELL, my friend of Henry Lowes,
Wit: John North, Elizabth Dashiell, James Smith.
25. 520

ROBERTSON, JAMES, Rector of Coventry Parish, Somerset Co.
28 Jun, 1748
2 Jan, 1748/9
To son ALEXANDER, "Tract Arcum."
To son THOMAS, my land down the river of Monocon, at the old plantation.
To son JAMES, land where I now live.
Remainder to be divided bet. the above 3 sons and MARY ROBERTSON.
Wit: Thomas Williams, John Baird, Thomas Denwood.   25. 521

BEARD, LEWIS, Somerset Co.   8 Oct, 1748
18 Jan, 1748
To bro. JOHN, pt. of tract "Beard's Advantage," Somerset Co.
To wife RACHEL, if my child dies without hrs., my wife to have land; name of child is not mentioned.
Wit: Arch Ritchie, James Laramur, Jesse McCabe.   25. 522

GRAY, JOHN, Somerset Co.   25 Dec, 1748
26 Jan, 1748
To son ALLEN GRAY, 2 tracts where he now lives.
Son JAMES GRAY shall make over to sd. son ALLEN GRAY,within 3 months after my decease, as to rights to the plantation whereon he now lives; if he refuses to do so, then I give to son ALLEN GRAY, my dwelling plantation.
To dau. ERIN MC GRAIN, tract whereon now she lives.
Wife JEAN, my dwelling plantation.
To dau. JENNETT GRAY, 1/3 pt. of my personal estate.
To grand-son JOHN GRAY, son of ALLEN GRAY, my clothing.
To ROBERT KING, SR., DAVID WILSON, NEHEMIAH KING, HENRY WAGGONER (or WAGGEAR), EPHRIAM WILSON,
Child.: ALLIN and JAMES GRAY; dau. ELLIN MC GRAIN.
Wife extx.
Wit: John Anderson, John Givens, John McGlamery.   25. 523

RICHARDSON, WILLIAM, Somerset Co.   3 Jan, 1748
              28 Jan, 1748
 To young. son JOHN RICHARDSON, my dwelling plantation, being a
tract called "Norwick," lying on the south side of Quantico
Creek, and desire Wilson Rider to have full charge of which,
while JOHN RICHARDSON becomes age 18, to be divided bet. 2 sons
BENJAMIN and JOHN RICHARDSON.
Wit: Wm. Austin, Wilson Ryder.   25. 524

GILLISS, ANN (late ANN LACKIE), Somerset Co. 7 Feb, 1748
                7 Feb, 1748
 In relation to a marriage contract, wherein THOMAS GILLISS of
Somerset Co. contracted before marriage, that the sd. ANN LACKIE,
to let her dispose of 500 pounds with her then own estate to such
purpose as she, the sd. ANN LACKIE, shd. think fit. According to
agreement, she made appointment as follows:
 To my only son NICHOLAS EVANS, 350 pounds.
 My husband pay unto my son-in-law THOMAS JONES and SUSANNAH,
his wife, 1 slave; use of moiety of half of tract devised to me
by my former husband ALEX LACKEY, whereon the sd. Thomas Jones
now lives, and at their decease, to the hrs. of sd. SUSANNAH and
son NICHOLAS, equally, at the discretion of Col. George Dashiell
and husband THOMAS GILLISS.
Wit: George Dashiell, Jr., Patience Hust, Joseph Dashiell.
               25. 526

GOSLEE, THOMAS, Somerset Co.   2 Feb, 1748/9
             13 Feb, 1748
 Member of the Church of England.
 To son SAMUEL, the plantation I now live on, which I desire
Graves Beardman to take unto his care my 2 daus. FRANCES and
ELEANOR.
 Graves Beardman, ex.
Wit: Daniel Dulany and Joseph Venables. 25. 527

COTTMAN, JOSEPH, Somerset Co.   27 Jan, 1748
             14 Feb, 1748
 To son JOSEPH, son JOHN, wife HANNAH, my lands in
Pennsylvania, which I had with my wife.
 Child.: JOSIAH, ESTHER, BETTY and JOHN, and the children
unborn.
Wit: Thomas Gillispie, Benjamin Cottman, Soal (Saml.?) Brereton.
               25. 528

HARRIS, THOMAS, Baltimore Co.   12 Jan, 1740
             20 Feb, 1748
 Wife MARY ANN HARRIS, extx.
Wit: Thomas Sheredine, Wm. Johnson, Wm. Duke. 25. 529

JACKSON, ISAAC, Baltimore Co.   10 Jan, 1748
             25 Feb. 1748
 To wife MARY, tract "Icols Ridge."
 To bro. JACOB'S 3 daus. PGNES (or AGNES), FEBY and EMILY,
Wit: William Hill, Wm. White, Samuel White. 25. 530

WILLMOTT, JOHN, Baltimore Co.   18 Feb, 1748
                                                  1 Mar, 1748
     To son JOHN WILLMOTT, tract "Lunsfield City," which I bought
of William Worthington, and tract "Rachel's Prospect," originally
called "Robert Forrest," and land adjoining William Parrishes,
"Rawling Road."
     To son ROBERT, pt. of tract "Rachel's Prospect."
     To wife RACHEL, dau. CONSTANT, wife of Wm. Cromwell, dau.
DINAH TOWSON, wife of Wm. Towson, dau. RACHEL, dau. HANNAH MOORE,
wife of James Moore, Jr., slaves.
     To son RICHARD, ann JOANES, now living in my house, 1 slave.
     To grand-son JAMES FRANKLIN, 5 pounds money.
Wit: Wm. Parrish, Joseph Taylor, Thomas Norris, Richard
Chenwerth.   25. 531

CAGE, JOHN, Queen Anne's Co.   ------------
                                                 19 Dec, 1748
Deposition of Richard Keiran, Jr., Queen Anne's Co. and of Esther
Keiran,, were at the house of John Alley, where a certain JOHN
CAGE of sd. county, laboured, but was then on his death bed, and
heard him make statement giving to sd. JOHN ALLEY, his estate.
Wit: Wm. Tilghman, the deposition of Wm. Keiran and John Alley,
Jr., of sd. county, state the same as above.   25. 533

EAGLE, WM., Queen Anne's Co.   7 Jun, 1748
                                                20 Feb, 1748
     To son WILLIAM, 100 A. in Kent Co. upon the Delaware, being
pt. of tract called "Rawlings."
     To son SOLOMON, 100 A., pt. of same tract.
     To son JAMES, after decease of my wife MARY, tract called
"Lamberts Addition."
     To son HENRY, 2000 pounds tobacco, after decease of my mother.
Son-in-law THOMAS FISHER, son-in-law ALEXANDER CHALMER, son
JAMES, and dau. MARY, my personal estate.
     Son James, wife MARY, exs.
Wit: Wm. Banning, Vincent Price, James Payne.
                                                25. 534 - 535

ROCHESTER, FRANCIS, Queen Anne's Co.   7 May, 1748
                                                 2 Feb, 1748
     To wife SARAH, son JOHN ROCHESTER, my now dwelling plantation
called "Winchester," 200 A.
     To son HENRY, 1 tract of 70 A. called "Lowden Hazard."
     To dau. ANN COMIGGES, 50 pounds money.
     To dau. SARAH FINDLEY, 60 pounds money.
     3 sons: JOHN, FRANCIS, HENRY.
Wit: John McConchin, John Holt, James Massy, Jr., James Meanor.
                                                25. 536

KINNIMONT, JOHN, SR., Queen Anne's Co.   14 Sep, 1748
                                                 2 Feb, 1748
     To son AMBROSE KINNIMONT, son JOHN, my land in Talbot Co.
Wit: Morris Giddens, John Harding, John Cole.   25. 538

BIRKHEAD, SARAH, Calvert Co.   25 Jan, 1748/9

BIRKHEAD, SARAH, Calvert Co.   25 Jan, 1748/9
                                       25 Jan, 1748/9
    To son-in-law LITTLETON WATERS and dau. ELIZABETH, his wife,
my land near Hunting Creek called "Stokely" 113 A., then to fall
to my grand-dau. ELIZABETH WATERS.
    To son-in-law LITTLETON WATERS, my slaves and money I may have
in England, and my stock at Herring Bay.
    To son NEHEMIAH BERKHEAD, 1 slave.
    To son SAMUEL BIRKHEAD, my grand-dau., SARAH WATERS, my
clothing.
    To son JOHN BIRKHEAD, shillings.
Wit: Sarah Rhodes, Jo Wardrop, Charles Graham.   25, 539

HARRYMAN, JOHN, Baltimore Co.   4 Feb, 1748/9
                                        8 Mar, 1748
    Tract "Richard's Forrest" divided bet. 3 sons JOHN, CHARLES
and THOMAS.
    Mentions: my 7 child., JOHN, CHARLES, THOMAS, dau. PRUDENCE
MITCHELL.
Wit: Elizabeth Dew, Elizabeth Jones, Walter Dallas.   25. 540

HENDON, HANNAH, administratrix, and widow of JOSEPH HENDEN, late
of Baltimore Co.   29 Jan, 1748
                                        8 Mar, 1748
    To daus.: ELIZABETH, HANNAH; sons: WILLIAM, JOSIAS, JAMES,
ISHAM, 100 A.
Wit: Charles Baker, Darby Henly (Henley), Sarah Henley.
                                          25. 542

ROBERTON, SARAH, Baltimore Co.   17 Dec, 1748
                                       8 Mar, 1748
    Daus. JANE, MARY, CLEMENCY; grand-child MARY BOND.
Wit: Robert Carvill (written in body of the probate paragraph as
Robert Carlisle and Erlich Erickson, 2 witnesses).
                                          25. 542

SERJANT, JOHN, Baltimore Co., gentleman.   19 Jan, 1748
                                        9 Mar, 1748
    To son-in-law JOHN YOSTEN GORSUCH (spelled 2 different ways),
land I now live on called "Wells Angle."
    To wife ELIZABETH SERJANT, possession of land during life, and
if son-in-law dies without hrs., then to my 2 sons SAMUEL and
BENJAMIN, and if they have no hrs., to son-in-law AQUILLA
GOSWICK's hrs., and if no hrs., then to daus.-in-law: ANN YOSTEN
GOSWICK, MARY ANN SERJANT and ELIZABETH SERGANT.
Wit: Samuel Sellers, Samuel Bowen, Henry Yosten. 25. 544

SPICER, THOMAS, Baltimore Co.   - - - - - -
                                       9 Mar, 1748
    Wife REBECCA.
    To son JOHN, land "Spicers Stones Hills."
    My 8 child.: JOHN, AUSTIN, SARAH, TEMPERANCE, EDWARD,
VALENTINE, ELLINER and THOMAS.
    Wife and Jonathan Henson, exs.
Wit: George Buchanan.   25. 545

MARIARTE, NINIAN, Prince George's Co.   10 Dec, 1748
                                           3 Feb, 1748/9
To MR. OSBURN SPRIGG, 150 A. tract "Darnalls Grove," now
called "Charlesses Folley."
Wit: James Edmonston, Tho. Hilleary, Thos. Belt, Wm.Chittam.
                                              25. 546

NEWTON, JOSEPH, Prince George's Co.   20 Jan, 1748/9
                                          23 Feb, 1748/9
Dau. SARAH and hrs.
Child.: MARY ANN, ELIZABETH, NATHANIEL, REBECCA, RACHELL,
MARGARET and SUSANNAH.
Bro-in-law Thomas Hillery, and Nenian Magnider (Ninian
Maynadier), exs.   25. 546

SHAW, JOHN, Charles Co.   3 Dec 1748
                                          29 Jan 1748
To wife ELIZABETH SHAW, Negro man named Sam and all my visable
estate.
At her death or re-marriage, then to be equally divided among my
children: JOHN SHAW, PHILIP SHAW, WILLIAM SHAW, JOSEPH SHAW,
CHARLES SHAW and ELIZABETH SHAW.
Wife ELIZABETH extx.
Wit: Thomas Hatton, Mathew Brooks, John Elgin(?)   25. 547

GREEN, Joseph, Charles Co.   8 Jan 1748/9
                                           1 Feb 1748
To wife JANE GREEN, extx. land, pt. of tract called "Greens
Inheritance" and other estate.
Wit: Sam. Hanson, Thos. Howard, Bennett Green, Tho: Jameson.
                                              25. 548

ADAMS, LUKE, Charles Co., carpenter.   17 Aug 1748
                                          25 Feb 1748
To bro. JOHN, land which my father devised to me in his last
will, which by this will the land was to be equally divided
betwixt him and me.
To bro. THOMAS, coat.
To bro. GEORGE, mare.
Mother, ELIZABETH ADAMS, extx., residue of estate.
Wit: Jas. Greend. Wood, William Thomas, Joseph Barker.   25. 549

MATHEWS, THOMAS, Charles Co.   Jan 1747/8
                                            9 Mar 1748
To be buried on the plantation where I now live and on the
hill near where my shop now stands.
To son MAXIMILIAN MATHEWS, Negro called Cesar, Negro girl
called Winnie, tract in Mattawoman called "Argyle," 156 A.; and
if without issue then to my dau. MARY MATHEWS.
To son WILLIAM MATHEWS, Negro man called David and his wife
Barrannuma.
To son THOMAS MATHEWS, Negro man called Aleleda and Negro boy
called Harry.
To son JOHN MATHEWS, Negro boy called Ignatius and a Negro
girl called Doll, and tract called "White Haven Dock," 200 A.;

girl called Doll, and tract called "White Haven Dock," 200 A.;
and if he should died without heirs then to dau. MARY MATHEWS.
If both tracts fall into her hands then she is to take her choice
and her sister THEODORA to have the other tract.
    To dau. THEODORA, Negro girl called Taby(?) and woman called
Mana.
    To dau. MARY Negro boy called David(?), Negro girl called
Brisey.
    To wife Negro man Homeda, Negro women called Joaney and
Phillis, Negro girls Lucey and Nell, Negro boy called Roger.
    My son in law JOHN SHORT to have authority to bind my son JOHN
MATHEWS in apprentice to some handicraft, trade or business.
Wife MARY and son MAXIMILIAN, exs.
Wit: Matthew Stone, Sr., Mathew Stone, Barton Stone. 25. 550

BOND, PETER, Baltimore Co.   18 Dec, 1748
                                              14 Jan, 1748
    To bro. WM. BOND; bro-in-law WM. ANDREW,
Wit: Alexr. Corbell (or Corbelt), Robert Dutton, Margaret Randon.
                                                       25. 552

DUKE, CHRISTOPHER, Baltimore Co.   17 Jun, 1748
                                              25 Mar, 1749
    Child.: CHRISTOPHER, SARAH, MARY FEMILLER, and CHARLES DUKE.
Wit: Thomas Stansbury, John Lord, Edmund Stansbury.
                                                       25. 553

FORTT, SAMUEL, Baltimore Co.   8 Jan, 1748
                                               4 Apr, 1749
    To wife, certain slaves.
    To dau. ELIZABETH, sons SAMUEL and BENJAMIN, and the young.
child or child., the 4th choice of slaves; eld. son to have his
choice.
Wit: Luke Trotton, Elizabeth Trotton, George Brammell.
                                                       25. 554

MARSHALL, MARY, Baltimore Co., widow.   23 Dec, 1748
                                               8 Apr, 1749
    To grand-dau. SUSANNAH HALL, dau. of son-in-law John Hall, my
lots.
    Mentions: my son-in-law John Hall of Baltimore Co.
    To nephew GEO. DRESBURY, known as GEORGE GOLDSMITH DRESBURY,
to AQUILLA HALL, son of Aquilla Hall, dec'd., personalty.
    To MARTHA GARRETSON, wife of George Garretson,
    To SUSANNAH HALL, my grand-dau., afsd. and if she die without
issue, then to son-in-law AQUILLA HALL, GEORGE PRESBURY and
MARTHA GARRETSON, wife.
    John Hall, son-in-law, ex.
Wit: Joseph Baley, Williamn Craig, Elizabeth Cook, John Kemp.
                                                 25. 555 - 556

WALLER, William, Baltimore Co.   27 Jan, 1748
                                              18 Apr, 1749
    Wife ELIZABETH.
    Son JOHN.

196

Wit: Daniel Durbin, Mary Mahon, John Heavin.   25. 557

BUNTON, SAMUEL, Talbot Co.   1 Mar, 1747/8
                                                24 Mar, 1748
   To wife MARY BURTON, dau. MARY, bro. JOHN (or JOHN BOUNTON).
Wit: Henry Burgess, Wm. Burgess, Absolem Turner.
                                                25. 558

LINCH, HUGH, Talbot Co.   8 Feb, 1748/9
                                                8 Apr, 1749
   To TERRANCE CONERLY , my son HUGH, to take care of him and
bring him up in Roman Catholic Religion; if TERRANCE dies before
my son is age 21, then JAMES CORBRIN have him.
Wit: R. Rawlinson, John Sisck, Ames Harris.   25. 559

HANSBURY, EDMUND, Prince George's Co.   18 Feb, 1748
                                                29 Mar,1749
   To son-in-law, MICHAEL COVLISALL, title to land called
"Chance," where on I live and if anything remains, to son-in-law
MICHAELL COOTS.
   Michaell Coots, ex. (Name also appears Michael Coutes).
Wit: Thomas Dawson, George Dawson.   25. 560

NORTH, ROBERT, Baltimore Co.   5 Apr, 1749
                                                5 Apr, 1749
   To dau. ELIZABETH NORTH, 500 A., conveyed to him by
Christopher and Nathaniel Gist (Guist), Baltimore Co.
   To sd. ELIZABETH NORTH, land in Jones Town, No. 16.
   To dau. ELLEN NORTH, the pt. where Nathaniel Gist lived., and
lots Nos. 8 and 9, 25 pounds sterl. left by her grandmother,
ELLEN NORTH, in my hands.
   To son THOMAS NORTH, 2 tracts "Browns Chance" and "Chivey
Chace," conveyed by George Brown in Baltimore Co.
   Wife CATHARINE NORTH.
   To son THOMAS, land.
Wit: John Stevenson, Benjamin North and Richard Chase.
                                                25. 561

SCRIVENER, RICHARD, Queen Anne's Co.   30 Dec, 1748
                                                23 Feb, 1748
   Wife MARGARET; eld. son JOSEPH, son RICHARD, son JOHN.
Wit: Joseph Sweatnam, Wm. Coventon, Nathaniel Wright. 25. 463

ROE, SARAH, wife of EDWARD ROE, Queen Anne's Co.
                                                24 May, 1748
                                                23 Feb, 1748
   To son SAMUEL, tract called "Tully's Addition" 150 A., now in
possession of my husband.
Wit: John Hamilton, N. Wright.   25. 564

ROE, EDWARD, Queen Anne's Co.   7 Feb, 1748
                                                3 Mar, 1748
   To son JOSEPH, land called "Roes Lain," 22 A. and "Ned's
Beginning," and pt. of "Sarah's Fancy."
   To son SAMUEL ROE, to have land, but if sd. JOSEPH does not

return, then desire some SAMUEL to have sd. land.
To SAMUEL, tract that I bought of Richard Benett.
To son THOMAS ROE, tract "Okenthorp," which I bought of John
Miller of 226 A. and "Roe's Chance," 247 A., and "Sarah's Fancy,"
lying in Tully's Neck.
My son JAMES ROE, bequeath to Nathaniel Curtis.
To son JOHN ROE, 100 A. "Norbourgh."
To SARAH COVENTON, dau. of Henry Coventon, land I bought of
Peter Hendsley, tract "Rachel's Desire."
To HENRY COVENTON, and RACHEL his wife, and at their decease
to be divided bet. EDWARD and MARY COVENTON, the son and dau. of
Henry and Rachel.
To son JAMES, 1 slave.
To son JOSEPH,
My child.: JOHN, SAMUEL, THOMAS, JAMES and RACHEL.
Mentions: Henry and William Coventon.
John and Samuel Roe, exs.
Wit: George Bennett,, James Knott, John Davis.   25. 565

COLLINS, JOHN, Queen Anne's Co.   10 Feb, 1748/9
                                         13 Mar, 1748
     To JOHN OFFLEY COLLINS, plantation where my son THOMAS
COLLINS, died.
     To dau. MABAEL SERTAIN; dau. CATHERINE CARMINE, her husband
Thomas Carmine; grand-dau. MARGARET COLLINS, dau. of Thomas
Collins, dec'd., JOHN COLLINS (COLLINGS ?), son to Barbery
Collings.
     Son-in-law JOHN SERTAIN, and Andrew Gibson, exs.
Wit: Wm. Rosebury, Gilbert Reed.   25. 569 - 571

CULLY, HENRY, Kingstown, Queen Anne's Co.   8 Dec, 1748 .
                                             30 Mar, 1749
     Wife CHRISTIAN CULLY.
     To MR. JAMES ASHBY, of St. Mary's Co., my lot No. 12.
     To bro. ANDREW CULLY, Newberry in Barkshire, 30 pounds sterl.
     To sister ANN IDNE, wife of Thomas Idne, in Balborough in
Wilkshire.
     To sister SARAH HARRELL, East Smithville, London, and in case
of death of my bro. or any of sisters, desire to be divided among
the child. of sister ANN IDNE, wife of Thomas, blacksmith in
Marlborough.
     Desire my will transmitted home to England, at the charge of
Mr. James Ashley (or Ashby).
Wit: George Primrose, Violet Primrose, Wm. Winchester.
                                              25. 571

WEBB, JOHN, Tuckahoe, Queen Anne's Co.   10 Feb, 1748/9
                                             19 Apr, 1749
     To wife GRACE WEBB, tract "Redford."
     To son WILLIAM WEBB, son JOHN WEBB, my 2 bros. JAMES and JONA.
NEALE, dau. GRACE; my 2 daus. RACHEL WEBB and SARA.
Wit: Hawkins Downes, Sarah Currey Pool, Richard Webb.
                                              25. 575

BOUNDS, JOSEPH, Somerset Co.

27 Oct. 1748
29 Nov, 1748/30 Mar, 1748

To wife TABITHA, and to SOFIAH RICHARDSON, son WILLIAM, land I bought of John Cooper "Barron Neck," and if no hrs., to son JESSY BOUNDS, son JOHN, dau. MARY, dau. BETTY.
Wit: Levin Dashill, John Cox, Mary McCape; Levin Dashiell.
25. 575

COVINGTON, THOMAS, Somerset Co.

10 Jan, 1748
24 Jan, 1748

Son JAMES, son NEHEMIAH, dau. PRISCILLAH, son THOMAS, and son SAMUEL, that they be left in care of their uncle Thomas Holbrook.
Mitchell Jones, ex.
Wit: Charles Leatherbury, Philip Covington, Richard Phillips.
25. 577

COTTMAN, BENJAMIN, SR., Somerset Co.

- - - - - -
- - - - - -

To son WILLIAM, son JOSEPH, dau. BETTY POLK (BETTY COTTMAN), THOMAS STOCKWELL, MARY STOCKWELL, SR., my plantation where on I live, bought of John Rhodes.
Give same to RACHEL STOCKWELL, dau. of sd. MARY, and if she die without hrs., give same to MARY STOCKWELL'S young. dau. of sd. MARY, and if she have no hrs., then to JOHN TUNSTALL COTTMAN, son of WILLIAM.
To ROCHILL STOCKWELL and MARY STOCKWELL, dau. of sd. MARY, SR.
...[incomplete]...
25. 578

ieaths in the Newspapers of Lancaster County, Pennsylvania, 1821-1830

Deaths in the Newspapers of Lancaster County, Pennsylvania, 1831-1840

ges and Deaths of Cumberland County, [Pennsylvania], 1821-1830

Maryland Calendar of Wills Volume 9: 1744-1749

Maryland Calendar of Wills Volume 10: 1748-1753

Maryland Calendar of Wills Volume 11: 1753-1760

Maryland Calendar of Wills Volume 12: 1759-1764

Maryland Calendar of Wills Volume 13: 1764-1767

Maryland Calendar of Wills Volume 14: 1767-1772

Maryland Calendar of Wills Volume 15: 1772-1774

Maryland Calendar of Wills Volume 16: 1774-1777

Maryland Eastern Shore Newspaper Abstracts, Volume 1: 1790-1805

Maryland Eastern Shore Newspaper Abstracts, Volume 2: 1806-1812

Maryland Eastern Shore Newspaper Abstracts, Volume 3: 1813-1818

Maryland Eastern Shore Newspaper Abstracts, Volume 4: 1819-1824

Maryland Eastern Shore Newspaper Abstracts, Volume 5: Northern Counties, 1825-1829
F. Edward Wright and Irma Harper

Maryland Eastern Shore Newspaper Abstracts, Volume 6: Southern Counties, 1825-1829

Maryland Eastern Shore Newspaper Abstracts, Volume 7: Northern Counties, 1830-1834
Irma Harper and F. Edward Wright

Maryland Eastern Shore Newspaper Abstracts, Volume 8: Southern Counties, 1830-1834

Maryland Militia in the Revolutionary War
S. Eugene Clements and F. Edward Wright

Newspaper Abstracts of Allegany and Washington Counties, 1811-1815

Newspaper Abstracts of Cecil and Harford Counties, [Maryland], 1822-1830

Newspaper Abstracts of Frederick County, [Maryland], 1816-1819

Newspaper Abstracts of Frederick County, 1811-1815

Sketches of Maryland Eastern Shoremen

Tax List of Chester County, Pennsylvania 1768

Tax List of York County, Pennsylvania 1779

Washington County Church Records of the 18th Century, 1768-1800

Western Maryland Newspaper Abstracts, Volume 1: 1786-1798

Western Maryland Newspaper Abstracts, Volume 2: 1799-1805

Western Maryland Newspaper Abstracts, Volume 3: 1806-1810

Wills of Chester County, Pennsylvania, 1766-1778